D1557296

MAKE MONEY WITH YOUR CAPTAIN'S LICENSE

HOW TO GET A JOB OR RUN A BUSINESS ON A BOAT

David G. Brown

International Marine / McGraw-Hill
Camden, Maine • New York • Chicago • San Francisco • Lisbon
London • Madrid • Mexico City • Milan • New Delhi • San Juan • Seoul
Singapore • Sydney • Toronto

Library of Congress Cataloging-in-Publication Data

Brown, David G. (David Geren), 1944–
    Make money with your captain's license : how to get a job or run a business on a boat
/ David G. Brown.
        p.   cm.
    Includes index.
    ISBN-13: 978-0-07-147523-5 (hardcover : alk. paper)
    1. Charter boat captains—United States.   2. Boats and boating—Chartering—
United States.   3. Small business—United States—Management.   I. Title.

    GV776.A2 B76   2008
    387.5'42—dc22   2007038396

1 2 3 4 5 6 7 8 9 10 11 12 13 14 15 16 17 18 19 20 21 22   DOC/DOC   0 9 8 7

ISBN 978-0-07-147523-5
MHID   0-07-147523-0

McGraw-Hill books are available at special quantity discounts to use as premiums and sales
promotions, or for use in corporate training programs. For more information, please write
to the Director of Special Sales, Professional Publishing, McGraw-Hill, Two Penn Plaza, New
York, NY 10121-2298.

Questions regarding the content of this book should be addressed to
International Marine
P.O. Box 220
Camden, ME 04843
www.internationalmarine.com

Questions regarding the ordering of this book should be addressed to
The McGraw-Hill Companies
Customer Service Department
P.O. Box 547
Blacklick, OH 43004
Retail customers: 1-800-262-4729
Bookstores: 1-800-722-4726

This book is printed on acid-free paper.

CONTENTS

PREFACE

Being on the water is almost addictive for some of us, and perhaps it is for you, too. Sometime between hooking the big one that almost got away and watching a colorful sunset from the boat, an idea that could change your life begins to form and slowly takes shape as you ask yourself an all-important question: "Why don't I do this for a living?"

Indeed, why not? Many people have found a way to turn what they love doing on the water into full-time jobs. Others turn their spare time into cash by working on the water on a part-time basis. This is especially true of the growing number of physically fit retirees who want to transform their passion into income. Working as the skipper of a charter fishing boat or a small passenger vessel may seem like a dream, but it is one you can make come true. This book will show you how.

Enterprising skippers have found all sorts of ways to earn money on the water, and some were pretty clever. Over my nearly two decades of teaching, I have taught more than 400 aspiring captains, most of whom were interested in operating traditional six-passenger charter fishing boats. However, some of my students had other ideas that raised eyebrows in some quarters, like the one who planned to purchase a Russian-made wing in ground (WIG) effect machine to ferry passengers at nearly 200 miles per hour to a nearby island.

WIG machines are airplanes with stunted wings. They fly on a cushion of air between the surface of the water and the wings, usually at a height of less than 50 feet. Because they need the surface of the water to operate, they come under both U.S. Coast Guard and Federal Aviation Administration regulations. Unfortunately, costs, regulations, and safety problems with sailboat masts kept my student from achieving his dream. The chapters that follow will help you avoid such pitfalls.

While researching this book I've talked to creative captains who do everything from running waterborne duck hunting services to carrying grieving families out to sea to scatter the ashes of a recently departed loved one. One of my former students is living aboard his boat and teaching sailing in the Virgin Islands. Another young man a few years out of high school got his master's license and then decided to make a real career on the water. After graduating from the Maine Maritime Academy, he landed what Mark Twain viewed as the best job in the world: piloting commercial vessels on the Mississippi River. Several of my former students deliver yachts for brokers and boat dealers.

Over the many years I spent as an instructor, I found a sizeable number of my students had no particular reason in mind when they set out to get their U.S. Coast Guard license. A few of them just wanted the accomplishment of gaining the required knowledge and had no intention of even taking the written exam. However, the majority of the men and women who patiently allowed me to explain the Rules of the Road or current vector diagrams were taking the first positive step to make a dream come true. Obtaining a license was not their ultimate goal but rather a waypoint on their course toward making money on the water as professional mariners.

The path to making a living on the water isn't an easy one, though, and you shouldn't expect it to be. There are six different U.S. Coast Guard licenses for vessels up to 100 gross tons. They range from the most basic one required of launch drivers to the far more demanding ones required of captains in command of larger vessels. In Chapter 1, I will go into more detail about the various licenses, the necessary requirements that must be met to obtain each one, and the types of vessels and areas of operation that each license covers. Other chapters will build on the information presented initially, with the view toward providing you with the knowledge you will need to realize your dream of becoming a captain.

As you learn more about the process, keep in mind that it takes most people several years to acquire the required knowledge and sea time to obtain the kind of U.S. Coast Guard license available to those with pleasure boat experience. One category allows you to operate a small uninspected vessel. It is often called a six-pack ticket, because it caps the number of paying passengers allowed on board at six. The other category, a master's license, allows you to operate inspected vessels carrying more than six people.

Once you have your license, you can begin building a career as a professional mariner. For those aspiring to go beyond a six-pack ticket, the next step typically involves some unpaid "riding for time" (see Chapter 2 for details) to qualify for an upgraded license. This route is usually for captains interested in working as employees for shipping companies or other enterprises. Entrepreneurs who start their own business frequently discover that it takes five years or longer for it to prosper.

Regardless of the path you choose, in my opinion the work is well worth the effort. If you are a U.S. citizen in good health and have clean driving and criminal records, you can earn the title of captain and make a living on the water. You may just find your own version of Mark Twain's best job in the world.

Over the years I've started and managed six entrepreneurial businesses. Currently, in addition to being a boating writer, I run a water taxi and excursion service on the Great Lakes, and I'm involved with the local juvenile court system using boating to help at-risk kids build character and achieve a sense of self-reliance. The biggest benefit from being captain of my own ship has not been economic. Honestly, I've kept my day job as a marine writer and wooden boat repair specialist throughout my career as a professional captain. The big reason is the short season where I live on the Great Lakes.

My best earning year as a captain was spent working for someone else at $20 per hour plus some benefits. My current water taxi business has yet to produce anything close to a living wage for my partner and me. However, our eyes are not on hourly income. We have plans for a larger operation, and the taxi business is just a stepping-stone along the way. So, I know from experience there are plenty of jobs that pay more and have better benefits, but I would rather spend my life on the water pursuing my passion instead of being chained to a desk.

Fortunately, while I haven't gotten rich, the money has been good enough to allow me to live as close to my dream lifestyle as it is possible to get. A big part of that dream has been being my own boss.

Along the way I have also enjoyed working as the captain of a large high-speed passenger ferry. The pay was better and there was a certain excitement about strangers addressing me as "Captain." However, regardless of what I do to make money as a professional mariner, my real motivation is to spend as much time on the water as I can. Running my own small passenger business accomplishes that.

As you read this book, you will meet other captains who are identified by first name only. They are real people, most of whom I know personally. To protect their privacy I have changed their names and certain other details. However, their stories, including their successes and failures, are true. I share their stories with you to provide a glimpse into the lives of professional mariners and to give you a better idea of what you can expect as you pursue your own dream of making a living on the water.

Whether you plan to work for an employer or start your own charter business, you will get the most out of this book if you have two characteristics I see in my successful students. One is a love of being on the water. The other is a dream that motivates your life.

My most poignant experience was teaching a man with ALS, often called Lou Gehrig's disease. He had no false hopes of recovery. His dream was simply to live life to the fullest, and that meant being out on the water. I last saw him strapped in a wheelchair aboard his sailboat calling tactics to his crew as they raced around the buoys. He was living his dream, and he would let nothing stop him, not even a terminal disease. The most successful of my students was a young man who started out with the intention of earning extra money to support his young family. He worked as a part-time captain during the summers until he was able (with help from relatives) to buy a 149-passenger excursion vessel in a highly profitable market.

The purpose of this book is to guide you around the economic and personal rocks and shoals you may encounter when trying to earn a living as a licensed captain. While much of the content of this book is about starting and operating a sole proprietorship, such as a charter fishing business, I have also addressed the possibility of working as a captain for a ferryboat company or a "headboat" fishing operation. Most licensed skippers do a bit of both during their careers. It is not uncommon for a captain to work for a larger company while getting the money together to establish a sole proprietorship. There is also good information about how to land a dream job on the water, something many of us aspire to.

In short, this book is meant for a wide audience of people who want to earn money on the water doing what they love most. Whether you are just starting out or are a captain on your third or fifth license renewal, I am confident you will find many useful ideas and plenty of essential information to make your dreams a reality.

CHAPTER I

U.S. COAST GUARD LICENSES

I n the United States, you need a license issued by the U.S. Coast Guard to carry passengers for hire on vessels operating in federally navigable waters: coastal, most rivers, and the Great Lakes. These areas of operation are important in terms of the license requirements because different licenses are restricted to operating in certain waters. The terms below are used to define where a license is valid:

- **Near coastal:** ocean waters not more than 200 miles offshore
- **Great Lakes:** the Great Lakes and tributary waters, including parts of the Calumet River and the St. Lawrence River to approximately Montreal, Canada
- **Inland:** the navigable waters of the United States inside the COLREGs line, excluding the Great Lakes but including some coastal areas such as the Intracoastal Waterway
- **Rivers:** any river, canal, or other similar body of water designated by the U.S. Coast Guard
- **Western rivers:** the Mississippi River and its tributaries, plus certain designated connecting waterways specified by the U.S. Coast Guard

A license pecking order exists within these defined waters. The list below illustrates why a license valid in near coastal waters is the most desirable:

- **Near coastal:** A skipper holding a license to operate in near coastal waters may also operate in the Great Lakes and in inland waters, which, for the sake of this discussion, include rivers. The near coastal license may have restrictions that require the skipper to operate in waters closer to shore than 200 miles off the coast. The near coastal license is the most desirable for the captain of a small passenger or charter fishing vessel because it is valid in the most areas of operation.

- **Great Lakes:** A skipper holding a Great Lakes license may operate in inland waters. However, the license is not valid for near coastal waters.
- **Inland:** A skipper holding an inland waters license may not operate in near coastal waters or in the Great Lakes. An inland license is only valid in the Great Lakes if it specifies that it covers both inland waters and the Great Lakes.

Most licenses are issued for either near coastal or the combined Great Lakes and inland waters. Before you apply for a job or start your own business, make sure the license you qualify for covers the waters upon which you will be operating.

It is important to note here that there are two general license tracks for prospective captains. One is to work for what is called an upper-level license. This track is intended for large commercial freighters and cruise ships. It eventually leads to a master's license that may ultimately have no restriction on the size of vessels. The upper-level license track is intended to be a lifelong career path. Few people enter this track late in life because progressing up the ladder from mate to captain can take decades.

This book is meant for people who seek a lower-level license. These are based on the tonnage of vessels where you earned your sea service, the coast guard designation for time spent gaining experience on the water. As mentioned, where you obtained your sea service—coastal, Great Lakes, or inland waters—is also important. Lower-level licenses are those that allow the skipper to operate a vessel under 100 gross tons. There are six licenses in this category. These divisions are designed primarily to meet the requirements of specific segments of the passenger vessel industry. Here are the four license designations:

- **Master:** (1) Inland steam or motor vessel; (2) near coastal steam or motor vessel. Either may be endorsed to allow operation of auxiliary sail vessels and/or commercial assistance towing vessels. With this license, you can operate U.S. Coast Guard–inspected vessels carrying more than six passengers.
- **Limited master:** With this license, you are highly restricted in waters of operation. A limited master's license is typically held by launch drivers operating U.S. Coast Guard–inspected vessels.
- **OUPV (operator of uninspected passenger vessel):** (1) Inland steam or motor vessel; (2) near coastal steam or motor vessel. An OUPV is also commonly called a six-pack license.
- **OUPV limited:** This license is typically held by launch drivers operating vessels that have not been subjected to a U.S. Coast Guard inspection.

Each of these categories is described below. Information about sea service and other requirements you must meet to obtain a specific license follows. The general rule of thumb is that the higher-level licenses in the under-100-gross-ton category are based on how much time you have spent on specific types of vessels in specific waters. More experience means you can increase tonnage restrictions on your master's license. Although generally outside the scope of this book, a lower-level license can be upgraded to a maximum of 1,600 tons. To do so requires sea time on larger vessels as well as additional U.S. Coast Guard–approved training in firefighting, radar, and shipboard safety.

MASTER'S LICENSES

A master's license is required for operating U.S. Coast Guard–inspected passenger vessels carrying more than six passengers, including passenger ferries, walk-on fishing headboats, dinner cruise boats, and whale watch vessels. Master's licenses are issued in three tonnage limits: under 25, under 50, and under 100 gross tons. The size of your initial license is based on the sizes and types of vessels you have operated. A 25- or 50-ton license can be upgraded to a 100-ton license by showing proof you have worked on larger vessels for the required number of days. In addition to tonnage, master's licenses specify the waters on which they are valid, as described previously.

ENDORSEMENTS

Two endorsements that extend the scope of your master's license may be added. Taking the test for either of them when you sit for your initial written exam avoids extra U.S. Coast Guard user fees and delays. The two endorsements are:

- **Sail or auxiliary sail:** allows you to operate a sailing vessel, such as an excursion schooner while under sail
- **Commercial assistance towing:** required if you intend to operate a towboat

A sailing endorsement requires at least 180 days of sea service on sail or auxiliary sail vessels for an inland master's license and at least 360 days for a near coastal master's license. Sea service days acquired prior to obtaining your license can be applied to this requirement. The commercial assistance towing endorsement does not require additional sea service beyond that needed for a master's license.

RADAR AND FIREFIGHTING SCHOOLS

Strictly speaking, there are no endorsements for passing firefighting or radar training if you hold a 100-ton or smaller license. These schools are only required for licenses for 200 tons and above. Even so, obtaining professional radar observer training is never a waste of money if your boat is equipped with radar. Radar training, particularly in collision avoidance, sets you apart from other captains and can help you get work driving ferries and other larger vessels.

On the other hand, firefighting training is expensive and only required for 200-ton and above licenses. Almost none of the skills learned apply to the firefighting equipment on smaller vessels. While knowledge of the nature of fire is always valuable, the cost of this training generally outweighs the benefits to holders of 100-ton or lower licenses. Both classes cost from $500 to $2,000, depending on the length and complexity of the curriculum. Mariners should study the course offerings to avoid buying more training than they need for their purposes.

PLEASURE BOAT TONNAGE

A boater with no formal maritime training or big ship experience can use days of pleasure boating to meet sea time requirements. However, pleasure boat experience almost always restricts applicants to a master's license under 25 gross tons. Tonnage will be explained further in Chapter 6, but for practical purposes gross tonnage (G.T.) measures the internal cubic volume of the hull, exclusive of cabin trunks and superstructure. Gross tonnage is always listed on the paperwork of a documented vessel.

The gross tonnage of state-registered boats is hardly ever calculated. Because no two boat models are the same, the gross tonnage of each must be handled separately. For pleasure boats, the following rule of thumb is illustrative:

- **25 gross tons:** up to a 36-foot cruiser
- **50 gross tons:** up to a 45-foot cruiser
- **100 gross tons:** up to a 65-foot motor yacht

Holders of under-100-ton master's licenses are able to captain U.S. Coast Guard–inspected vessels (see Chapter 6). These include ferryboats, walk-on fishing headboats, water taxis, harbor excursion boats, and so forth. A master may also operate an uninspected six-pack charter fishing boat.

OUPV LICENSE

The operator of uninspected passenger vessel (OUPV) license limits the holder to carrying six or fewer passengers. Because of this passenger restriction, the OUPV is often called a six-pack license. An OUPV license is limited to vessels of 50 tons or less, and it cannot be used to operate an inspected vessel (see Chapter 6) even with six or fewer passengers aboard. You need a master's license or a limited master's license to operate U.S. Coast Guard–inspected vessels.

Because of these restrictions, it makes good business sense to avoid the OUPV. You have far more opportunity to make money with a master's license even if your original plans are to operate only a six-pack charter fishing boat. Foreign nationals are the only exception to this economic rule. A legal immigrant who is not a U.S. citizen may obtain an OUPV but is barred from holding a master's license.

LAUNCH OPERATOR

The limited master's and limited OUPV licenses are the least desirable for professional mariners. Commonly called the "launch operator" class, they are intended for people who operate boats that pick up and drop off passengers in yacht club mooring fields or who work for marinas, formal camps, and educational institutions. The OUPV limited license is for six or fewer passengers, while the limited master license allows operating U.S. Coast Guard–inspected vessels. Both limit the holder to a very specific route, sometimes just the water inside a yacht club's harbor. These licenses are so limited in scope as to be an impediment to the growth of a water-related business or finding employment outside the route stated on these licenses.

LICENSING REQUIREMENTS

Licenses do not come for free. Most aspiring captains attend one of the approved licensing schools. The coast guard charges user fees for approving candidates and issuing licenses. In addition, the applicant must pay for a medical examination, drug test, and training in first aid and cardiopulmonary resuscitation.

Typical Cost of U.S. Coast Guard Licenses

Basic OUPV Class	$750
Upgrade to Master	$350
Drug Test	$90
Medical Examination	$150
First Aid, CPR	$60
U.S. Coast Guard Fees	$190
Total Cost:	$1,590

In addition to being a U.S. citizen (for a master's license) and having the required sea time, all applicants must have a clean driving record and be free of criminal convictions. Applicants must pass a limited physical examination and take a urinalysis test to detect the use of illegal drugs. These and still other requirements are discussed next.

SEA TIME

Most applicants self-certify their days of sea time aboard their own boats. Proof of ownership of the boat in which days of service are claimed must accompany the application. You must provide a signed letter from the owner or operator of any other boats on which time is claimed. The U.S. Coast Guard application contains a special form and detailed instructions for claiming sea time.

To obtain a near coastal master's license, you must have acquired at least 720 days of sea service, and 90 of those days must have been within the preceding three years. Half of the total number of days of sea service (360) must have been in the ocean or in near coastal waters. Up to 360 days of inland sea service can be included in the total number of days. If you meet these requirements and your time was acquired in sailing vessels, you already qualify for the sail and auxiliary sail endorsement.

To obtain an inland master's license you must have acquired at least 360 days of sea service, and 90 of those days must have been within the preceding three years. The sea service required for the OUPV inland and near coastal licenses is the same as the requirements for the inland master's license.

A "day" of sea time is supposed to be eight hours on the water, but it can include preparing to get under way and cleaning up after a voyage. A single calendar day can only be used once. If you spend eight hours on your boat, then another eight hours on a friend's boat, the total is still only one day of sea time. A "day" can never be counted twice whether on your boat or on any combination of boats or waters.

DRIVING RECORD

Applicants must sign an authorization allowing the coast guard to examine their driving records. Conviction for operating a motor vehicle under the influence of alcohol or drugs may prevent the coast guard from issuing a license. Waivers can be obtained under some circumstances and are decided on a case-by-case basis.

CRIMINAL RECORD

Applicants must allow the coast guard to search for any criminal convictions. Fingerprints are taken and checked against national databases of known criminals. As with a bad driving record, a criminal conviction may prevent issuance of a license unless waivers are obtained on a case-by-case basis.

DRUG TEST

Applicants must be tested drug-free within the past six months or be currently enrolled in a random drug-testing program accepted by the coast guard. See Chapter 7 for drug-testing requirements.

MEDICAL EXAMINATION

This is simply a physical exam performed by the applicant's physician at the applicant's expense. The U.S. Coast Guard has three primary areas of interest: vision and color blindness, hearing, and high blood pressure.

FIRST AID AND CPR TRAINING

For an initial license, applicants must show proof they have passed a class in first aid and have been trained in cardiopulmonary resuscitation (CPR). Most people take classes offered by the Red Cross.

PROOF OF CITIZENSHIP

An original Social Security card is required, along with a picture ID driver's license. The rules have been tightened on documents that can be used to prove citizenship. The only acceptable documents are notarized birth certificates, certificates of citizenship, certificates of naturalization, and U.S. passports.

EDUCATION AND TESTING

Until a few years ago, all applicants had to spend a full day taking a four-part test at one of the 17 U.S. Coast Guard regional examination centers (RECs). It is still possible to take this test at any REC. However, the more popular route is to take an approved course from an accredited school. Proof that an applicant has passed an approved class eliminates the need to test at an REC.

If you elect to take an approved class, be sure it leads to the license you need. For instance, many classes say you will receive a 50-ton license but neglect to mention that it will be an OUPV and not a master's license. There is usually an additional class fee for obtaining a certificate showing you have passed an accredited master's license course. Upgrading an unintentional OUPV license once it has been issued adds expense and complication to starting your business. License schools typically charge from $550 to $750 for an OUPV course and an additional $250 to $350 for the required class to upgrade to a master's license.

Not all approved schools offer endorsements such as commercial assistance towing or auxiliary sail. If possible, you want to obtain both your master's license and applicable endorsements at one time. This avoids paying duplicate coast guard fees for re-issuing your amended license.

It is possible to self-study for the coast guard examination and take it at an REC. Perhaps the best book to aid in this process is *Get Your Captain's License* (3rd ed.) by Charlie Wing. It is published by International Marine and is available through bookstores everywhere. Wing has organized his book following the organization of the written coast guard test.

BEYOND THE LICENSE

Whether you attend an approved class or use Wing's book, it is a happy moment when the examiner hands you that piece of paper and says, "Congratulations, Captain." All those weeks of study, the late-night sessions with tide tables, and those hours spent with navigation light flash cards have paid off. You are a licensed, professional mariner. You check that your name is actually on the document. "Thanks," you mutter as you try to restrain your excitement before heading to an appropriate celebration. It's easy on that first day to overlook the big new question you face: What are you going to do with that license?

For most license holders the answer is "earn money," but that is only half the story. The underlying question is: How? A license only allows you to operate a vessel for commercial purposes. It is up to the holder to find a way to make that license profitable. The first thought most people have is to turn their own boat from an expensive hobby into a tax-deductible business. There is nothing really wrong with keeping a few dollars out of the hands of Uncle Sam's tax collectors as long as you do it legally. The problem is that all too many new skippers find out that, as Chapter 5 will show, dodging the tax man is more complicated and expensive than they thought.

HOBBY OR SERIOUS?

Full tax consequences will be discussed in later chapters. For now, the important thing is to consider how your intentions will influence the outcome of your maritime venture. A hobby business is run primarily for enjoyment, with income and profit being secondary concerns. A hobby business is usually done on a sporadic basis almost at the whim of the owner. When it comes to anything related to boating, a hobby business almost always spends more money than it brings in.

A profit-motivated business, on the other hand, is started and maintained for the purpose of economic gain. This does not mean that you intend to become a tycoon with a fleet of boats in ports around the world. A profit-motivated business can consist of a single boat that you run commercially only on weekends. The key thing is that you intend to have more money in your bank account at the end of the tax year than you did at the start. Achieving this goal takes knowledge, planning, and hard work.

If your motivation for getting a captain's license is to run a hobby charter fishing service, aside from knowing how to catch fish, all you really need to know is that hobby business expenses can be deducted up to the amount of the income they produce.

Economic Rocks and Shoals

Few charter boat or small passenger vessel captains get into trouble at sea. The rocks and shoals that trap unwary skippers are those of bookkeeping, cash flow, and tax reports. All too often, the grand dream ends with a prematurely worn-out boat and a smaller bank account. That's what happened to Cap'n Joe. That's not his real name, but I'm sure he would prefer anonymity. He decided to transform his personal fishing boat into a six-pack charter operation.

During the euphoria that comes while starting a new venture, Joe willingly drew down his savings account to upgrade the boat's life jackets and other safety gear to meet U.S. Coast Guard standards. Then he purchased a bunch of personalized cups, key chains, and ballpoint pens to hand out at fishing shows. Cap'n Joe's credit card took the hit for buying booth space at those shows and for the hotel rooms and restaurant meals.

The first summer brought "hot" fishing. The phone rang and the customers came. Joe began feeling confident in his business. After all, his gross income far exceeded the costs of gasoline, insurance, and dockage. He thought he was profitable. At the end of the year, however, his accountant showed him a different picture. When all the expenses were added in, the boat had cost more to operate and maintain than it had returned in income. There were no profits. Business was up during the second year, but so were expenses. Cap'n Joe had forgotten that increased operating hours meant bigger maintenance and repair bills. Again, the accountant had bad news.

Fishing interest dropped in the third year because of bad weather. Still, Joe's customers caught fish and he was enjoying himself. By the end of that year, though, the old boat was showing signs of hard use, and Joe found himself wrecked on those dangerous economic shoals. He could not continue without either expensive repairs or a new vessel. Yet he did not have the cash on hand to pay for either option. His credit cards were still maxed out by start-up expenses. The trade-in value of his old boat was not enough to make a sizable down payment on a new one. Joe faced bigger monthly loan payments than his charter operation could handle. He was effectively out of business.

This sad state of affairs is not the inevitable result of Joe's earning a captain's license. Rather, it was the consequence of starting a business without doing what is called due diligence, a term covering everything from market research and sales promotion to cost analysis and a multiyear budget. Due diligence also includes looking deep into yourself. Do you have the risk-taking personality of an entrepreneur? Or are you better suited to working for someone else and keeping your pleasure boating a private affair? These two options are open to the newly licensed captain. Some license holders choose to do both. Joe fixed up his old boat and still runs a few charters every season, but he mostly works as a paid captain on a headboat run by a local marina.

CHAPTER 2

BECOMING A PAID CAPTAIN

F or some new captains, the risks and challenges of operating their own business pose steep hurdles, and the best way for many to learn about and gain confidence in commercial operations is to work for someone else. Being a hired gun allows you to learn how to deal with things as diverse as handling unruly passengers to passing an annual coast guard inspection. Limited financial resources and family responsibilities may also be factors in a decision to hire on as a captain rather than starting your own business as a sole proprietor. There are a variety of jobs open to skippers with the right license and experience.

AVAILABLE POSITIONS

Upgrading to at least a 100-gross-ton license pays economic dividends. The bulk of high-paying jobs for captains are on vessels larger than 50 gross tons. This includes scheduled ferry lines, most dinner cruise ships, and many harbor tours. That said, there is still plenty of work available for holders of licenses below the 100-ton benchmark, if you are willing to search it out. Few jobs for captains are advertised in the newspaper. In fact, they are seldom advertised anywhere. It is up to you to ferret out employment by becoming familiar with the operations near your home. Here are some of the most common opportunities:

Business to Consumer
- Dive boat
- Parasailing

- Towing services (SeaTow and others)
- Fishing guide

Business to Business

- Small towing service
- Industrial diving
- Marine construction
- Mooring service

YACHT DELIVERIES

The cost of trucking boats wider than 12 feet can be astronomical, making it attractive to deliver a boat by water. Many insurance companies require a licensed master for these trips. You can find these jobs by becoming friendly with boat dealers and yacht brokers in your area. It may take a while before you get your first trip, but once "inside," look for continued work. Payment starts at $100 per day and goes up depending on the complexity of the voyage and any additional crew the captain may need to hire.

SEA TRIALS

Regulations allow a bona fide salesperson to take customers on demonstration rides. However, many boat brokers and used boat dealers employ licensed captains to handle sea trials conducted for potential buyers. Using a licensed captain allows the sales staff to concentrate on selling boats. It also avoids the problem of the customer being intimidated by the salesperson. As with yacht deliveries, you can find these jobs by making friends with brokers and sales agents. Minimum payment is usually $50, but it may be more depending on the size of the boat and the amount of time involved.

FISHING HEADBOATS

Fishing boats that take walk-on anglers are known in the trade as headboats or party boats because the owners charge by the head, as opposed to operating on a chartered basis. Most headboats can handle from 24 to 49 passengers. They take people offshore fishing for a specified period of time. The best way to break in is as a mate. Don't be put off by the fact that mates are not always paid. Many are, but a large number of mates are unpaid except for the tips they earn from customers. If the fishing is good, a helpful mate can earn as much as the captain. Get the confidence of the owner and soon you'll be a fill-in skipper. Eventually, you'll be on the regular rotation of captains. Payment may be by the hour or by the trip. Hourly salaries of $15 to $25 are common. Day rates start at $150.

WATER TAXI SKIPPER

Water taxi operations are not the highest paying but usually need extra skippers. Most water taxi skippers collect the money and entertain the passengers as well as drive the boat. A good line of patter can earn handsome tips, making up for the low hourly wage. To get a job with a private water taxi company, find the owner and ask about potential job opportunities. Government-operated services may have more complex hiring practices involving formal job postings. Taxi captains are usually paid by the hour. Rates start at $10 to $15 per hour, but good captains on popular routes can receive tips equal to their hourly pay.

HARBOR TOUR CAPTAIN

This job requires detailed local knowledge as well as an appropriate license. On smaller tours, the captain narrates. This makes having the gift of gab helpful. Harbor tours come in all sizes, from six-pack operations to 149-passenger inspected vessels. Pay rates for smaller vessels where the captain is tipped are similar to water taxi operations. Larger vessels usually follow the pay schedules of local fishing headboats.

PASSENGER FERRY

Few ferry companies or state governments will give a command to a brand-new captain. Most hire prospective captains as deckhands or mates. This allows the individual to learn the company's policies while the company assesses the employee's potential. Upward movement can be slow if the current crop of captains is young. Better prospects can be found at a company with lots of older captains on the payroll. Payment varies and depends on the status of the employee. Part-time captains are usually paid by the hour based on the local prevailing wage rate. Full-time captains receive annual salaries from $35,000 to

$80,000. The size of the vessel and the local wage rates determine how much a full-time captain can earn.

EXCURSION AND DINNER CRUISE CAPTAIN

These companies usually have a higher turnover of personnel than ferry lines. Still, expect to hire on as a mate and work your way up. New captains usually get the least desirable runs, like the Tuesday morning breakfast tour that requires getting up early for only a few paid hours on the water. The best way to get involved is to be available any time to scrub decks or greet guests. Becoming an integral part of the team will pay dividends down the road. Wages on vessels that carry fewer than 150 passengers are similar to those paid on local fishing headboats. Captains of vessels that carry more than 150 passengers generally receive about the same pay as local ferry skippers.

"DUCK" DRIVER

"Ducks" are those famous amphibious DUKW assault vehicles of World War II and their later derivatives. These "boats on wheels" are popular around tourist attractions in Baltimore, Branson, Memphis, Stone Mountain, Seattle, and Boston. Depending on the number of people the "duck" can carry, you may also need a commercial driver's license (CDL) to drive on the highway as well as at least a 25-ton master's license. Information on CDLs can be obtained from state driver's license bureaus.

SCHOONER CAPTAIN

This work was confined to New England for generations, but excursion schooners are now showing up along the East and West coasts, in Florida, in the Caribbean, and in the Great Lakes. Most require a minimum 50-ton license and all require a sailing endorsement. Apply directly to the company operating the vessel. Most start new captains as deckhands until they have experience in the vessel. See www.sight sailing.com for the website of a typical excursion sailing operation. Wages vary widely based on the location of the business and on the size and purpose of the vessel. Hourly rates starting at $25 are common for commercial vessels.

GAMBLING SHIP CAPTAIN

You really have to know somebody on the inside to get one of these cushy jobs. Many states require gambling ships to be under way when the slot machines are ringing, though the vessels never travel very far and are not designed to weather storms. In some areas, the ships are large enough to stay beyond the three-mile international limit, allowing gambling without interference of state laws. However, getting patrons to and from the ships requires transportation and many companies use 150- to 300-passenger shuttles for this purpose. Most of the shuttles are under 100 gross tons.

OFFSHORE SUPPLY VESSEL (OSV)

This used to be a haven for 100-ton licenses, but companies are increasingly asking for 200-ton skippers. The work involves taking workers and equipment to offshore oil rigs in the Gulf of Mexico. You will need at least a near coastal license and will also have to work at least six months as a deckhand, but the time served as a deckhand can be used to upgrade your 100-ton license to the required 200 tons. Additional OSV license and watch standing training and a radar endorsement are needed as well. See www.americancrewing.com for some additional details and wages.

VESSEL SURVEYOR

A master's license is not needed to be a surveyor, but holding one can be a valuable credential in this business. Customers are reassured by the title "Captain" before your name. Surveying requires a superior knowledge of boat construction and maintenance, particularly if you plan to work on inspected vessels. Break into this business acting as a "go-fer" for a working surveyor while taking courses from schools that offer studies in marine surveying to pass the various accreditation tests of the three national professional surveyor associations. See Appendix B for schools that offer courses in marine surveying and other useful websites about job placement services.

PERMANENT YACHT CAPTAIN

This is the hardest job to get and keep. Most yacht captains are hired by personal referral. A good way to break in is to advertise your services as a "day captain" to boat owners who want to enjoy the party without worrying about operating while consuming adult beverages. Get your name known in harbors frequented by crewed yachts. Be gregarious. Above all, become friends with other full-time yacht captains, because they will be first to know when a new job is about to open up. Check www .rentacaptain.com for more information. Married couples where one is a licensed captain and the other a gourmet cook are in high demand.

While glamorous, this job requires long hours of polishing and painting when you are not driving the boat. You may have to live aboard or be away from your home for weeks at a time. Professional yacht captain jobs usually last no more than five years. Over time, owners often feel their captains become too much a member of the family, and they prefer the clearer distinction between captain and owner. When this happens, they look for a new "stranger" to take command of the yacht.

INSTRUCTOR

A surprising number of people buy boats of 40 feet or larger and don't know how to drive them or how to operate the complex electronics on board. Freelance captains provide these buyers with a crash course to bring them up to speed, holding their hands as they learn about their new boats. This work takes patience, a cool head, and a friendly personality. The pay is not the best but tips from clients can be rewarding. As with most yacht-related jobs, get to know boat salespeople and brokers who can refer clients to you.

Instructor-cum-Delivery Captain

Ron W. has been sailing for most of his adult life. He obtained his 25-ton master's license about 10 years ago when he retired from the railroad. His first intention was to take people sailing on sunset cruises. Almost from the beginning a large number of his customers came for sailing lessons instead, and Ron quickly aligned himself with a sailing school to capitalize on the situation. His teaching business increased and led to additional opportunities. It turned out that the school was operated by a sailboat dealership that often sold boats that needed to be moved to their new owners. Before long Ron was making more money doing delivery trips than he was from his six-pack sailing lessons. He admits that he would not have found steady work delivering sailboats without first proving his seamanship to the yacht broker.

RIDING FOR TIME

The majority of former yachtsmen who become licensed masters qualify for 25- or 50-ton licenses. However, most employers require 100-ton masters, even for smaller vessels. It may not be fair, but that's the system. The way to get around the problem is to "ride for time" on vessels that will qualify you to upgrade your license to the required tonnage.

I went this route. My first license limited me to 50 tons, so I began serving as an unpaid mate on a local interisland ferry. By the end of the summer I had the required number of days of sea time to upgrade to a full 100-ton license.

Note that riding for time is often unpaid work—or unpaid in terms of money. The boat line knows you need the license upgrade and, frankly, takes advantage of your situation. This is a grand old nautical tradition. Even the unlimited masters who sail the big ships find themselves riding for time occasionally. It happens most often when a license holder needs a few more days at sea to meet renewal regulations set by the U.S. Coast Guard.

A Two-Captain Family

Diane B. and her husband met and courted while sailing his sloop. His job of driving a survey vessel required holding a master's license. She went to school with him and they became a two-captain family. As a full-time school teacher, Diane had her summers free. She started working as a mate for a river tour and dinner cruise line. What she calls her "gift o' gab" quickly made her the favored tour guide. By the third year she had upgraded her original 25-ton license to 100 gross tons and was the primary captain on the company's smallest vessel.

SEA TIME LETTERS

No matter what job you hold, there is one bit of record keeping that should never be overlooked. At the end of each operating season, or once a year, you must obtain a letter from your employer listing your days of sea time. This letter should be typed on the company's letterhead and signed by the owner, president, or whoever is in charge of hiring captains. It should indicate the number of days of sea time you acquired during that season or year. These letters should be as simple as possible with few extraneous details. For example:

Joe Doaks (Social Security number) worked for this company from (date) to (date), and during that period of time acquired (number) days of sea service on (vessel name), (official number), (gross tonnage).

If you worked on a number of vessels, list their individual names, documentation numbers (official numbers), and the gross tonnage. Breaking down your days of sea time on each vessel is not usually required. Keep this letter (or letters) with your license so it will be available when it comes time to renew. Make sure that the company official signs the letter. It is not good enough for a secretary to sign and initial the document.

License Leads to Surveying

Tom P. obtained his 50-ton license with an eye toward operating fishing charters after selling his small business. Before the fishing charter business got started, he was asked by a boat dealer friend to do a couple of yacht deliveries. Through this work he learned from customers that qualified surveyors were in demand. He attended a school for surveyors in Florida and then returned to the Detroit area, where he apprenticed. Today he makes a comfortable retirement income from surveying. Tom also works for me as a fill-in water taxi captain and still does yacht deliveries. His dreams of a fishing charter business are all but forgotten.

INSURING YOURSELF

If you work for a company driving a company-owned boat, you will be covered under its liability insurance. However, the same is not true if you accept a freelance boat delivery job or agree to give boat-handling instruction on a customer's boat. This is why you become a named co-insured on the owner's policy before you take on the work. Because of what insurance companies call "reinsurance treaties," you cannot buy insurance to cover another person's boat. For practical purposes this means you cannot insure a delivery customer's boat under a policy that you purchase. The problem of insurance occurs any time you are hired as a private contractor to operate another person's vessel under your license.

This quirk in insurance policies is really one of those bureaucratic blessings. You should not be insuring your customer's boat. The customer should be insuring you as captain, which is the situation generally favored by insurance companies. The solution is to ask your customer to have you listed as a "named co-insured" under his policy. The process is simple. The customer calls his agent with the request to put you on his policy as captain. In most cases you will have to supply a copy of your license as proof it is current. The agent should issue your customer a letter stating you are now named on the policy. You should secure a copy of that letter before beginning the voyage.

Some insurance companies charge a small fee to issue this letter. Becoming a named co-insured has two benefits. First, you are now covered by your customer's policy for liability and damage. Second, it becomes difficult for the customer to sue you over damage since he is effectively suing himself.

WHERE ARE THE JOBS?

There are thousands of jobs out there for captains, enough so that those who want to should have few problems finding full-time work, at least during the summer season, if not year-round. Just bear in mind that very few of these jobs are ever advertised in newspapers. What's a captain to do?

STAY IN CONTACT

Maintain a large circle of friends within the industry. A tip from one of those friends may be the only way to learn about a specific job opening.

The best way to know about job openings is to have a network of friends already working at various companies. Make an effort to keep in contact with the friends you make within the industry. Work to keep the channels of communication open. You never know when a friendship will pay off in a job offer. Over the years two of my students have become managers of ferry lines. Both are now hiring captains, often from among the friends they made while attending my class. In the case of my water taxi business, we have pulled nearly all of our captains from students in our classes.

The secret is that to get a job in the industry you first have to be part of the small passenger vessel community. This is very much of an "old boys school" profession even though an increasing number of women are becoming one of "the boys." Like it or not, most jobs are never advertised. They are offered. When a boat line needs a new captain, the person doing the hiring usually starts by asking licensed masters he already knows. Generally, the job will be offered first to someone working as a mate on one of the company's boats or for the competition.

Who I Hire

I've been hiring water taxi captains for about a decade now. Most years we need two or three skippers in addition to me and my partner. Some work only on the busiest weekends, while others handle our daily lunch service to local restaurants. We look for mature captains who are at ease with all kinds of people. Over the years we have employed several school teachers who were also licensed captains. For a while we had a captain serving as a second mate on large ships but wanted something to do between voyages. Perhaps our most successful skipper (in terms of tips) was a retired business executive.

KNOW EMPLOYERS

Small passenger vessel companies tend to have a nontraditional organization. Learn the quirks of the company before approaching it for a job.

Some companies have very formal hierarchies while others have no visible organizational structure. Getting hired requires you to adapt the way you approach the company to fit with its hiring methods. You should also know the daily business cycle. For instance, trying to talk with the boss of a headboat fishing operation early in the morning is bound to fail. He will be too busy loading bait and ice, selling tickets, and helping people board his boats. Instead, come back midmorning when the boats are out and not much is happening around the docks.

Large, multivessel companies and governmental agencies usually have a more formal approach to hiring. You will need to fill out an application; then, if you're lucky, you'll be asked to meet the potential employer in a formal job interview. The proper methods vary. A few companies want everything on paper through the mail. Increasingly, employers are looking toward all-electronic applications via e-mail or through forms posted on the company's website. Don't guess. Find out how the company expects to see your application and follow the instructions and procedures to the letter.

WORK AS MATE

Good-paying captain jobs on larger vessels are harder to find than other positions in the industry, but every boat line needs trained help. Become part of the team and your turn will come.

No matter how competent and well-trained you are, to a prospective employer you are an unknown commodity. The employer has a lot of money invested in its vessels and entrusts passengers' lives to the skill and prudence of the captains it hires. There is a natural desire to get to know potential captains over an extended period of time before putting them in command. This is why so many companies promote from within. The best way into the pilothouse is often "up the hawse pipe" by starting out in a menial job and working your way up.

YACHT CAPTAIN JOBS

Captaining yachts is a business with its own set of rules. For a beginner with no contacts, the best starting point is with a crew placement agency.

See Appendix B for a listing of crew placement agency websites. From the pictures on these sites, it is obvious this industry prefers attractive and physically fit people in their 20s over less attractive and physically fit people who are older. Don't let this scare you off, but do keep the image factor in mind before deciding to sign with a crew placement agency.

Do not register with an agency until you have spoken directly with a placement agent. You need to know exactly what the agency can and cannot do to help your career. Also, the agent may have tips about how you can tailor your résumé to the existing yacht market. Most agencies can handle résumés sent by e-mail and many prefer this type of delivery. Reputable agencies will check out your credentials and verify them. The industry standard is for crew agencies to charge the yacht owners for finding the right crew members. Beware of agencies that charge an up-front fee to list your résumé.

Captains need to have local knowledge of the ports and marinas frequented by their employers. It pays to work as a mate long enough to gain the required knowledge. One yacht captain I know has his own "little black book" in which he keeps the names and phone numbers of diesel mechanics, butchers who will deliver on the spur of the moment, and dockmasters. He remembers each of these people with a card during the holiday season.

In the United States, the yacht capital is Ft. Lauderdale, Florida. Hundreds of private yachts with full crews use this city as their home port but only during certain months of the year. Most yachts are away cruising the Caribbean and other foreign ports during the winter months. They head north to New England for the summer. This means the fleet is gathered in Ft. Lauderdale for only a few weeks in April and May and again in October. These are the peak hiring months.

Yachts these days are growing in size, with many more than 100 gross tons. For a newly licensed 100-ton master, this means spending at least a year as a mate riding for time. Crew members in yachts over 100 gross tons are typically required to have STCW95 certification, and some jobs require a yacht ratings certificate. A good starting point for information about working on yachts is the Maritime Professional Training website: www.mptusa.com.

JOB HUNTING TOOLS

Just as you would not try to fix an engine without a set of socket wrenches, you need tools to look for work. The traditional job hunting toolbox consists of a business card, a résumé, and a cover letter. For licensed captains, the final tool in the box is a copy of your license. Due to the relatively small size of most passenger operations with vessels under 100 tons, the hiring practices of this industry tend to be informal. You may not need any of these conventional tools to get hired by a water taxi, or you may need very formal materials for a job with a large corporation or government agency or through a yacht crew placement service.

BUSINESS CARD

Everyone knows that most business cards get tossed away. Still, it is proper business etiquette to present your card to a prospective employer. Making up business cards is no longer time-consuming or expensive thanks to prescored blank cards and computerized word processing. Avoid the tendency to add a bunch of fancy graphics. All that's needed is your name, contact information, and details about what license you hold.

Jack Matelot
Master, 100 Gross Tons
Great Lakes & Inland
Aux. Sail, Power, & Com. Assist Towing

111 East 11th Ave
Anyplace, ST 00000

(888) 555-5555
email@email.net

Within much of the ferry, dinner cruise, and harbor tour industry, it is best not to use the title "captain" or abbreviate it on your card. Claiming the title if you do not actively command a vessel is considered presumptuous. However, within the sport fishing industry, the title "captain" is always used to differentiate professionals from amateurs. Because computer-generated cards are so inexpensive, it is possible to have cards with the "captain" title and cards without it. Choose which one to use based on your research into the likes and dislikes of each employer.

Don't forget the back of your business card. Nothing prevents you from putting a limited sales pitch there. You might consider listing the sizes and types of vessels you have commanded or other information about yourself that makes you stand out from the pack.

RÉSUMÉ

The networking nature of the business reduces the importance of traditional résumés. Still, a one- or two-page outline of your training and experience can be useful. Avoid putting too much information on paper. You may have worked long and hard for that doctorate in underwater basket weaving, but someone looking for a captain isn't interested. They need to know the types and sizes of vessels you have commanded and the waters on which you have local knowledge.

Career counselors say that résumés should contain strong keywords. This advice is based on the fact that big corporations use computerized scanning programs to analyze résumés and pick out the ones to be read by human beings. Companies hiring 100-ton-and-under captains do not use such sophisticated equipment. Even so, the language you use is important. There is no list of the 20 best keywords for a captain's résumé, but the list below will provide you with some commonly accepted rules:

- **Words in ad:** Include words and phrases from the job ad in your résumé or cover letter. If the ad says the applicant should be "good with people," then say that you are "good with people."
- **Use jargon:** Jargon is the language specific to a given industry. Don't overdo trying to sound like an old salt, but it can help to use familiar coast guard abbreviations or industry phrases where appropriate. For instance, you can describe yourself as a "100-ton master" even though in reality your license says "under 100 gross tons."
- **Golden words:** All passenger vessel employers want to hire people who are interested in growing the business or who have good communication skills, especially with the public.
- **Don't be modest:** State your training and (most of all) accomplishments with pride. Remember, it's not bragging if you can prove you did it.

Brand Yourself

In business, branding is the process of creating a unique identity for a product or service. Career advisers say you should apply the same process to yourself as a job applicant. Instead of being a generic license holder, you want potential employers to think of you as Captain Joe. The experts suggest that the first paragraph of any résumé should be a branding statement designed to make you stand out from the other, run-of-the-mill applicants, something along the lines of:

> **Highly motivated 100-ton master with impeccable safety record seeks command of fast, interisland ferries on which he (or, she) can use skills and experiences honed in the fishing, water taxi, and harbor tour industries.**

A branding statement should be one or two sentences. State exactly who you are and your job goal. This may be the only part of your résumé that gets read during the initial selection process. Often, it is only after you get on the short list of potential applicants that the full details of your résumé receive a careful reading.

Essential Résumé Contents

- Contact information: full name, mailing address, e-mail address, and telephone numbers (home and cell)
- Branding statement
- License information: gross tonnage, applicable waters, and endorsements
- Experience: type and size of vessels operated and previous employers with job descriptions

COPY OF LICENSE

Include a copy of your license, both front and back, with each résumé. Color is not necessary. Attach these to your résumé as proof that you hold the license you claim. Always have extra copies of your license available. Most employers will want a copy on file. You will also have to post a copy on each of the vessels you operate.

Something often overlooked on a coast guard license is the issue number. Your first license will have a numeral "one" designation. Each five-year renewal increases that number consecutively, which means an employer can estimate your professional career by multiplying the issue number by five. If you are on issue two or beyond, it can pay to mention that in your résumé. If you are still in your first issue, just don't mention it.

COVER LETTER

A cover letter always goes with a résumé sent by regular mail. It becomes the e-mail message to which your résumé and scans of your license are attached when sent via the Internet. Think of your cover letter as a sales pitch for your services. It should never be longer than one page. There are several guidelines to a successful cover letter:

- **Address it to a person:** Find out who will be making the hiring decision and send your cover letter and résumé to that person's attention.
- **Describe the job:** Tell the recipient of your package exactly what type of job you are applying for. If you are responding to a newspaper help-wanted advertisement, quote the job description given in the advertisement.
- **Promote yourself:** Tell the recipient exactly why you are the person the company should hire.
- **Action:** Indicate what action you intend to take. The best thing to do is indicate what day and time you will call for an appointment. Allow the recipient 10 days to two weeks to prepare for your follow-up call.

The same cover letter cannot be sent to every potential employer. Tailor the contents of your letter based on your study of the company and its needs. In promoting yourself, it helps to quote a former boss who has had great things to say about your job performance. If you have some particularly hot piece of information about yourself, consider putting it into a handwritten postscript.

ADVERTISED JOBS

Although I have stressed that most jobs for captains aren't advertised, some of them *are*. Large corporations often use newspaper advertising to prove they intend to obey all nondiscrimination laws governing hiring practices. Government agencies are often required by law to post jobs and have an open period of up to 90 days for applications. In North America, most of these jobs will be seasonal. Help-wanted ads usually start appearing a month to six weeks before the starting date for the job.

As with other employment ads, most appear in the Sunday editions of major newspapers. They are also published in trade publications. Finding a help-wanted ad for a captain's job can require a bit of searching. Few papers have a "Captains Wanted" category. Start looking under headings such as "Professionals" or "Drivers."

There is an art to reading the "helps" in newspapers. Even the few brief sentences in most ads tell you a great deal about what the employer expects. The three ads below are real, although the actual companies have been disguised. The text is exactly as it was printed. If you know how to read between the lines, you can learn more from a short ad than you might think.

> **25T Captains with commercial assistance towing wanted. Chicago and Bar Harbor. Popeye's Towing. Apply: captain@popeyetowing.xxx.**

Popeye's Towing is obviously a company that services broken-down pleasure boats. This is obvious by the requirement that all applicants hold a commercial assistance towing endorsement on their minimum 25-ton licenses. Popeye's has two locations, so the job offered may not be near your home. Applications should be sent by e-mail.

> **Harborfront Now Hiring! 50-ton captains and mates. Must have good personality with people. Call for appointment. No walk-ins. (888) 555-5555.**

In this second ad, Harborfront is looking for masters holding 50-ton licenses. The mention of a "good personality with people" tells you this is a tour boat or water taxi. The captain has to interact with passengers. Harborfront is more formal in its application process. You must call for an appointment. The person doing the hiring does not want to be interrupted by people who just show up at the door.

> **Rockbottom Sound Tours is accepting applications for 100-ton captains for tour boat operation. Position requires two years operating similar**

vessels. Background in boat maintenance preferred. Customer service and public speaking experience necessary. Apply at www.rockbottomsoundtours.xxx.

Rockbottom probably already has a candidate in mind for the position. Note the requirement for experience on "similar vessels." The only way to get that sort of experience is to work in Rockbottom's fleet. So the job will probably be offered to a current employee. This ad is probably just to show proof that the company attempted to reach all qualified applicants. Don't be discouraged. There is still a job opening here. Promoting from within means Rockbottom really doesn't need a captain but rather is seeking a new mate to replace the person it just promoted.

RESPONDING TO AN ADVERTISED JOB

Follow the directions in the ad. Do not get creative. Many employers automatically reject applicants who do not follow instructions. Many companies now require you to fill out an electronic job application online rather than a paper form. Follow that requirement even if you do not have a computer. Borrow a friend's or go to a nearby library to use one of its public computers to e-file your application.

IN-PERSON VISIT

There is never any harm done by asking for work. Getting to know the person who does the hiring can put you at the top of the list for the next job opening. On the other hand, you may only get as far as a secretary who will curtly inform you of the proper way to approach the company. Either way, you have gained valuable information by visiting a potential employer.

You probably won't get a captain job on your first appearance. If the employer likes you, however, there's a good chance you'll be offered work as a mate or deckhand just to keep you around. The hardest thing for a small passenger vessel company is to acquire and retain qualified, trained people. Once you get on the payroll you can put the so-called grapevine to work. A company's need for a new master becomes conversation around the coffeepot among working captains. Often the grapevine gets the word out before the company even knows that one of its captains is going to move to another job.

Smaller companies usually require an in-person cold call. You just walk in and ask about job openings. The reason for this direct approach is simple. The owner usually does the hiring but only when not working on boats or doing paperwork. If you are standing there, he will stop work long enough to shake hands and talk. Don't expect more than a five-minute conversation. A more formal appointment may follow if the company has any job openings.

APPOINTMENTS

A formal appointment for a job interview is normal if you are selected as a candidate for the job after you respond to a help-wanted ad. The usual recommendations apply: arrive early but no more than 15 minutes early. Have your cover letter, résumé, business card, and a copy of your license with you. Put all of this paperwork in an envelope large enough so that the paper does not have to be folded. Write or type the interviewer's name and company name on the envelope.

A day or two before the interview, spend time watching the company's boats in operation. You might even buy a ticket to go for a ride. When the interview comes, this firsthand experience will let you talk knowledgeably about the company's operation. Nothing you can do will impress a potential employer more than demonstrating your interest in his or her business.

THE INTERVIEW

Professional job recruiters pay a lot of attention to the body language of candidates. Not too many ferryboat operators know or care anything about how you hold your arms or cross your legs. But they do know the way a successful captain looks, and you had better look like someone the employer wants as a captain when you step through the door. Try to be a walking version of the company's job description. Walk erect without slouching, have a strong handshake, and speak without hesitation. A few more tips are listed below:

- **Don't fidget:** Keep still during the interview even if you are nervous. One way to hide nervousness is to have something in your hand. Bring a notepad to hold if you need to.
- **Maintain eye contact:** Looking into the eyes of the recruiter helps form a bond between you that will help you get the job,

but do not stare fixedly at the other person. Shifting your gaze from the eyes, to the ears, and then to the shoulders of the interviewer will avoid a "deer in the headlights" appearance. Don't look around the room or out the window.

■ **Never slouch:** Slipping into a classic couch potato slouch gives the impression you are at best lackadaisical and at worst lazy. Neither impression will help your career. Sit fully back in the seat of the chair so you are almost forced to maintain an upright posture. It is possible to use the chair as a prop to make yourself appear more eager and attentive. Angle the chair slightly so you can lean on one arm as you talk to the interviewer. This will give you the body language of someone extremely interested in the process.

COMMUNICATION SKILLS

Your goal in any interview is to sell yourself. Nervousness can get in the way. Many people become chatterboxes when they are under pressure. The result is they give too much information when answering questions. More often than not, this results in talking yourself out of the job. Always give a complete answer to any question, but don't elaborate any more than necessary. If you take more than two breaths to give an answer, you are probably talking too much.

The other end of the communication spectrum is the applicant who becomes almost catatonic during the interview. Once again, this is usually the result of nervousness. No matter how difficult it is, make sure to answer every question you are asked with a complete sentence. Maintaining eye contact actually makes it easier to speak to someone, even a stranger. It may also help to pretend you are talking to your best friend instead of the interviewer.

One way to overcome nervousness is to ask questions about the company and its operations. This helps you avoid chattering or being too quiet. By asking questions you indicate an interest in the company, which in turn shows the interviewer that you genuinely want the job.

ABOUT THE MONEY

Specialists who coach top executives on how to apply for jobs tell their clients never to bring up the subject of salary and benefits early in the interview. If possible, let the company representative broach this subject. Most employers will ask, "How much do you need to take this job?" Applicants are typically afraid to ask the going rate for the job, so they mention a lower wage that is readily agreeable to the company representative. Instead of answering with a dollar amount, it is acceptable to ask, "How much are you offering?"

You should already know where the negotiation is going to end because you should have checked out what the company pays starting captains before you applied for the job. Pay rates for government agencies are public record. Companies do not have to reveal what they pay, but people working within the industry always have a good idea. This is another case where a network of friends helps.

PUFFERY AND EGO

A good captain must demonstrate a firm belief in his or her abilities. The pilothouse is no place for timid people and employers know this. But they aren't looking for captains with overinflated opinions of themselves. Your goal is to appear confident but not ego-driven. The one absolute rule of job applications and interviews is to never claim training or experience that you do not have. Most employers do some background checks beyond just those required by U.S. Coast Guard antidrug regulations. Sooner or later inflated claims of experience or lies about training show up. When they do, the person responsible is invariably discharged.

WHAT TO WEAR

Except when passengers are aboard, wearing a work shirt and blue jeans is the industry norm. For the interview, wear the same type of clothes as the company's workforce. To get your wardrobe right, during your pre-appointment research pay particular attention to what the employees are wearing, particularly the people who work in the front office. Blue jeans and a button-down casual shirt are usually acceptable, but don't wear anything stained or with holes in the knees. T-shirts are also not recommended. Your favorite artwork may be offensive to the person doing the hiring.

CHAPTER 3

CAPTAIN AS ENTREPRENEUR

Accordint to the U.S. Small Business Administration (SBA), the biggest obstacle new entrepreneurs face is underestimating the difficulty of starting a business. Statistics show that 50 percent of all new businesses fail in the first year. A whopping 95 percent fail within the first five years. Vessel operators face more than the ordinary entrepreneurial problems of finding customers and controlling expenses. They also have to face the vagaries of weather and mechanical breakdowns. Whether they operate a six-passenger fishing boat or a 149-passenger ferry, owning a marine business is definitely not for the faint of heart.

Owning and operating such a business may not be right for your spouse and children, and that's something you should consider as you make your plans. The successful entrepreneur is a self-starter, a go-getter. From an American view, you might consider a successful entrepreneur as the iconic pioneer with a rifle slung over his shoulder while he plowed the fields. The hearty pioneers were not lone mountain men. They were families, and they prospered because husbands, wives, and children worked together. Whether you are a male or female captain, keep the picture of the pioneer family in mind as you start your marine business, because the new venture will affect everyone close to you. Without full family support, your entrepreneurial endeavors are likely to fail.

In its advisory materials for starting a business, the SBA points out the importance of family in success or failure. "It's important for family members to know what to expect and for you to be able to trust that they will support you during this time," the agency advises. "There may be financial difficulties until the business becomes profitable, which could take months or years. You may have to adjust to a lower standard of living or put family assets at risk in the short term."

PERSONALITY TRAITS OF AN ENTREPRENEUR

Even if you do have family support, having a strong desire to take people fishing doesn't mean you are cut out to run your own charter business. You may be better off running a headboat for someone else. Being an entrepreneur requires a special kind of personality as well as a number of specific skills. Take stock in yourself before investing a lot of your own time, energy, and money into a private business. The following test was adapted from questions originated by the SBA to help potential entrepreneurs find out if they are made of the "right stuff."

TEST #1 ENTREPRENEUR PROFILE		
QUESTION	YES	NO
1. Do you possess strong willpower and good self-discipline?		
2. Do you prefer following the instructions of others?		
3. Is your family in favor of this project, and will they go along with the strains they will bear?		
4. Do you put off making decisions? Does decision-making come hard for you?		
5. Can you stick to a job even when things are not going as well as expected?		
6. Do you enjoy competition?		
7. Do you enjoy being around people and dealing with them?		
8. Are you ready to lower your standard of living on a temporary basis for the good of your business?		

Give yourself 3 points for answering "yes" to questions 1, 3, 6, 7, and 8 and "no" to 2, 4, and 5. Deduct 3 points for answering "yes" to questions 2, 4, and 5 and "no" to questions 1, 3, 6, 7, and 8. Scoring: below 12, consider working for someone else; 12 to 18, you're a possible entrepreneur; 21 to 24, you fit the profile!

Don't be discouraged by a low score on this test. It is intended more to guide you in making decisions about your career as a licensed mariner. Not everyone has the personal traits that make for a born entrepreneur. This does not mean you cannot be an excellent captain, and keep in mind that all of us change as we age and what wasn't right at a given time may be at another. The results of the test only apply now. Take the test again after reading this book and see how your answers may change.

Reading business-oriented inspirational books like this one is also a great way to buck up your courage. Undoubtedly the most successful of these books is *Think and Grow Rich* by Napoleon Hill. It contains the collected wisdom of more than 500 entrepreneurs. Enrolling in one of the many business entrepreneur courses described below may also change your attitude about risk-taking and your ability to handle decisions. These classes are offered by most junior colleges as continuing education and don't translate into credits toward a degree. You can also develop your skills as an entrepreneur just the way you taught yourself to dock a boat: through practice and perseverance. Successful entrepreneurs demonstrate a set of learned characteristics:

RISK TAKER

Those who succeed at running their own businesses do not fear taking risks. Risk takers are far from gamblers. A gambler depends on luck for success and finds excitement in the turn of a card or the roll of the dice. By comparison, a risk taker knows that good luck comes to those who plan and prepare for it. Risk takers see opportunity in any situation, form plans to take advantage of those opportunities, and then execute those plans. They turn risk into opportunity.

Several years ago a national bird-watching conference came to town. Until then I had never really thought much about looking for birds. An hour wandering around the conference exhibits opened my eyes to the need for a birding cruise on the Portage River that flows through my town. Not two miles upstream the marinas and condominiums disappear into woodlands, mud flats, and creeks. I learned the area is a bird heaven that is on a red-tailed hawk migration route, has a nesting colony of blue herons, is favored by Canada geese, and is home to nearly two dozen pairs of bald eagles.

Attendees at the conference wanted to get close to those birds, and I realized that they could not without a boat. They were finding spots off the road to do their bird-watching, often more than 100 yards from the nearest nest. I figured they'd be interested if I could put them smack in the midst of the birding action, and I was right.

At the time nobody was providing eco-tours on the river. That meant starting a passenger cruise would be risky business. Adding to that risk, I realized that servicing the shallow, muddy backwaters meant a special boat would be needed. Risky business? Sure. But instead of risk I saw opportunity in the hundreds of bird-watchers attending the conference.

SELF-STARTER

There is no boss telling an entrepreneur what to do and when to do it. You have to be self-motivated to succeed.

Once you start your boat business, it will be entirely up to you to organize your time, develop new business, and follow through on details from business cards to engine maintenance. One surprising aspect of self-motivation is that it is largely a learned behavior. You can organize your life so that getting things done becomes almost second nature. Most successful entrepreneurs use punch lists and other techniques to keep track of daily tasks. It almost becomes a game for them to see how soon each day they can get through their to-do lists.

My recognition that a bird-watching cruise opportunity existed did not make anything happen. If those cruises were to become reality, I knew that it was up to me to act. At the time, I had a comfortable job running the yacht race program for a major yacht club. That gave me more than enough to do when combined with my other pursuits. It was tempting to drop the whole bird-watching idea and continue plodding along as I had been for a couple of years. But in the past I had started two magazines and helped put a party cruise line on the water, and each effort was born of a vision I had about an opportunity I believed I could turn into a business enterprise. The bird-watching cruise opportunity was too tempting to pass up.

PERSEVERANCE

Successful entrepreneurs demonstrate a strong drive to achieve and are goal-oriented people. No business runs itself. Most sole proprietors report spending 60 or more hours a week growing their business. To start my eco-tour venture I needed a boat that could practically push its way through a wet handkerchief. My wallet permitted only a used pontoon boat that had seen better days. When I found the right boat and began the operation, I soon found I was working very long hours to get the whole thing moving.

At 5:00 A.M. each morning I was rounding up sandwiches, breakfast pastries, and coffee for the day's adventure. By 7:00 A.M. we were on the water seeking loons, snowy egrets, great black-back gulls, and eagles. At about 2:00 P.M. I would be thanking my guests as I ushered them off the boat. Changing from my white captain's shirt into work clothes, I then spent an hour or so cleaning up the boat. Most days I also had a couple of hours of boat or engine maintenance to do to be ready for the next morning's adventure.

Today, the water taxi business that grew out of those eco-tours is solid enough that I can hire a real mechanic to work on my boat's engine when necessary. I still do most of the boat maintenance, but I do it while my second boat under the command of a hired captain is making money for my company. It took six years or so to get my business to the point where my workday approximates eight hours during our operating season.

CREATIVITY

To succeed you will need to be innovative and unafraid of trying new ideas. It isn't necessary to compose music like Mozart or paint like Picasso to be an entrepreneur, but you do need to have the curiosity to find innovative solutions to problems. Making my eco-tour business a reality required finding some creative financing. I had to involve the seller of the pontoon boat as a lender. Considering that we were total strangers I had to do a bit of creative talking. The boat was on a trailer, but my Volkswagen Rabbit was not a suitable tow vehicle. I traded a load-leveling hitch for the use of an oversized pickup truck, and I'd solved the tow vehicle problem.

Dockage is always a problem for a commercial operation. None of the marinas would allow a commercial passenger vessel because of parking problems and liability considerations. It didn't take me long to find a waterfront restaurant with a section of wharf too shallow for its customers to use. I agreed to give the restaurant all of the food catering business in return for free use of that shallow dock. Creative financing had kept my out-of-pocket expenses to under $3,000 by the time the first passengers set foot on the boat.

PEOPLE SKILLS

In most start-up marine operations you will be your own sales force, customer relations department, and hospitality staff. In addition, you will have to negotiate with bankers, marinas, and cranky mechanics. All of these interactions require good people skills. There is no room for a bad attitude.

By now it should be obvious that my bird-watching cruises got started on other people's money and using other people's property. I had to convince at least a half-dozen people to get involved with my dream, which took good people skills on my part. River cruising by its nature requires going past the same scenery twice, once going upriver and again coming back down. Once the first eco-cruise left the dock, I discovered the need for the ultimate people skill: hospitality.

Every magician practices a line of patter, the spiel that goes along with the illusion. What you hear sounds spontaneous, but it is carefully rehearsed for maximum effect. I found the same technique worked with my bird cruises. My patter was based on making passengers feel like they were old friends getting a special tour of the river not given to ordinary people. Along the way, I had a few stock jokes. "Over there is where the barge sank in 1932," I would say. Heads would swivel to view an empty stretch of water. "You didn't expect to see it, did you?" I would ask. "It sank; there's nothing to see."

While the joke may not be all that funny, it was a part of my talk and people seemed to enjoy it. Consider these angles as you deal with the public. People like to be entertained, and sometimes a captain has to put on a stage hat to make a business enterprise viable.

TOLERANCE

Not everything will go as planned. You won't be able to live up to your own demands. Other people will fail to perform. Whatever happens, to be successful you have to roll with the punches and keep going.

After two extremely successful seasons with the eco-tours, the city decided to do some economic revitalization. The on-street parking used by my customers was transformed into wide brick walks studded with trees in a process called "streetscaping." My sign was torn down and a request to put it back up was refused because of new zoning laws.

In short, in the name of economic revitalization the government walled me off from my customers and took away their parking. June was cold and July was even colder when it came to my cash box. I wanted to kick someone. However, anger never does any good. Instead, I searched for a new route for my boat. By late July my operation had a new home in a nearby city. Today it has grown into a two-boat fleet, and we are actively seeking a larger third boat to break into corporate and wedding charters.

REQUIRED SKILLS

Creativity, perseverance, and tolerance are general requirements for all entrepreneurs. In addition, every type of business has other requirements, such as specialized education or licensing. In your profession, a U.S. Coast Guard license enables you to carry passengers for hire. This license is designed to ensure that captains have a working knowledge of the Rules of the Road, navigation, and safety at sea. However, it takes more than seamanship to keep a marine business going. You have to be as handy with a wrench and a screwdriver as you are with calculators, spreadsheets, and business management techniques.

Earlier you took a short test to see whether you have the personality to be a successful entrepreneur. This next test is designed to see whether you possess the skills and tools necessary to operate a commercial vessel. You're not alone, though. You should have family support and the support of hired help when it is needed.

Most start-up charter fishing skippers, for instance, have the tools and knowledge to keep their boats running, but they often lack the ability to keep their financial records in order. Often, the spouse possesses these skills so that as a couple they are able to keep the whole business functioning. Like the first test, this one will help you identify potential strengths and weaknesses that you should be aware of before you start your business. The more "yes" answers on this second test, the better your chances are for success.

TEST #2 YOUR SKILLS AND EXPERIENCE		
SKILL AND EXPERIENCE	YES	NO
1. Do you possess the mechanical skills to perform repairs and maintenance on your boat?		
2. Do you possess the tools necessary to make repairs?		
3. Do you have the basic business skills needed to operate a start-up company?		
4. Do you have the office equipment (computer, fax machine, etc.) to successfully run a business?		
5. Have you ever held a job as a manager or supervisor?		
6. Have you had any formal business training?		
7. Do you have the special knowledge required for your particular business (fishing, ecology, etc.)?		
8. Are you willing to go back to school to learn new skills needed to operate your business?		

It is possible to hire bookkeepers, mechanics, and even someone to answer the telephone. Unfortunately, few start-up businesses have the working capital to pay for these services. Instead of spending money, the entrepreneur has to revert to what is euphemistically called "sweat equity" to get things done. In other words, the owner of a new company wears a lot of hats. He or she goes from being captain of the ship into bookkeeper, mechanic, or booking agent mode. Working overtime is not enough, however, if you do not know what you are doing. Learning what you need to know from the outset is an important step in starting a successful new business.

LEARNING NEW SKILLS

Getting the new skills you will need to operate a successful business is not hard or expensive. Look to your local junior or community college. These institutions are springing up across the country as an alternative to the traditional four-year university. The courses are designed to provide high-school graduates with useful skills in fields where a traditional degree is not required. In addition, a junior college allows students to earn the first two years of a university degree at a lower cost, and it also offers enrichment courses open to the general public that don't count as credit toward a degree.

The courses open to the public are usually offered once or twice a year. They provide information on all aspects of a new start-up from financing to taxes. The sessions are an excellent way for you to meet representatives of various government agencies that may be helpful. Here are a few classes you may want to consider.

Basic Bookkeeping

Most small businesses keep their own records of income and expenses, in addition to tracking accounts receivable (money people owe you), inventory, sales and marketing results, and business growth or decline on an annual basis. Taking a bookkeeping class to give you an understanding of how to keep your own books and how to avoid costly pitfalls is a good first step, though you may benefit from more complex business classes as well.

At the very least, though, accurate bookkeeping is the best defense against a tax audit, and it will provide you with a realistic view of your cash flow to determine whether you are working in the black (making a profit) or whether you are working in the red (losing money because you spend more than you earn; this is also known as deficit spending). Look for a course that explains how to keep track of your income received, expenses, and uncollected payments from customers.

If your state or local government imposes sales tax on services, you will also want to learn about collecting this money and making payments to the government. A large number of small businesses go broke because they spend sales tax money owed to the state on operating expenses, and when the taxman comes calling, the owner doesn't have the money to pay up.

Computer Skills

These days everything from bookkeeping to finding and keeping clients is done on computers. Learning how to operate the necessary software is essential. Look for classes that provide an understanding of how the Internet can help promote your business. The easiest way to keep financial records is on a computer using prepared accounting software such as Peachtree or QuickBooks. Classes in computerized accounting usually focus on one brand of software, so purchase yours only after taking the class to get the right brand and version. Home accounting programs do not contain all of the tax, accounts receivable, and report functions needed to fully understand your business.

In addition to an accounting package, you will need a word processing program to write letters and prepare other printed documents. Low-cost programs to prepare mailing labels or print business cards are also helpful.

Marketing

A few colleges offer classes in how to promote your business through the process of marketing, which is far more than just buying advertising. It is well worth learning as much about sales, marketing, advertising, and public relations as you possibly can. A class is a good way to get started, and there are many excellent books on these subjects in your local library. Read some of them to augment what you learn in the class.

You can lose big money by buying the wrong ads. You have to know which publication will reach your target audience, and, once you've identified a potential publication, you have to decide whether the cost for the space will result in enough actual sales to justify the investment. You have to know whether you want a display ad (an ad on a page) or a classified ad (text only or text with photo in the classified section). Consider the free boating magazines distributed at marinas, bait shops, and chandleries as good places to start. The rates are relatively low for display ads, and people do read these publications.

As I said, marketing means more than simply buying ads and waiting for the phone to ring. Advertising must be part of a larger effort. Try to get yourself written about in the local newspaper by making a personal appearance, by giving a free fishing trip to a charity as a prize, or by sending news releases out about upcoming events. This is called public relations or free media.

Direct-mail coupons cost a fair amount for postage and printing, but they do get results, depending on the nature of your business. Of course, you should begin building a mailing list at the start of your business. Your existing clients are the first ones to include, but try to come up with other ways to get names and addresses. Some businesses send newsletters to customers and potential prospects or special offers limited only to those receiving the direct mail.

Signage, billboards (outdoor advertising), promotional events, sponsorship of charity events—the list of what you can do to promote your business is extensive. The most important thing to remember is to come up with a marketing plan that includes more than just buying ads and to take small steps first and track the results of your efforts. A savvy marketer and self-promoter is far more likely to succeed, whereas someone who does very little in this area is far less likely to prosper. Start with the classes and the books and have some fun with it. See Chapter 9 for more details on marketing your business.

Auto Mechanics

Mechanical engine problems are the most common reasons why boats break down. Continuing education classes in automotive engine repair are available through many high schools and most junior colleges. While marine engines are different from their automobile counterparts, the techniques and tools used to repair them are the same. A good course in engine mechanics provides the basic training needed to keep your vessel running.

Marine Mechanics

True marine mechanic classes are scarce compared to automotive instruction. However, if a nearby junior college offers classes in marine engine and drive repairs, take them. The money and time will be well spent. A single lost day of peak season operation can cost more than the tuition for these classes. Even if you never turn a wrench, knowing what goes wrong and how to fix it will help you get the most for your money when dealing with marine mechanics and repair shops.

Costs for college-level training vary. A single night class on how to start a new business is usually free at a junior college or adult school program held in your town. Longer, more in-depth courses may cost several hundred dollars. There is a tendency to see those dollars as wasted because they do not apply directly to getting on the water. The opposite is true. You will have a far better chance of earning enough money to stay "out there" if you have the knowledge and training to keep your business functioning properly.

CHAPTER 4

RESEARCHING YOUR BUSINESS

N
o competent skipper steams full speed into unfamiliar water without consulting a chart. The risks of running aground or encountering other dangers are too great. Prudent captains study the best way to approach a new harbor by learning the landmarks and the positions of key aids to navigation before heading in. Whenever possible, local knowledge is obtained from another mariner familiar with the area.

You need to apply the same level of caution and the same level of effort in terms of study when you begin planning the start of your own business. If you can do it when operating your boat, you can certainly do it when laying the foundation for your new life as an entrepreneur. The first step starts with research—and plenty of it.

ON MARKET RESEARCH

This may sound a little scary, but before I go into specific details on how you can find the best route to your new business, there's something I have to tell you: market research is important, but sometimes it doesn't work. Knowing how to respond in that worst-case scenario is worth a few words of explanation, and perhaps the best example I can use to illustrate my point is the Ford Motor Company in the late 1950s and in the mid-1960s.

Fortune 500 companies never go into a new type of business or launch a new product without studying the market first. The objective of the research is to determine whether the idea for the business or product is viable. Sometimes the results of the research are surprising when it turns out that many apparently good ideas simply do not fulfill enough need in the marketplace to justify pursuing them.

A prime example of market research gone bad is Ford Motor Company's introduction of the Edsel in September 1957. The car was supposed to represent the cusp of automotive innovation, but it turned out to be more marketing hype than anything else. It was also more expensive than similar cars from competing manufacturers, and, in short, the public rejected it. That was quite a blow to Ford, which had spent many millions on its development.

Ford learned its lesson. The company's next big introduction was the sporty Mustang in 1964, which was designed to appeal to the burgeoning youth market resulting from large numbers of baby boomers coming of driving age. The Mustang was economical and attractive, and buyers were offered a wide variety of options that made it possible to almost customize it according to individual preferences. The response was impressive. The Mustang created its own niche in the automotive market called (in honor of the horse on the Mustang's grille) "pony cars." In its first year of full production, more than 400,000 Mustangs were sold.

There are some important lessons to be learned from Ford's fiascos and triumphs. First, mistakes in business cost money. Ford was a big enough corporation to survive the multi-million-dollar debacle of the Edsel, but few entrepreneurs have pockets that deep. Bad market research that leads to establishing a business that fails to meet demand in the marketplace almost always leads to economic hardships for the entrepreneur and his or her family. In some cases, it results in bankruptcy. But, like Ford, everyone blunders from time to time. You may make mistakes, too. The trick is to never make the same one twice and to avoid making any if you possibly can.

In business, if you find yourself embarked on a path that is obviously not working out financially, you must not be afraid to cut your losses after carefully assessing your situation. Ford did not try to save the Edsel, even though its market research indicated it should have been hugely successful. Once it had obviously failed, Ford dropped the line and went on building other cars, and it made heaps of money on the Mustang. Entrepreneurs often have such an emotional attachment to their projects that they keep throwing good money after bad, and that just makes things worse. Businesses exist to make money. When that doesn't happen, or stops happening, you must have the courage to cut your losses and find a more profitable way to spend your time and money.

An initial failure doesn't mean you have to give up entirely. You may just have to change your focus. Sadly, many entrepreneurs faced with a failing business overlook the seeds of success buried within their foundering enterprise. Everything gets trashed, including those seeds.

I learned this lesson the hard way when I walked away from a business unrelated to boats. About 30 years ago I was trying to keep publishing a regional magazine despite a lack of capital to grow the business. Advertisers told us that our circulation was too small for them to want to buy advertising space, but they liked our production and design work, and a few asked if we could do booklets and pamphlets for them.

Even though the brochure work was profitable, I was so discouraged by the failure of the magazine that I got out of the business, giving away some elements to another entrepreneur. He went into the business of producing brochures and other materials for museums and visitors' bureaus. That part of the business continues making money today, without me, under the management of a more visionary owner.

FINDING YOUR BUSINESS ROUTE

Commercial enterprises are broadly divided into manufacturing, retail, and services. We all understand these divisions. Our boats were manufactured by companies that transformed raw materials into watercraft. Boats are manufactured products, and the dealer or broker who sold you yours is in retail. When something goes wrong with our boats, we call service companies to make repairs. On the water, a service business can provide transportation, entertainment, leisure pursuits such as fishing, instruction, towing, diving, and much more.

There is a big difference between an engine repair service business and operating a passenger vessel. As the name of our branch of the service industry implies, direct interaction with the customer also makes small passenger vessels a part of what is known as the hospitality business. We must be both a service provider and host or hostess to our customers. It is no exaggeration to say that happy customers are the products of the hospitality industry. This component of success is the most overlooked aspect of passenger vessel operations. Whether you want to go fishing, run eco-tours, or serve dinner afloat, the first requirement is to satisfy your customers. This process starts by identifying an unfulfilled customer need (market research) and then filling that need beyond your customers' expectations (service).

Open any book on entrepreneurship and you will see a chapter or two on the broad subject of market research and segmentation. The idea is quite simple. In order to sell your service, it is necessary to tailor your efforts to those people (market segment) who are most likely to purchase the service you wish to offer. The critical first step in any business is identifying the overall market and then segmenting the market into a tightly defined group of customers that you can reasonably service.

I call the process of market research for a passenger vessel "route finding." This odd name comes out of something I noticed when I first entered the business. Success in the passenger vessel industry never seems to come from painfully building a business in the middle of nowhere. Instead, profits flow from tapping into a pre-existing need.

For instance, you won't sell many tickets on a sightseeing boat that cruises in places where people don't already go to see the sights. Bar Harbor in Maine is an excellent example. Tens of thousands of people visit there every year as part of a trip to Acadia National Park. The sightseeing cruise boats in the harbor benefit directly from Acadia's popularity. That particular spot may already be saturated from a marketing perspective. In other words, others beat you to it. However, the example still makes my point. Go where the people are and give them something they want and choose a location that's not already saturated. This is easier said than done, but savvy professional mariners continue to do it all the time.

Likewise, you can't sell fishing charters in an area where the fishing is bad or where the species of fish aren't desirable. My personal passenger vessel epiphany was that to succeed I would have to find a route serving an existing public need and then fulfill it. This has become my first rule for identifying a profitable business route for a passenger vessel.

Rule 1: Find an existing customer base and develop a business to capitalize on that group of people.

My successful eco-tour route allowed people to see from the water a variety of bird-nesting areas they had already come to see on land. My boat allowed them to venture into the midst of that wildlife habitat and to view it from a different, more exciting perspective. Until the boat tour, their bird-spotting had been from muddy riverbanks or from the side of the road. The birds were often several hundred yards away.

Note that I did not invent bird-watching in the area. Bird-watchers were already "flocking" there during the spring and fall migratory seasons. Customer demand already existed. My birding tours were a logical outgrowth of existing bird-watching activity on the river. Potential customers were already waiting for a boat that would take them into the backwaters where they could not drive or walk. All I had to do was fill that existing need.

Another example of the concept of fulfilling an existing need is my current water taxi route. Our two boats travel only 984 feet from one bank to the other of the Maumee River. However, on one side there are several major hotels and concert venues. On the other, there are the five best restaurants in town, but walking by way of the nearest bridge involves a hike of more than a mile through city traffic. The need for a shortcut across the river existed even before I boarded my first passenger.

Rule 2: Provide the service your customer wants, not the service you want to provide.

In a way, this rule is just a restating of Rule 1 but worded for a different purpose. Many beginning entrepreneurs make the egocentric mistake of thinking that what they like will appeal to everyone, but that's not necessarily so. Most people prefer prime rib, but McDonald's proved the money is in selling hamburgers to people who don't have time for a sit-down dinner.

Hauling passengers 984 feet across a river and then doing it again 80 or 90 more times in an afternoon is grueling, mindless work. What makes it attractive is that on good days as many as 1,500 people want to take that short ride. I would rather be doing harbor cruises, but only a handful of people want that service on our river. So I find myself setting the unenviable record for river crossings just to have the privilege of counting the money.

Traditional market research usually does not need to take into account the infrastructure required for a business to succeed. Paved streets, water, electricity, and telephones are assumed to be available almost everywhere. Routes for passenger vessels only exist in specific areas. This is the biggest difference between researching a retail business and a passenger vessel. No market exists for a boat where there is insufficient infrastructure. The need for such things as parking spaces for passengers and a suitable dock is so critical that they must be taken into account during the market research phase—the route-finding process.

Rule 3: Customers must have easy access to your business. If they come by car, there must be adequate parking nearby at a fair price.

As I mentioned earlier, after two successful years of doing eco-tours on the river, a municipal revitalization program eliminated the area where my bird-watching customers parked their cars. It was a bitter blow, but it taught me another key to developing a successful route: passengers must be able to get to your boat. People travel by car. So, with few exceptions, a boat business must have nearby parking lots that charge reasonable rates. The rule of thumb in retailing is that people want to park within sight of your front door. Shopping malls sometimes exaggerate their front entrances by making them so large that even outlying parking places still appear to be within sight of the door.

An advantage of my water taxi route is that hotel guests who make up a large percentage of my passengers are not concerned with parking. They either arrived by air and do not have a car in town, or they have parked their car in the hotel garage. Few of my passengers park in the downtown garages and come across the river for dinner. People will pay for parking but not if they then have to pay an additional fee for the water taxi. Who can blame them? It is cheaper to drive across the river where parking is free. Of course, that negates any need for my water taxi service.

Rule 4: You must have long-term control over your permanent "home" dock and any other piers necessary to your business.

No Home Port

Carl and Bill had been sailing buddies since college. It seemed only natural to turn their mutual hobby into a business. So they pooled their resources and purchased a gorgeous 74-foot schooner that could carry up to 49 passengers. They became so engrossed in getting their dream trucked across the country that they neglected the key issue of where to dock the boat. Once the boat arrived, they started looking for a place to put it. They ran into a wall of open palms asking for money. They discovered that the perception among marina owners and city officials was that commercial vessels can afford to pay almost any price for a place to dock. The trouble was that Carl and Bill had spent their last dime getting the boat in the water. There was no up-front money left in the kitty for dockage.

I have learned this lesson well. Today, my company has a long-term contract to manage the docks that our boats operate from. This means we have to supply "dock boys" (half are girls, but the customers don't always notice) and charge fees to transient pleasure boats visiting the restaurants. Managing the docks is little more than a break-even proposition, but the contract to manage the docks is pure gold because it gives us total control over our wharfage.

The accompanying business route assessment checklist is intended as a guideline for assessing your potential passenger vessel business. It contains those elements that I have found critical. You may add to or alter the list to meet your needs. The purpose of this checklist is to force a critical assessment of the proposed route in terms of potential success. We'll discuss all of these items briefly immediately below and then examine some of them in greater detail later.

ROUTE ASSESSMENT CHECKLIST			
ITEM	GOOD	AVERAGE	POOR
1. Route has existing purpose			
2. Existing customer base			
3. Competition in market			
4. Home dockage available			
5. Long-term control of dock			
6. Customer parking nearby			
7. Departure area visibility			
8. Amount of surrounding activity			
9. Surrounding activity prices			
10. Length of season			

1. **Existing purpose:** As noted, if you intend to go fishing, the route should provide lots of fish. If eco-touring is the plan, the route must have lots of scenic habitat with abundant wildlife.
2. **Customer base:** It is expensive and difficult to draw people somewhere they do not regularly visit. A profitable business finds ways to tap into existing groups of potential customers, particularly if those groups return year after year.
3. **Competition:** This is a two-edged sword. Competition means many businesses are spending money to promote the area in which you plan to operate. That makes your job easier. However, there are only so many customers for any type of passenger service. Too

much competition means that everyone gets too small a share for profitability. See below for further discussion of this topic.

4. **Home dockage:** Even the smallest six-pack charter boat needs a home dock where customers can board. Few marinas or yacht clubs permit commercial operations from their docks. It is necessary to find a home dock that allows commercial boarding.

5. **Long-term dock control:** Businesses build from year to year. It is impossible to obtain the growth necessary for profitability if the home dock is constantly changed. You must gain long-term control over your main point of departure in the form of a long-term lease or some other type of contract.

6. **Customer parking:** As noted, customers must be able to park nearby at a reasonable price.

7. **Departure area visibility:** Signs are great, but the vessel itself is the cheapest advertisement. The best route is one that provides dockage where the boat can be seen. In addition, the route should go past potential customers watching from shore.

8. **Surrounding activity:** Customers have only so much money to spend at one time. Your business is competing for those dollars with gift shops, restaurants, museums, miniature golf courses, and every other business on shore. Even anglers go out for dinner or buy souvenirs for the kids. If people come for shore activities, a water business may fail unless it becomes a natural extension of the existing tourist attraction. If it does, the surrounding activities can actually work to your advantage. People may come to your area to visit a wax museum, relax in a riverside park, or see a show at the civic center, but if you're visible and offering the right service, you might get their business, too.

9. **Surrounding activity prices:** It is no secret that the cost of living rises or falls with location, as do the prices for various forms of entertainment like those in Rule 8. Your business has to be structured so that it can make a profit within the limitations of the prevailing prices of tourism-related activities within the area you serve.

10. **Length of season:** It can come as a shock to discover how few profitable days there are in one year. Where I live on the Great Lakes, the big money season starts on June 15, when school lets out,

and it ends on Labor Day. That means a successful passenger business has to make a profit in just 75 operating days encompassing only 10 weekends. Subtract points for rainy days.

Importance of Long-Term Commitments

An interisland ferry line was started by a group of local investors on the Great Lakes. Rather than tie themselves into a long-term contract, they elected to go on a month-to-month basis for their dockage at the "money island" of their route. Things got into a fine mess when the start-up costs exceeded the passenger ticket revenues and a monthly dock payment was forgotten. One morning their captain was refused permission to dock when he pulled in with a load of passengers. Needless to say, a ferry line without a destination can't survive.

COMPETITION

Be especially wary if you discover what appears to be a route for a new boat line on which there is no competition. The lack of competition in a market may indicate that there is no money being spent in that venue. Businesses do not survive long where there is no income. If you think a competition-free situation is too good to be true, you are almost certainly correct.

Competition is something that must be taken into account when starting a new business, even though this factor is completely out of your control. Beginning business operators tend to overemphasize their competition. They turn it into some dreaded ogre with the power to hoard all the customers and money in the market. Few competitors are that big or that powerful. Even the giant retailer Wal-Mart still has competition. The fact of the matter is that good competition actually makes your company stronger and helps enlarge the overall market.

Be wary if your competition controls the wharfage you need to be successful. For instance, my company controls the "money dock" on the restaurant side of the river. We welcome anyone but reserve the right to charge commercial vessels fees for each passenger landed or picked up. A competing water taxi company would be forced to increase the gross income of my company, helping my bottom line. That is not a recipe for successful competition against my boats.

VISIBILITY

It is becoming increasingly more difficult to keep a passenger vessel operation visible to the public. This goes well beyond just people seeing your boat. It involves the overall process of keeping your business in the minds of potential customers. If they cannot "see" you in their mind when they think of the services you offer, you probably will not get their money.

Three factors are against you. The first is the cost of advertising. The other is the trend toward antiseptically clean waterfronts where commercial operations are forced to hide from view. The third problem is related to the second, the growing number of antisign regulations in port cities. Keep in mind the need for high visibility of your boat when analyzing the possible success of a new route. An invisible boat is a money-losing boat. The public has a demonstrated lazy streak. Most people won't seek out a new business that is off the beaten track.

THE ACTION

People congregate where there is a lot happening. The desire for "action" explains the three-ring circus. It is also the driving force behind the success of tourist destinations like the Wisconsin Dells, Pigeon Forge, Branson, and Orlando. Action and excitement encourage visitors to stay extra days and spend more money.

Few people choose to visit sleepy backwater towns and even fewer choose to stay overnight. This is true even of places just off major interstate highways. When picking a route, it is best to find a home dock in a busy tourist location. No matter how scenic or quaint, avoid a quiet location in "drive-through" country, unless you have a huge advertising and public relations budget. As a small business owner, it is always more profitable for you to follow the money rather than to make the money follow you.

The cost of dockage in a prime tourist area can be high. In some cases, dockage may cost more than fuel and other operating expenses. Your start-up business may not be able to afford the monthly or seasonal charge. It may be possible to negotiate a payment schedule you can afford. For instance, you may offer a per-passenger fee in place of part or all of the monthly charge. This arrangement makes the dock owner a "partner" in your venture. It is in the best interest of the owner to make sure you have the visibility and customer access for success.

SEASON

Regardless of where your business is located, the length of the season is determined by the number of days during which a sufficient number of customers exist to make serving them profitable. Depending on the nature of your business, a location in a warmer climate usually lengthens your season, whereas a location in a colder climate shortens it. But the weather isn't necessarily the only key factor. Other factors that determine when and how long customers will be present in your market are important as well. There are slow times in Florida, just as there are slow times on the Great Lakes and along both coasts in the United States.

For example, the weather in New Jersey is nice in June, but the action on the waterfront doesn't really pick up until the kids get out of school for summer vacation. July and August are peak months for the beach crowd, and these months are among the most profitable for fishing businesses, both for headboats and for private charters. The same goes for tour boats operating on Barnegat Bay, a scenic and shallow body of water nestled behind New Jersey's barrier islands.

Don't expect the actions of people to be rational. Charter captains discover that even fishing has seasons that aren't necessarily related to the behavior of the fish. In western Lake Erie, the customers come seeking walleye during the spring and fall. Plenty of fish can still be found in midsummer, but the number of anglers decreases because of habits learned by their fathers 40 years ago, when Lake Erie was recovering from its "dead" period of the late 1950s and the 1960s. The relatively small population of walleye back then meant that summer was too unproductive for most anglers to spend money hiring a boat. That is no longer true, but those old habits remain.

My bird-watching cruises had the same seasonality. Birders follow the migratory habits of their feathered friends. The estuary served by my boat is on one of the largest flyways of the North American continent. This means that during spring and fall a huge variety of geese, ducks, and shorebirds pass through. They are accompanied by flocks of birders with binoculars and notepads on which to document sightings. The two big attractions of my cruise were the blue heron nesting colony and a half-dozen pairs of American bald eagles. Both are active all summer long, but the flocks of birders disappear for a very good reason. During the summer the overall number of bird species declines. It becomes less likely for an individual observer to add to his or her personal "life-list" of birds spotted.

It is virtually impossible for a single small business to change the habits of its customers. Instead, the business must adapt to the customer base. Charter fishing skippers often follow the fish up or down the coast during seasonal migrations. Innovation can pay dividends. On the Great Lakes, some skippers actually move their operations—boats and all—from Lake Erie in the spring to Lake Michigan during the summer months. This allows them to tap the walleye segment of the market during the early season and the Coho salmon anglers in the summer. Fall sees them trailering their rigs back to Lake Erie for late-season walleye and fall perch fishing.

My solution was to change from six-hour birding cruises to two-hour eco-tours during the summer months. This shorter trip appealed more to the summer tourists and even some local residents. My summer customers seldom brought binoculars and none carried a life-list diary. They just wanted a couple of hours on the water seeing interesting scenery and to perhaps get a glimpse of a bald eagle.

RESEARCHING A BUSINESS ROUTE

In business school they talk a lot about market research. Think of this as precruising a route by checking the chart for rocks and shoals along the way or reading the pilot book to discover any vital information not printed on the chart. Sometimes the chart and books will convince you to alter your course or change destinations. The same thing happens when you properly research a business. Sometimes major changes have to be made to your plans before the first customer is welcomed. Just as navigators have charts, there are lots of sources for information to guide your business plan. These are listed in the accompanying table, and some are addressed in greater detail later.

BUSINESS CLIMATE INFORMATION SOURCES	
SOURCE	INFORMATION AVAILABLE
State fish and game commissions	Guide licenses; most popular species of fish; most popular areas to fish; predictions of fishing in future years; number and distribution of charter boats; restrictions and bag limits
Charter captain associations	Number and distribution of charter fishing boats; most popular species of fish; problems with local game wardens or other law enforcement
Local tourism bureaus	Estimated size of local tourism market; increase or decrease in number of visitors; most popular tourism activities; free or low-cost promotion of your business
Chambers of commerce	Scope and size of local business activity; issues with local government; general business activity; networking with other local businesses
Public libraries	Small business start-up materials in reference section; past copies of local newspapers for news about your industry; local histories
State divisions of watercraft	State regulations on six-pack charter boats; registration of documented vessels; state environmental regulations

PUBLIC LIBRARIES

These venerable institutions are gold mines of business information. The reference section of most big-city libraries will have an extensive collection of books and information on starting a new business. In one place you will find state laws and regulations as well as publications from the federal Small Business Administration. A local public library in the port where you plan to base your operation may have annual reports and other publications of the visitors' bureau or chamber of commerce. If so, you can study them without losing your anonymity. Looking through the past year's issues of the local newspaper should give you a clear picture of the political climate and any legislative issues that may impact your business.

TOURISM BUREAUS AND CHAMBERS OF COMMERCE

Small passenger vessel companies fall into the travel and tourism industry. This is true as much for a charter fishing boat as it is for a water taxi or a dinner or excursion boat. One of the first things to assess, therefore, is the general tourism business climate where you intend to base your operation.

Two organizations can provide information about the health of the local travel and tourism industry. One is the local chamber of commerce. The other is the local travel board or convention and visitors' bureau. The chamber is a private organization of businesses, while a regional bureau will likely be an arm of local or state government. Both can provide a wealth of information about the number and types of travel-related businesses. You may also be able to get some idea of the annual number of visitors and data about the money they spend locally.

Not all places are equally attractive to a new business. Some areas are growing in popularity, while others are beginning to lose their attractiveness. Some local governments have adopted restrictions that discourage new businesses. Trends are more important in assessing the tourism business climate than current statistics. As a rule, you are looking for an area where the number of potential customers is rising while local restrictions on business remain static or are being removed.

Beware of sharing too much information about your plans with either the chamber or the bureau. The chamber as an organization may be helpful, but many of its members will be your competition after you go into business. The same is true of the visitors' bureau. It will already be working closely with the passenger vessel companies operating in the vicinity. It is quite likely that any details you divulge about your planned business will be communicated to your competition by nightfall.

Early on, you may want to confine your contact with either organization to asking for published annual reports and other documents on the local travel and tourism industry. Wait until you are ready to announce your new business to the public before asking more in-depth questions.

ASSOCIATIONS

Groups of charter captains or passenger vessel operators exist to promote their specific segments of the market. A few are closed societies that actually work to keep new businesses from starting, though this is rare. Most industry groups welcome new members and provide sources for information you will need in planning your new operation. While the individual members may be your worst competition on the water, the organization can be a gold mine of valuable information and friendships. Of particular value are the programs many of these associations offer that are designed to meet U.S. Coast Guard drug testing regulations.

YOUR TARGET CUSTOMER

A neophyte charter captain is likely to claim everyone who wants to go fishing as a customer base. This naive view of the actual customer base seems logical because a fishing boat wants to attract people who like to fish. In reality, customers are too complex for such a simplistic approach.

Not every angler is looking for the same fish. Some want the bass that lurk in quiet freshwater lakes, while others want the striped bass of coastal salt water. Two completely different fish attract a totally different set of anglers. On the Great Lakes near my home, charter captains know there is a difference between customers who want to catch walleye and those who fish for yellow perch. Each different type of angler represents a *segment* of the overall fishing market.

MARKET SEGMENTATION

Big companies consider market segmentation as a strategic tool for allocating their resources. They use a variety of complex statistical measurements such as "cluster analysis" and "factor analysis." These are combined with demographic research into the sex, age, and personal interests of potential customers. Done on the level of Wal-Mart or General Motors this is expensive business for professionals. However, it is possible to do effective market research on your own for very little money. Most of the time all you have to do is listen carefully to what your potential customers say they want.

When I started my bird-watching cruises, I assumed that every birder would want to ride my boat. Not so. The overall population of bird-watchers broadly divides into two different groups. I discovered the differences between these two groups while trying to market my cruises for the first time.

The occasion was a convention where I purchased an exhibition booth. At first, people were curious but not motivated. So I began to listen to their conversations. Some were talking about life-list numbers. Others were discussing the coastal estuary habitat where my boat operated. Instead of promoting my boat, I listened. What I heard was that bird-watchers are not all alike. From their conversations I realized there were two different groups of people visiting my table, each group with a separate set of customer needs.

There is a segment of the bird-watching market that only seeks new birds to add to their life-list. This is a personal list of all the various species of birds spotted by an individual. Some people have thousands of birds on their lists and are constantly seeking new ones to add. The other large segment of bird people is more interested in the habitat and lifestyles of the different species. In other words, they don't want to just "see" the birds, they actually want to "watch" them. Just like different bird species, the habits of these two types of birders differ considerably.

The life-list birder:

- is constantly on the move, searching new territory
- is primarily interested in recording as many birds as possible
- is often a solitary bird spotter, avoiding groups because they tend to scare shy birds away

The habitat and lifestyle birder:

- prefers to go where the birds live and wait to see what they do in everyday activities
- observes birds carefully and lengthily and is not satisfied with a quick glance at yet another species to add to a life-list
- tends toward small group activities with shared spotting, often traveling in pairs with friends or spouses

Listening to my customers allowed me to define them into relatively homogeneous subgroups. In everyday language, I had segmented my market by discovering that birders with a primary interest in life-list numbers are not good candidates for a boat ride. On the other hand, those birders who are primarily motivated by a desire to enjoy wildlife are hot prospects as customers. I had segmented my market. This allowed me to eliminate from my marketing efforts those people who weren't going to purchase my service. From that moment on, I could apply all of my resources to reaching the hot prospects.

Market segmentation is an economic necessity even for a small start-up business. Advertising a fishing charter, bird-watching cruise, or any other small passenger vessel service to the entire population of the country is cost-prohibitive. There are 300 million Americans, most living too far away or having no interest in your particular offering. Even advertising to everyone in your *city* is a waste of money. Like it or not, they are *not* all realistic potential customers. Segmenting the market allows you to focus your precious advertising and promotion dollars on those people most likely to be customers.

MARKET PRICE

There is an old saying that proves true in pricing a product: "It's not the money, it's the amount." People expect to pay for a boat ride. However, customers have a preset notion of how much they expect to pay. They will buy without objection if your price is within their internal guidelines. Sales drop off dramatically if the price is too high. Most new entrepreneurs are surprised to discover that too low a price can decrease sales. Marketing experts call the response of buyers relative to the cost "price sensitivity."

Everything from shoes to fishing charters has a market price. In reality, this is a price range. For instance, in my part of the world a half-day fishing charter has a market price range of between $350 and $450. A round-trip ferry ride to the offshore islands is $30. Water taxis charge from $3 for a one-way ticket to $5 for a round-trip ticket. These numbers are not the same everywhere. The market price in major tourist destinations or international fishing hot spots is considerably higher because the demand is greater. There are two good indicators of market prices in your area:

- **Competition:** The prices set by directly competing businesses will have established market price for your area.
- **Similar services:** If you do not have direct competition, check the prices of similar services. In my water taxi, the prices of downtown parking are my guide. I know that my price must be at or below parking garage charges or my customers will be better off driving.

Market price also changes both seasonally and over the course of years. Nobody discounts a $450 fishing charter in spring when the walleye are running in my area. However, the same trip can be had for $350 or less in the dog days of July and August when fishing demand falls. The price rises in the fall as the fishing gets "hot" again.

Ferryboats sometimes offer discount coupons (example: two-for-one) during the cold spring and fall seasons but never during the peak summer vacation months. Year to year, prices tend to rise as long as the demand remains strong but not always. My water taxi business is currently threatened by completion of a new bridge with wide walkways perfect for sauntering across the river. I may have to decrease the ticket price once the bridge opens if I expect to compete with the free sidewalk.

Pricing your services too high will obviously drive away customers. Not so obvious is that you always lose money by charging too little. If you charge less than what customers will pay, the difference is lost revenue. Even less obvious is that customer price sensitivity is based on perceived value. They expect to pay a certain amount. If your price is too low, they subconsciously think something must be wrong and your service must be substandard in some manner. It comes down to perceived value. People are most likely to purchase if the price is equivalent to the perceived value of your product. See Chapter 9 for more information on marketing and pricing.

CHAPTER 5

PLANNING AND FUNDING YOUR BUSINESS

Now is the time to pull off our sea boots and slip into a pair of banker's wingtips. This chapter is all about planning and the numbers, and the work is just as critical to your success as your ability to navigate, catch fish, or entertain passengers. No one would start to build a boat without a blueprint, and the same is true with a business. For real success you need a plan. Without one, the results are not likely to be worth your time, money, and effort. Remember the five Ps of business: **P**roper **P**reparation **P**revents **P**oor **P**erformance.

The idea behind a business plan is to force you to think about the future in an orderly, systematic fashion. To build a comprehensive plan you have to consider not just the "upside" of income but also the "downside" of expenses. A business plan also allows you the freedom to try a variety of different approaches to your idea to find the one most likely to succeed. Banks and investors will want to examine your business plan in detail before handing over any cash.

STRUCTURING YOUR BUSINESS

One of the first things you have to decide is the legal status of your new business. There are a variety of accepted structures for a business depending on its anticipated size and capitalization. This choice is often dictated more by federal and state tax laws than it is by the service you plan to offer. You should seek professional accounting and legal advice before making your choice of structure. Your decision will reflect not only your personal desires but also the manner in which you plan to fund your new venture.

For instance, if you want to attract investors you will probably pick a corporate business structure. Investors are people who give venture capital to a start-up business with the expectation of making a profit. In return, they expect some sort of equity in the company. Usually this equity is in the form of ownership through being a partner in a partnership or through stock in a corporation. Getting venture capital requires that you give up some of your ownership rights. However, few real investors have any desire to run your business unless you demonstrate a lack of skill or commitment. They want you to do the daily work.

Talking about venture capital is heady business, but few such investors exist who are interested in small passenger vessel operations. The risks are too high, there is not enough glamour in the investment, and the potential returns are too low. More likely you will have to turn to "angels" for start-up capital. Unlike investors, angels put money into start-up companies because they believe in either the people or the idea. Unlike a true investor, an angel does not automatically expect to make a return on the money put into the company. For instance, a parent or other relative usually invests simply on the basis of family ties and not on the merits of the business.

Beware, however, that family relations can be a powder keg in the middle of the business. All too often the money changes hands with no formal written agreement. A few months or years later, both parties may have different interpretations about the management of the business, the return of the money, or the sharing of profits. That's when the feud begins.

Dysfunctional Family Affair

My friend Tom had a very successful business that disappeared during a family squabble in which all parties came out losers.

Tom had done well over a lifetime in business. When his daughter and son-in-law came to him with the idea of running a combination interisland entertainment cruise and ferry service, he didn't think twice about putting up the money. From the beginning, he considered that his money gave him control over the daily operation of the fledgling company. Before long, the father-in-law and husband were at odds over almost everything. Their relationship deteriorated as fast as the business prospered. In the end, the feud exploded into total failure of both the venture and the marriage out of which it had grown. The company had succeeded but the people had not.

Whether you are dealing with family angels or hard-core venture capitalists and bankers, it pays to formalize your business plans and to structure your company properly. The word *structure* in a business sense refers to the legal nature of the business. It can range from a sole proprietorship to a full-fledged corporation with several intermediate steps between.

SOLE PROPRIETORSHIP

The majority of captains who start their own charter fishing or water taxi operation go into business by collecting money from passengers. This sort of business that occurs by default is known as a sole proprietorship. This type of business is the easiest to start because there are few forms to fill out or legal requirements. If you go into business with your own money, no partners, and no stockholders, you are a sole proprietorship. All your income from the business will be taxed as "regular income" on your IRS 1040 tax form Schedule C. You do not file a separate income tax report for your business.

The biggest disadvantage of a sole proprietorship is unlimited legal liability. You are personally responsible for all debts of the business, including legal claims and judgments. Another problem with a sole proprietorship is obtaining money. Few investors will back such an enterprise simply because the venture is dependent upon one person. Backing a sole proprietor amounts to a personal loan, not a business investment. Banks will only consider your income and assets in granting loan applications. Sole proprietors generally do not have enough asset equity to obtain the needed funding from a bank.

Most six-pack fishing captains can obtain a personal loan to cover the cost of a boat without a formal business plan or structure beyond sole proprietorship. Banks will usually lend on a boat as long as the borrower's income is sufficient to cover the monthly payments. This means you have to keep your "day job" to finance your new business. A more formal approach that includes a business plan is necessary whenever the business has grown beyond a simple sole proprietorship.

PARTNERSHIP

A partnership (often called a general partnership) exists when two or more people share in the ownership of a business. Most partnerships grow out of two (sometimes more) people realizing they share a business dream, but they need each other's support to set up the business. Legally, it is just a two-person version of a sole proprietorship with some additional consequences. In a partnership, you become responsible for the actions of your partner. If your partner goes into debt in the name of the partnership, it is your debt as well.

LIMITED PARTNERSHIP

This type of business is sort of a halfway step between an ordinary partnership and a corporation. In most cases there is one partner who has the power to make management decisions. The other partners are really investors. Unlike in a regular partnership, however, their risk is limited to the amount of their investment, hence the term *limited partnership*.

Special legal paperwork is needed to form a limited partnership. In most states you obtain the required forms from the Attorney General's office. A filing fee ($50 to $500 depending on the state) is required before limited partnership status is granted. After that, it may be necessary to file annual state reports and state or federal income tax forms not required from a sole proprietorship.

CORPORATION

This is the structure most people think of when they discuss businesses. A corporation is chartered in a given state and has a life separate from the people who form it. Corporations can "live" for a hundred years or more. They do not dissolve when ownership changes hands. As far as the law is concerned, a corporation is much like a person. It can enter into contracts, be sued, and be taxed. Shareholders in a corporation are usually not liable for the company's debts beyond the value of their stock. Your business will undoubtedly need to be some form of corporation if you plan to raise a large amount of venture capital.

All for-profit corporations are chartered in the same way by the Secretary of State's office in any given state. For tax purposes, the U.S. Internal Revenue Service (IRS) recognizes several different types of corporations. The type of corporate structure you choose can have a profound impact on the cash you take home. Two corporate tax structures are commonly used for smaller businesses:

- **Regular or "C" corporation:** This is the standard corporate structure. After being chartered, a board of directors raises funds by issuing stock. Stockholders get a distribution of the after-tax profits. Under IRS regulations there is no limit on the number of years a "C" corporation can claim losses. In contrast, there are specific limits on the amount of time that sole proprietorships, partnerships, and limited liability companies can claim losses.
- **"S" corporation:** Profits distributed to investors are not taxed at the corporate level but only as personal income. This means that profits are only taxed once, so more money winds up in your pocket. Also, if you operate at a loss in your first year, that loss can be passed through as a deduction on your personal income tax. An "S" corporation is intended to be a small, closely held operation with few investors. As the company grows, it may become advantageous to change to a "C" corporation to attract new investors by selling more stock.

A corporation is a legal entity that can continue to exist long after the original investors are gone. With certain restrictions, corporations can issue stock to raise operating capital. And investors enjoy protection from personal liability for liability claims against the corporation. Despite these advantages of incorporating, there are considerations that make this choice less attractive.

Corporations require a great deal of paperwork. A corporate federal tax return must be prepared and filed, there are state forms to fill out, and annual corporate franchise fees must be paid to every state in which the corporation does business. There are also serious tax considerations, which will be discussed when I cover limited liability corporations a little later.

You don't need to hire an attorney to incorporate in most states, but it is probably a good idea. You can usually download all of the necessary forms from the Internet; they should be available from the office of your Secretary of State. All you have to do is fill in the blanks with appropriate responses and send the completed form with a check for the franchise fee. As will be discussed, attorneys are needed for other purposes when forming a corporation, but you can fill in the forms yourself and maybe save an hour of billable time.

LIMITED LIABILITY COMPANY (LLC)

The newest form of business structure, the LLC combines the limited liability protection of a corporation with the tax benefits of a partnership. Laws governing LLCs vary from state to state. Generally, an LLC may not have more than two of the four characteristics that define a corporation. These include:

1. Free transferability of ownership interests
2. Continuity of life
3. Limited liability to the extent of assets
4. Centralization of management

Free transferability means you are not prohibited by the LLC bylaws from selling your portion of ownership to another person. Unlike a corporation that can "live" virtually forever, an LLC must have a defined time limit on its operations. At the end of the specified time limit, the LLC will cease to exist unless the partners vote to extend the time limit. A major attraction of an LLC is the ability to protect the personal assets of the owners from being attached as the result of lawsuits or failure of the company.

Formation of an LLC is more complex than an ordinary general partnership or a sole proprietorship. Obtaining legal advice is prudent before forming an LLC. A key factor in their popularity is that LLCs are most often taxed as partnerships. This means business profits are taxed only once as regular income to the recipients. In some corporate forms of business the profits can be taxed twice, once at the corporate level and again as personal income.

Characteristics of Business Structures

	SOLE PROPRIETORSHIP	GENERAL PARTNERSHIP	LIMITED PARTNERSHIP	LIMITED LIABILITY CORPORATION	"C" CORPORATION	"S" CORPORATION
Ownership	One owner	Unlimited number of partners	Unlimited number of partners	Unlimited number of "members"	Unlimited number of shareholders	Up to 75 shareholders; one class of stock
Liability of Owners	Owner liable for business	All partners have full liability for the business	General partners have full liability; limited partners have no personal liability	Most of the time no personal liability for the business	Most of the time no personal liability of shareholders for the business	Most of the time no personal liability of shareholders for the business
Management	Owner/Operator	Partners manage equally	General partner manages under partnership agreement	Per the agreement among the "members"	Board of directors and company officers	Board of directors and company officers
Funding	All funds from owner	Partners contribute all funds	Funds contributed by the partners	Funds contributed by the "members"	Usually from sale of stock to stockholders	Usually from sale of stock to stockholders
Taxation	Owner's personal taxes	Each partner's personal taxes	Each partner's personal taxes	Each partner's personal taxes	Corporation pays taxes before distributing profits, which are taxed again as personal income	Corporation is not taxed; profits taxed as personal income of recipient
Documents	DBA filing	Agreement signed and filed with local clerk of courts	Limited partnership certificate; Limited partnership agreement	Articles of organization; Operating agreement	Articles of incorporation; Bylaws; Resolutions of the board; Stock certificates; Stock ledger	Articles of incorporation; Bylaws; Resolutions of the board; Stock certificates; Stock ledger; IRS and state "S" corporation election

PROFESSIONAL ADVICE

Everyone who is successful in business has an attorney and an accountant. You need their advice on what sort of business structure is right for your operation. A wrong decision at the start could have profound consequences years later. This is especially true if you go outside your family "angels" to find new stockholders or partners.

Depending on your corporate status, state and federal laws govern whom you can ask to purchase stock, how many stockholders you can have, and what paperwork must be filed with governmental agencies. Some choices, like electing to be an "S" corporation, are a one-time event, so the decision cannot be taken lightly. At tax time, an accountant is your best defense against an IRS audit. Even more important, a good accountant should find enough deductions to pay the cost of preparing your taxes.

The above information is presented for the purposes of acquainting the reader with the various business structures available. It is not meant as legal or accounting advice. Do not start a business without legal and accounting experts on your team.

YOUR BUSINESS PLAN

There is no single proper form for a business plan. These documents are tailored to fit the purpose and needs of the authors. Large corporations may create plans running to thousands of pages. An experienced entrepreneur may launch a new sole proprietorship business with a simple statement of purpose and a pro forma business projection. Most small passenger vessel companies require a plan that falls somewhere in between these extremes.

Do not make the mistake of thinking you need a business plan only to obtain a bank loan or find investors. Spending the time and effort to write a business plan will help you achieve success even if you never intend to go beyond a sole proprietorship. A good business plan grows and develops as you research and cultivate your ideas. In fact, a good plan forces you to make changes by stimulating additional research into the various elements of the plan. Each change should inspire other changes. Roll with this process and update the rough draft of your plan as often as necessary.

There are dozens of business plan software programs available to help you in the writing process. Most have boilerplate wording you can possibly use as you tailor the business plan to your specific needs. The advantage of these programs is that they force you to answer all of the questions an investor or banker might ask about your endeavor.

The disadvantage is that most canned programs are intended for retail and service businesses quite different from operating a passenger vessel. You will have to do some creative adapting to make most software suit your purpose. Some people find that using canned business plan software speeds the job along, but they export the document into a word processing program for the final editing process.

Another alternative is to create the document from scratch using your computer's word processing software. Within this document make individual pages corresponding to the broad topics outlined below. Do not get too fancy with fonts and graphics. This document is not for entertainment. The people who read it will probably think that too much color in a business plan is hiding a lack of serious research.

Photographs, tables, and other illustrations may be necessary to explain your ideas or the business. Keep them as simple as possible. Use color sparingly to enhance understanding. Use 12-point Courier type with single line spacing. Set the margins at 1 inch on all sides. If you intend to bind the plan into a folder, the left margin may be increased to accommodate the binder.

Every business plan contains the same general material, although it can be arranged differently to fit the specific company. First-time entrepreneurs should have a page in their business plans for each of the following topics. A sample business plan is included in Appendix A.

COVER PAGE

Keep the cover simple. Other than keeping the inside pages protected, the only purpose of the cover sheet is to identify the contents of the business plan. It may also carry the name of the bank or lending institution if you are seeking a vessel mortgage. Make a new cover page for each person to whom you distribute the plan. That way, nobody knows your list of names except you. Be sure to include your name, address, phone number, and e-mail address.

TABLE OF CONTENTS

The value of the table of contents to the person reviewing your business plan is obvious. However, do not overlook this page as a way to help you organize your thoughts as you prepare your business plan. As you glance down the table of contents, make sure you have included all of the necessary written sections and the required financial data. Make sure that the titles on the table of contents match the titles on each section page, and double-check that the page numbers shown on the table of contents match the actual pages where the information can be found.

STATEMENT OF PURPOSE

This is a "what" section of the business plan explaining to the reader the purpose of the document and the nature of the envisioned enterprise. In short, it should answer the important question: "What does the preparer of this business plan envision for the endeavor?"

Do not confuse the purpose of the plan with the reasons for going into business. A plan is written either as a guide for the development of the business or to obtain a bank loan or venture capital. Most new captains start sole proprietorship charter fishing or similar one-boat operations. A business plan for this type of structure guides the owner's efforts through the tumult of starting a business.

If your business plan is also meant to help you raise funds through a bank loan or from investors, do not be shy about saying so. A business plan is not a request for charity. You are offering a banker or investor an opportunity to make money from your business, so state up front how much money you need and what you plan to do with it.

DESCRIPTION OF BUSINESS

This is the other "what" section of the plan. It should answer the important question: "What purpose is served by this business?"

The previous section was composed of brief descriptions and terse sentences. This one should describe in detail the overall industry and how your endeavor fits into that big picture. It candidly discusses the potential strengths and weaknesses of your new business.

Be honest. Anyone familiar with business knows there are always risk factors and problems that can cause a start-up company to fail. Writing down your weaknesses also helps you focus attention on them. Beginners at this process are often surprised at how many negative factors they face.

Fortunately, they also discover that exposing these weaknesses is the first step to finding solutions. A long list of negative factors often transforms itself into positive solutions that can be presented with pride in this section of the business plan. The hidden benefit in this process is that it costs a lot less money to solve problems before you go into business than after you are up and operating.

OPERATIONS

This section answers the important question: "How is the company going to operate its boat (or boats)?" This is nuts-and-bolts stuff, where you explain which boat (or boats) you have chosen and why. Even if you are just converting your private craft into a six-pack commercial operation, make it sound like the choice was made after due deliberation. Explain how you plan to maintain the equipment. The operations section also includes the physical handling of passengers from ticket sales to boarding policies and safety briefings. If you do it on the water, it should be discussed in this section of the business plan.

LOCATION

This section answers the important question: "Where is the business located and why was that location chosen?" The old joke about house values is that they depend upon three factors: location, location, and location. This is just as true about a water-oriented business. A charter fishing business will have a hard time surviving in Death Valley. Choose your home port carefully and then carefully explain the reasons for that choice in this section of your business plan.

MARKETING

This section answers the important question: "Who is your market?" It identifies your customer base and how you will advertise or promote your business to this group of people. The typical small business entrepreneur overlooks this critical component of a successful company. Without a marketing plan, too much money is spent trying to attract people who will never purchase the service while buyers who will purchase the service are often overlooked.

Put your market research into this section. Prove to the reader that there really are enough potential customers to support your proposed business. Show that the customer base is large enough for your company to grow and prosper. Explain how you intend to reach customers with information about your new boat service. Explain your pricing structure and how it maximizes profits without unduly discouraging business.

COMPETITION

This section answers the important question: "Who is your competition?" Never make the mistake of thinking that your idea is so unique it has no competition. Even if nobody is offering DUKW ("duck") rides or parasailing in your area, if you start either business you will still be competing against fishing charters, video games, and ice cream parlors for the entertainment dollars spent by potential customers. Carefully examining your competition will help you develop business strategies to offer services that other boats do not offer.

MANAGEMENT AND PERSONNEL

All the people associated with your new company deserve credit for their efforts. Write a two- or three-paragraph biography of each person. Stress the relationship of their experience to the proposed business and why it is an important ingredient for its success. Include the people you hire, such as attorneys and accountants, if you have a continuous working relationship with them.

CAPITAL EQUIPMENT LIST

Banks and investors often want to know the type and value of capital equipment the company owns or will own when the business plan is implemented. The list includes a description, the original purchase price, and the current market value of each item. Capital equipment in this context generally means the big stuff like boats, outboard motors, trucks, and real estate that can be attached by creditors for nonpayment of debts.

Think twice before including your own personal property on this list. Once you put it into the venture, it cannot be taken back without tax consequences to the business or to you personally. If you do put your personal property into the business, be sure to include the value of those items as "paid-in capital." This establishes your investment in the company for tax purposes should you ever sell it.

FINANCIAL PRO FORMA

Accounting has been called the "dismal science" in part because as a job it lacks excitement and in part because when you crunch the numbers the results are often rather dismal. It is a lot harder to make money than most people realize. You will find it helpful to bookmark the sample business plan in Appendix A and refer to it as you read this section of the book.

A "pro forma" is a prediction of what you expect your company to do but presented as if it were an actual accounting of at least five years of operation. Creating a five-year set of financial numbers is a tedious and time-consuming process. Don't even think of doing it with pencil and paper. The same software that writes your business plan can be adapted to a boating business. Some small business accounting packages have pro forma capabilities. For the most accurate results, you can build an interactive spreadsheet on a spreadsheet program. This last option takes extra time, but you can customize everything to your specific needs.

The frustration of crunching numbers is often used as a justification for preparing only a one- or two-year pro forma. Traditionally, a pro forma prepared for banks or investors looks forward three years, but even a three-year projection is hardly worth the effort. Here's why.

Most start-up businesses have enough capital to get through the first couple of years. The expectation is that the project will be profitable from the start, so there will be money available later on. However, by the third or fourth year the initial capital has been used up, but the business usually has not yet maximized its profits. The result is an unforeseen cash crunch in the third or fourth year of operation that to the unwary entrepreneur seems to come out of nowhere. That's why you need to take the time to do a five-year pro forma, in anticipation of the potential cash crisis that may come along in the third or fourth year of your business. You need to think ahead and prepare for any financial storms that may arise.

Thus, a realistic business plan addresses the almost inevitable need for a second infusion of capital in the third or fourth year of a company's operation. This money can come from family and friends or from a second mortgage on your home (not recommended). It may even be an arrangement with creditors such as the marina to accept late payments until the cash crunch is over. No matter how you do it, getting past this troublesome period in the life of your business will take some financial creativity.

Big businesses use accrual accounting techniques. These pair expenses against income only when the actual cash is received. You are better off doing your pro forma on what is called a "cash" basis. This means you list income when it is received and expenses when they are paid.

The traditional business plan gives all projections for the first year by month. The second and third years are given by quarters. Monthly projections may continue into the second or third year until the company is shown to be making a profit. I adjust this traditional format by doing at least five-year projections by year only. In my area, the profitable season of operation is short enough to allow me this luxury. In reality, I experience only two "months" each year: summer and winter. Money comes in during the summer and goes out during the winter. A single pro forma for each year suffices. This would not be true in a year-round business such as a retail store.

Nearly all business plans include the following pro forma financial information:

- Source and application of funds
- Balance sheet
- Income and expense statement
- Break-even point analysis
- Cash flow

Sources and Application of Funds

In simple terms, this is a table showing where your firm will get its money and then how that money will be spent. This will be the first page a banker or investor will study if you are seeking either a loan or venture capital. It tells them how much of the funding they will be providing in comparison to what you are bringing into the company, and it shows how you plan to use the total funding to greatest benefit.

Sources of funds include the following:

- **Paid-in capital:** This is money or *capitalized assets* that you bring into the business as the entrepreneur. Paid-in capital generally cannot be removed from the business, so it serves as a measure of your belief in the project.

- **Loans and mortgages:** This is money you receive in return for a promise to repay. Typically, it comes from a bank or other formal lending institution. A friend or relative may also lend your company money.

- **Stock sales:** If you incorporate, your company may sell shares of stock to investors. These sales are subject to complicated state and federal regulations and should not be undertaken without legal counsel.

- **Revenue:** Once your business begins operating it will generate a "revenue stream." This money flows into the business and becomes available to fund growth after current expenses are paid.

Application is the fancy word for how you plan to spend the money. It includes everything from purchasing a boat to buying bait. One application start-up entrepreneurs overlook is holding some money in reserve against the day when things don't go according to plan. Applications of funds include the following:

- **Capital assets:** Everything you purchase for the company is an asset. This category includes your boat (or boats), tools and equipment, computer, charts and publications, etc.

- **Initial inventories:** Service businesses such as passenger vessel operations seldom have inventories. This category is primarily for the goods purchased for resale by a retail store. If you plan to sell fishing tackle, snacks, or even hats and shirts, these items would be considered inventories.

- **Working capital:** This is a catchall category for all of the expenses that do not purchase hardware. Advertising, fuel, insurance, dockage, repairs, and similar expenses come out of working capital.

- **Contingency reserve:** This is money set aside for the time when things go wrong. A reasonable reserve is considered prudent. Too much money held in reserve tells a banker or investor to put less money into your business.

Balance Sheet

Accountants consider a balance sheet as a snapshot of a company's financial situation on a certain date. For a start-up company, this is usually considered to be the first day of operation. This report gets its name from the fact that the company's assets are "balanced" against its liabilities. Any difference between the two is considered "owner equity." It represents the company's net worth. If assets are greater than liabilities, the company has a positive net worth. The other situation, with liabilities greater than assets, means a negative net worth and may signal trouble.

Banks must have collateral to make a loan. The positive net worth of the company represents that collateral. Banks and other lending institutions are usually prevented by regulation from making loans to companies with negative net worth. The reason is that such a business technically has no collateral against which to borrow. All of the assets are offset or exceeded by accounts payable.

Income and Expense Statement

This is the page of most interest to you as the business owner. It shows the projected income and the projected expenses. The difference between the two is profit or loss. Most small boat businesses have only a single income stream. This is the money generated from ticket or charter sales. Other possible revenue can be generated by selling prepackaged snacks, souvenirs, or other items. Expenses fall into two categories:

- **Cost of sales:** This category includes all of the variable expenses required to generate income. For a boat, they can include such things as advertising, fuel, maintenance, crew wages, etc. Entries in the cost of sales category rise or fall with the number of trips you run and the income you generate.

- **Operating expenses:** These are the fixed expenses of a business. Dockage, winter storage, inspection fees, insurance, loan payments, and similar items fall into this category.

Break-Even Point Analysis

In business, break-even point describes a level of income that precisely matches the company's expenses so that there is a zero balance. This means no profit and no loss. Knowing your break-even point is as important as keeping track of your fuel when operating offshore. With fuel, you know how much you need to reach port. That amount changes with the weather and wave conditions.

Similarly, the break-even point is your port in a business and your available cash is your fuel. You need to know at all times if your cash will last until you reach your break-even point. Just as wind and waves affect the rate of fuel consumption in your boat, changes in your expenses or ticket prices affect the break-even point for your business.

Let's examine a six-pack charter fishing business to see how this works. The basic idea is to add the annual fixed and variable costs together, then divide the figure by the income per trip to see how many trips it will take to break even.

$$\text{Fixed Costs + Variable Costs =}$$
$$\text{Total Costs/Income per Trip = Break-Even}$$
$$\$5,000 + \$3,500 = \$8,500 / 350 = 24.3 \text{ trips}$$

This particular operation has a $350 per trip income at a break-even point of 25 trips (the 24.3 must be rounded up to a full trip since you can't operate three-tenths of a trip). But what happens if the number of trips goes up or down? As the number of trips decreases, the cost to operate each trip goes up because the fixed costs of keeping the company in business are spread over fewer trips. Conversely, increasing the number of trips spreads the fixed cost over more trips and the total cost for each goes down. For the operator of this hypothetical charter service the initial implication is obvious. The boat must go fishing a minimum of 25 times a year at $350 per trip to break even.

SIMPLIFIED BREAK-EVEN POINT ANALYSIS (HYPOTHETICAL)							
FIXED COSTS	VARIABLE COSTS	TOTAL COST	NUMBER OF TRIPS	OPERATING COST PER TRIP	TOTAL COST PER TRIP	INCOME PER TRIP	PER-TRIP PROFIT (LOSS)
$5,000	$1,740	$6,740	12	$145	$562	$350	($212)
$5,000	$2,610	$7,610	18	$145	$423	$350	($73)
$5,000	$3,500	$8,500	24	$145	$350	$350	Break-Even
$5,000	$4,350	$9,350	30	$145	$312	$350	$38
$5,000	$5,220	$10,220	36	$145	$284	$350	$66
$5,000	$6,960	$11,960	48	$145	$249	$350	$101

Cash Flow

Income flows into the company's checking account and then out to pay expenses. Any remaining funds are profits. This process is called "cash flow." In theory, the incoming cash is always equal to or greater than the expenses that have to be paid. When this is the case, the cash flow is said to be "positive."

Things are not always so simple in real life. For instance, dockage is usually paid in the spring before the company has generated any income from customers. This produces "negative cash flow" because more money went out than came in, and the deficit must be offset by funds taken from contingency reserves, bank loans, or your wallet as the sole proprietor. An honest cash flow projection helps you prepare for periods when you are spending more than you take in. After the first year, you should be setting aside reserves to cover months when the flow is negative.

BUSINESS RATIOS AND OTHER CALCULATIONS

Something my personal spreadsheet program computes is a table of business ratios, which I will explain in a moment. I created this table as a quick guide for comparing one possible business scenario against another. As vital as business ratios are to the management of my affairs, I generally do not include them in any business plan I give to a potential banker or investor. After all, I know the ratios are positive or I would not be presenting the plan. I also know the banker or investor will compute these ratios for themselves, and it's better for me if they do some work to discover that my proposal really does have merit. Besides, they tend to trust their own computations.

Here are some important business ratios:

- **Debt to equity ratio:** This compares the total equity of the owners to the amount of debt (usually loans) carried by the company. A 1:1 ratio indicates debt equals equity. Most small businesses have 2.25:1 ratios, meaning that a bank or other outside lender has put $2.25 into the company for every dollar the owner has invested.
- **Current ratio:** This is the amount of liquid assets available to cover immediate debts such as loan payments or fuel bills. Some noncash assets can be included if they are easily turned into cash. A 2:1 ratio of current assets to debt is the minimum most banks will accept.
- **Quick ratio:** This ratio measures the amount of cash assets against immediate debts. A lower ratio is acceptable here, but it should still exceed 1:1.

All of the above ratios can be calculated for a start-up company. Some other ratios need a year or so of history to be meaningful. These include the following:

- **Return on assets:** This compares the annual gross income against the total assets of the company.
- **Return on equity:** This is a similar comparison of the annual gross income against the total amount of investment in the company by the owners.

Two other calculations need to be done in the business plan and then monthly and annually throughout the life of the company:

- **Working capital:** This is the subtraction of total current expenses from the total current assets, giving a measure of the company's liquidity. Working capital can be thought of as the money you have to help grow the business or to meet unexpected expenses. It tends to be artificially high at start-up and decreases to a low level about three years into the business before rebounding, if the company remains viable.

- **Net worth:** This measures the cash value of the company. It requires subtracting the total liabilities, including long-term loans, from the company's total assets.

CHAPTER 6

CHOOSING YOUR BUSINESS BOAT

I t should be obvious that there is some sort of magic in the number of six passengers. This magic grows out of long-standing U.S. Coast Guard regulations that divide the fleet of small passenger boats into two groups: inspected and uninspected. An uninspected vessel can carry up to six passengers. Inspected vessels typically carry seven or more passengers. An OUPV, or six-pack, license allows only the operation of an uninspected vessel, while a master's license permits the operation of either type.

A lot of OUPV license holders overlook the fact that they can never operate an inspected vessel with passengers on board, even if the number is limited to six. This limitation is a strong reason for either never obtaining an OUPV or upgrading to a master's license as quickly as possible. *Upgrading* is the general term for improving a license in terms of increasing the allowed tonnage or moving from OUPV to master.

As a professional captain you will almost always be hauling people. With the exception of supply vessels that work in the offshore petroleum industry, the majority of cargo work is done by vessels of more than 100 gross tons and thus falls outside the scope of the captain's licenses covered in this book.

A 100-ton master's license is no longer enough to work on tugboats or towboats. In response to several accidents involving barge tows hitting bridges, the U.S. Coast Guard has instituted new tug and towboat license requirements that require extended sea time in that occupation. By default, hauling passengers has now become the work of captains holding lower-level master's licenses of 25, 50, or 100 gross tons, or those holding OUPV licenses. We will focus primarily on passenger operations for this reason.

COMMERCIAL OPERATION

You might ask whether you really need a captain's license at all. Might it be possible to run your sportfishing boat as a business under the radar of the coast guard and thus avoid all kinds of regulation, business taxes, professional liability, and so on?

PASSENGER DEFINED

Shouldn't who a passenger is be easy to define? The short answer is no, it's not. About two decades ago, U.S. Coast Guard regulations gave no clear-cut dividing line between "for-hire" passengers and purely social guests sharing the expenses of a boat ride. Some districts interpreted the word *passenger* to apply only to people who purchased a ticket to ride a vessel. Other districts applied it to fishing buddies who shared expenses with the boat owner for a day on the water. On December 20, 1993, President Clinton signed into law the Passenger Vessel Safety Act of 1993 (Public Law 103-206). This law finally established the clear definition of a *passenger*. It can be found in Title 46 of the U.S. Code of Federal Regulations.

---

46 CFR Subpart 24.10

Definitions of Terms

Consideration means an economic benefit, inducement, right, or profit, including pecuniary payment accruing to an individual, person, or entity but not including a voluntary sharing of the actual expenses of the voyage by monetary contributions or donation of fuel, food, beverage, or other supplies.

Passenger means an individual carried on a vessel, except

(1) the owner or an individual representative of the owner;

(2) the master;

(3) a member of the crew engaged in the business of the vessel who has not contributed consideration for carriage, and who is paid for onboard services.

Passenger-for-hire means a passenger for whom consideration is contributed as a condition of carriage on the vessel, whether directly or indirectly, flowing to the owner, charterer, operator, agent, or any other person having an interest in the vessel.

Stripped of all legal gobbledygook, this means fishing buddies can share expenses for fuel, food, and even bait and not be considered as passengers for hire. The same exemption would apply to a Sunday picnic cruise with relatives up the bay, or an evening sunset sail with old friends. The key element in all of these scenarios is that the people involved are friends and the boating trip is intended to be a social event.

Things change when the social aspect disappears and is replaced by the expectation of what is known as "consideration" under the regulations. Quite obviously, a person buying a ticket on a fishing boat or water taxi is a passenger-for-hire. The same applies to some other situations that are not so clear.

For instance, a salesperson who takes customers out on his or her boat for the purposes of establishing more cordial business relationships has an expectation of "economic benefit" in the future. Therefore, even though no business is transacted on the boat, those passengers are still considered as for-hire and the salesperson must have a captain's license to conform to current regulations, or a licensed captain must be hired for the trip.

Of course, this means that thousands of voyages every year are technically illegal. Someday, somebody will pay a big price for ignorance of the law. Most insurance policies have provisions that prevent payment of claims arising from illegal commercial operation.

Despite these new regulations, it is still possible to split legal hairs over the definition of *for-hire*. Leave that sort of haggling to the sea lawyers. The penalties for making the wrong decision can be severe. Without a license, you may be liable for civil fines and even criminal prosecution if death or injury results from a voyage that is later determined to fall within the for-hire category, even if you believe that was not your intent. The sales representative taking customers fishing mentioned above is an obvious example. Although the customers may be friends, he or she has the expectation of economic gain from the relationship.

Even if you escape legal sanctions, your noncommercial yacht policy liability insurance may not cover an injury to someone the insurance company views as a passenger-for-hire. Only a commercial policy covers passengers-for-hire. To qualify for commercial insurance you will have to hold a U.S. Coast Guard license and operate a vessel that at least meets the safety requirements of an uninspected passenger vessel (see below).

U.S. COAST GUARD REQUIREMENTS FOR COMMERCIAL VESSELS

A lot of U.S. Coast Guard regulations come into effect once consideration (usually money) is exchanged and a voyage becomes for-hire. The idea behind these regulations is that the public has a right to a higher standard of safety from commercial operations than from private boat owners engaged in social activity. The regulations governing the operation of small commercial passenger vessels fall into four broad categories:

- **Manning:** The U.S. Coast Guard licenses operators and masters of commercial vessels and sets the minimum number of crew that must be on board when passengers are being carried. Members of the crew must meet certain standards of training and must be enrolled in a drug testing program.
- **Safety equipment:** All boats, commercial or not, are required to carry safety equipment such as life jackets, distress signals, and fire extinguishers. Requirements are more strict for commercial vessels. Improved life jackets, fire suppression, bilge alarms, and other devices are specified, depending on the size of the vessel and its route.
- **Hull and machinery:** Carburetor backfire flame arrestors and bilge ventilation requirements apply to all commercial vessels. In addition, vessels carrying more than six "for-hire" passengers must be inspected by the coast guard. They also must

meet strict stability guidelines. Inspected vessels are restricted to specified waters while carrying passengers for hire.

- **Documentation:** (46 CFR subchapter G) U.S. Coast Guard regulations require all U.S. commercial vessels admeasuring more than five gross tons to be documented. (See below for a discussion of admeasurement.) Documentation is the process of enrolling the vessel in the U.S. merchant fleet. It is a federal process conducted by the coast guard and highly regulated by both U.S. law and international treaties. It requires a complete and unbroken chain of title from the original builder right down to your hands. Without that chain of title the vessel cannot be documented.

Duck Boat Dilemma

Jim G. ran afoul of documentation requirements when he started a business to take duck hunters out on a marshy bay. He had a perfect "mother" boat in a 1940s vintage steel netboat built for commercial fishing. He planned to put individual hunters in layout boats launched from this steel craft. His problem was the boat had been built by a company that went out of business before he was born. Using the simplified admeasurement formula, his mother ship came in at 5.3 gross tons. Because there was no original "carpenter's certificate" and the chain of title had gaps, the coast guard refused to document the vessel. Jim's duck hunting plans were put off a full year while he wrangled with officials. In the end, he argued that a long-form admeasurement as done on big ships would probably have resulted in a number under five tons. Therefore, he claimed, the boat did not need documentation. Perhaps the officials were tired of arguing with him, because they agreed.

ADMEASUREMENT

Commercial vessels are traditionally sized by either *gross tonnage* or *net tonnage*. Both are a measurement of internal cubic volume, not weight. (The term *ton* as a unit of cubic volume goes back to the practice of measuring vessels by calculating the number of *tuns*, or wine casks of a certain size, that could be loaded into a ship's hold.) The system of calculating either type of tonnage is known as *admeasurement*. Today, an admeasurement ton is defined as 100 cubic feet of volume by either of the following metrics.

- **Gross tonnage** is based on the total volume of the vessel's enclosed spaces. This is the measurement that is used to describe the largest vessel a licensed captain may operate.

- **Net tonnage** is based on the vessel's presumed earning capacity and is always less than gross tonnage. Space for engines, crew accommodations, and voids is deducted from gross to get net tonnage. Net tonnage is not used to describe the size of vessel a licensed captain may operate.

Three systems of admeasurement exist. Two of them are suitable only for vessels rating more than 100 gross tons, so are not applicable to this book. The third, the *simplified measurement system*, can be used on vessels under 79 feet in overall length, any vessel operated only on the Great Lakes, or any noncommercial pleasure craft. Under the simplified measurement system, the overall length, breadth, and depth of the vessel are multiplied together. The product of this multiplication is then divided by 100. A coefficient is then applied to get gross tons. For a power-driven vessel, the coefficient is 0.67; for sailboats it is 0.50. For the purposes of this calculation, length, breadth, and depth are measured as follows:

- **Overall length:** This is the horizontal distance between the foremost part of a vessel's stem to the aftermost part of its stern, excluding pulpits, swim platforms, and other attachments.

- **Overall breadth:** This is the horizontal distance taken at the widest part of the hull, excluding rubrails.

- **Overall depth:** This is the vertical distance taken at or near amidships from the bottom inner skin of the hull upward to an imaginary line drawn across the boat from gunwale to gunwale. It excludes trunks, cabins, and deckhouses.

Measurements are taken in feet and inches to the nearest half-inch or in feet and tenths of a foot to the nearest 0.05 of a foot. The coefficients applied at the end of the formula adjust for the differences in the typical hull shapes of powerboats and sailboats. Because of these coefficients two boats of the same basic dimensions may admeasure quite differently.

Powerboat example:

Length 38'

Breadth 16'

Depth 7'5"

$38 \times 16 \times 7.5 \times 0.67 = 30.6$ gross tons

Sailboat example: (same dimensions as powerboat)

$38 \times 16 \times 7.5 \times 0.50 = 22.8$ gross tons

Net tonnage for a powerboat under simplified admeasurement is 80 percent of its gross tonnage. For a sailboat, net tonnage is 90 percent of gross tonnage.

U.S. Coast Guard Acronyms

Like all military organizations, the U.S. Coast Guard loves acronyms. Mariner licensing and vessel inspection issues are handled by the local coast guard marine safety office, or MSO. The regional examination center (pronounced "wreck-center") where you obtained your license is part of the MSO, as is the OCMI. This acronym stands for officer in charge, marine inspection. It is a generic term applied to any employee, civilian or military, of the U.S. Coast Guard who inspects commercial vessels. The OCMI is the person you will interact with on issues involving vessel questions. The local MSO issues a certificate of inspection, or COI, to qualified vessels.

Some things are referred to by their location within the U.S. Code of Federal Regulations. You may hear an OCMI refer to "Q-specs." This means the specifications governing a specific item as published in 46 CFR subchapter Q. A "T-boat" is any small passenger vessel with a capacity of under 150 passengers. A "K-boat" carries 150 or more passengers.

Domestic Voyages

All of the material presented in this book is only applicable to domestic voyages. This means trips to and from U.S. ports or on the Great Lakes to and from U.S. or Canadian ports. International voyages come under regulations of both the U.S. Coast Guard and the International Convention for Safety of Life at Sea (SOLAS). SOLAS requires additional training standards (including training in lifeboat operation, firefighting, radar observing, and watch standing) beyond those required of captains holding a coast guard–issued master's license.

UNINSPECTED PASSENGER VESSEL (SIX-PACK) CHARTERS

The category of uninspected passenger vessels, and the OUPV or six-pack license, was established for the charter fishing industry. In the beginning it was more of a registration procedure than a real test of skill or knowledge. Individual commercial fishermen would occasionally supplement their incomes by taking groups of anglers to offshore fishing grounds. Over time this episodic spare cash activity grew into full-time employment for many skippers. Today, the licensing requirements for an OUPV are nearly the same as a lower-level master. Even so, vessels carrying fewer than six passengers (hence the term *six-pack*) still do not require formal hull and equipment inspections by the coast guard.

Being uninspected does not mean that a six-pack vessel is free of regulation. It just means that the operator is responsible for maintaining the required equipment in serviceable condition at all times. Even though the boat is not inspected on a regular basis, from time to time the coast guard does make compliance checks of uninspected vessels. (See U.S. Coast Guard Boardings for the language of the pertinent federal regulation.) Penalties for noncompliance range from reprimands to fines. At the least, the voyage of a vessel in noncompliance will be terminated, and the boat must remain docked until the violation is corrected to the coast guard's satisfaction.

U.S. Coast Guard Boardings

46 CFR Subpart 26.15

Boarding

§26.15-1 May board at any time.

. . . officers of the coast guard may board any vessel . . . at any time such vessel is found upon the navigable waters of the United States. . . .

Compliance examinations of uninspected vessels may be conducted at the dock or at sea. Coast guard vessels are clearly marked and all personnel will be in uniform. The boarding officer will address the master, owner, or operator, and explain his or her mission.

DISPLAYING LICENSES

You must have your OUPV or master's license on board and available "for immediate production" to any coast guard boarding officer. Some (but not all) marine safety offices (MSO) recognize the damp atmosphere aboard a small vessel can be destructive to valuable papers. Check to see if carrying a copy of your license on board is acceptable, provided that you have your original ready for "immediate production" on shore at your home marina. Do not assume this option is available until you have confirmed it with the local MSO. If you must carry your license aboard, keep it inside a watertight plastic pouch. Do not laminate the license.

STATE REGULATION

Uninspected passenger vessels may also be regulated by state watercraft laws. For instance, the Michigan Department of Natural Resources has a mandatory charter boat inspection program. U.S. Coast Guard operator licensing for commercial vessels trumps state boat operator license requirements on federally navigable waters. A state license may be required on nonfederal waters. Also, even on federal waters, states may require charter fishing skippers to hold a guide's license. The number and diversity of state regulations make it impossible to list all the various requirements here. Be sure to check with state watercraft and fish and game authorities before you establish a six-pack business.

SIX-PACK MANNING STANDARD

There is no statutory minimum number of crew for an uninspected vessel. Practically, that number is one person, the licensed operator required by law. Economics force most six-pack boats to be one-person operations, although there is no legal impediment to prevent carrying extra crew. Many saltwater charter fishing captains carry a mate to help with cutting bait, setting up customers' fishing tackle, and cleaning up at the end of the voyage. Mates typically are unpaid, except with tips from customers. Still, even unpaid mates must meet federal drug testing requirements.

The drug testing requirement has eliminated one traditional way of getting around the six-passenger limit. Some captains in years past boosted the number of customers they carried by designating the seventh paying passenger as "crew" for the duration of the voyage. This can no longer be done. According to the drug testing regulations (see Chapter 7), before anyone can be considered as crew they must have taken a drug test and their employer must have received a report stating that the results came back negative for any illegal substances. This process takes a minimum of several days, so it is impossible to pick someone as crew on the morning of a fishing trip without risking draconian fines for violating drug testing regulations.

EQUIPMENT REQUIREMENTS

Uninspected passenger vessels must carry all of the required equipment for a noncommercial motorboat of equivalent size. In addition, they must upgrade certain items and carry additional lifesaving gear, as listed below. While the boating industry uses the term *personal flotation device* (PFD), some coast guard regulations still call these devices *life preservers*. Here is some of the safety equipment you need to carry on board:

- **Life preservers:** A vessel carrying passengers for hire must be equipped with one U.S. Coast Guard Type I life preserver for each person on board. Suitable child-size life preservers are required when children are carried. Each life preserver must have retro-reflective material attached to the upper portion in the area of the wearer's shoulders. Life preservers must be stowed where passengers have easy access to them. In addition, all child-size preservers must be stored separately from those for adults.

- **Life preserver lights:** Lights must be attached to all life preservers carried by six-pack vessels engaged in ocean, coastwise, or Great Lakes voyages. These are generally battery-powered pin-on lights.
- **Ring buoy:** All six-pack vessels 26 feet and longer must carry an approved ring life buoy. These come in either international orange or white and may be 20, 24, or 30 inches in diameter.
- **Fire extinguishers:** This is the subject of extensive regulations and is addressed separately below.

The U.S. Coast Guard makes changes to the required equipment from time to time. It is up to you to know the latest regulations. Two expensive items have been discussed as possibly being required equipment on uninspected six-pack vessels in the future. One is an emergency position indicating radio beacon (EPIRB). This is a radio transmitter that automatically sends a distress call if the boat sinks. The other item is automatic fire suppression in the engine compartment using either inert gas or carbon dioxide. Inspected vessels already must have fire suppression and carry EPIRBs on routes other than rivers.

FIRE SAFETY REGULATIONS FOR SIX-PACK BOATS

The same U.S. Coast Guard–approved B-I and B-II fire extinguishers used on pleasure boats are acceptable on uninspected passenger vessels. While not required, those installed on commercial vessels should be tested and tagged annually by a fire extinguisher service company. To be legal, each fire extinguisher must be stored in a type-approved bracket. Letters are used to indicate the type of fire an extinguisher can put out:

- **Class A:** wood, paper, bedding, etc.
- **Class B:** oil and burning liquids
- **Class C:** electrical fires

U.S. Coast Guard–approved hand-portable fire extinguishers are all rated for at least Class B fires. They come in three sizes: B-I, B-II, and B-III. Of these, only types B-I and B-II are normally found on pleasure boats. The higher numbers are for larger fire extinguishers. Fire extinguisher markings can be confusing because a single unit can be approved for different types of fires in different size classes. For instance, a fire extinguisher marked "Type A, Size II, Type B:C, Size I" is considered a B-I extinguisher.

An approved fixed or permanently installed fire system uses either carbon dioxide or another inert gas to extinguish flames. The best-known inert gas fire suppressor, Halon, was banned years ago because of environmental concerns, but some old systems are still legally in use. New systems rely on different gases that do not deplete the Earth's ozone layer. The system triggers automatically when it detects fire and is interlocked with the engine ignition system. Triggering the system immediately shuts down the engine to prevent the firefighting gas from being sucked through and discharged out the exhaust. A manual override system allows the boat operator to restart the engine after it has been determined that the fire is extinguished.

COMPARISON OF APPROVED FIRE EXTINGUISHERS (§25.30-10(c))				
CLASS OF FIRE	FOAM (GAL.)	CARBON DIOXIDE (LB.)	DRY CHEMICAL (LB.)	HALON (LB.)
B-I (Type B, Size I)	1.25	4	2	2.5
B-II (Type B, Size II)	2.5	15	10	10

MINIMUM NUMBER HAND-PORTABLE FIRE EXTINGUISHERS (§25.30-20(A)(I))		
VESSEL LENGTH	NO FIXED SYSTEM	WITH APPROVED FIXED SYSTEM
Less than 26'	1 B-I	0
26' to less than 40'	2 B-I or 1 B-II	1 B-I
40' to 65'	3 B-I or 1 B-II and 1 B-I	2 B-I or 1 B-II

Other fire-related regulations that apply to commercial passenger vessels include the following:

- **Backfire flame control:** (§25.45-1) All inboard engines that use gasoline for fuel and are equipped with a carburetor must have a backfire flame arrestor. This device must be stamped with the basic U.S. Coast Guard approval number 162.015.

- **Ventilation:** (§25.40-1) Boat manufacturers are required to install ducts to clear explosive gasoline fumes from boats with inboard gasoline engines. Boats built after 1980 must be equipped with one or more power exhaust blowers to remove potentially explosive fumes from the engine compartment.
- **Cooking fuels:** (§25.45-1) The only fuels permitted aboard uninspected vessels carrying passengers for hire are alcohol, fuel oil (no. 1, 2, or 3), kerosene, wood, or coal. Tanks for kerosene or fuel oil must be separated from the stoves that they serve, be vented to the outside air, and have an outside fill.

SAFETY ORIENTATION

Before getting under way, every six-pack skipper is required to give a safety briefing to the passengers on board. This is the small vessel equivalent of a lifeboat drill on big cruise ships, or the pre-takeoff safety instructions on airliners. Four items are specifically required in this briefing:

- Stowage locations of all life preservers
- Proper method of donning and adjusting life preservers of the type(s) carried on the vessel
- The type and location of all lifesaving devices (life rings, etc.) carried on the vessel
- The location and contents of the emergency check off list

EMERGENCY CHECK OFF LIST

This coast guard requirement of uninspected vessels is the one most six-pack skippers unwittingly violate. Yet, there is absolutely no getting around the wording of the regulation. "The operator *shall* ensure that an emergency check off list is posted in a conspicuous, continuously accessible place to serve as a notice to the passengers and a reminder to the crew of precautionary measures which may be necessary in the event of an emergency situation." The regulations even specify the wording of the check off list.

46 CFR 26.02-2(b)

Sample Emergency Check Off List

Measures to be considered in the event of

(a) *Rough weather at sea or crossing hazardous bars*

- All weathertight and watertight doors, hatches, and airports closed to prevent taking water aboard.
- Bilges kept dry to prevent loss of stability.
- Passengers seated and evenly distributed.
- All passengers wearing life preservers in conditions of very rough seas or if about to cross a bar under hazardous conditions.
- An international distress call and a call to the coast guard over radiotelephone made if assistance is needed (if radiotelephone equipped).

(b) *Man overboard*

- Ring buoy thrown overboard as close to the victim as possible.
- Lookout posted to keep the victim in sight.
- Crewmember, wearing a life preserver and lifeline, standing by ready to jump into the water to assist the victim back aboard.
- Coast guard and all vessels in the vicinity notified by radiotelephone (if radiotelephone equipped).
- Search continued until after radiotelephone consultation with the coast guard, if at all possible.

(c) *Fire at sea*

- Air supply to the fire cut off by closing hatches, ports, doors, and ventilators, etc.
- Portable extinguishers discharged at the base of the flames of flammable liquid or grease fires or water applied to fires of combustible solids.
- If fire is in machinery spaces, fuel supply and ventilation shut off and any installed fixed firefighting system discharged.

■ Vessel maneuvered to minimize the effect of wind on the fire.

■ Coast guard and all vessels in the vicinity notified by radiotelephone of the fire and vessel location (if radiotelephone equipped).

■ Passengers moved away from fire and wearing life preservers.

Regulations allow you to add information related to your specific vessel to the official check off list. Even if some of the measures are somewhat impracticable (for example, on an uninspected vessel with a single crewmember, the captain, it is clearly not a good idea for the crewmember to jump off the boat to rescue a person who has fallen overboard), nothing should be deleted from the required wording unless deemed unnecessary by the office in charge of marine inspections (OCMI).

This document must be posted on the vessel, which may present a problem in a wet environment. Laminating your list is one solution. Large sheet lamination offered by office supply stores will generally give six months to a year of continuous protection. The checklist can be printed from your computer, but keep in mind that the colored inks of inkjet printers fade rapidly in sunlight. Black ink does not, but most inkjet inks will run when wet. Laser printer inks do not run or smear even when the paper is soggy. Some boats have no suitable mounting surface for a checklist. The OCMI can give an exemption to this requirement, but you must make a formal request.

VHF MARINE RADIO

Although a VHF marine radiotelephone is strongly advised for six-pack boats, there is no federal requirement to carry one. If you voluntarily install a marine radio, it must be operated under the regulations established by the Federal Communications Commission (FCC).

A station license for your boat is not absolutely required unless you plan to cross into Canadian or Mexican waters. The same is true of a personal operator's license. Applications for both licenses come packed with new radios and are available from marine electronics dealers.

INSPECTED VESSELS

Vessels carrying more than six passengers for hire must be inspected every year by the U.S. Coast Guard. Hull inspections are also required on varying schedules. There is no way around it, and there is no escaping the host of rules and regulations. A master's license imposes no statutory upper limit on the number of passengers you can carry, which gives you some flexibility. The number of passengers is determined by the size and stability of each individual boat. In theory you could operate an inspected vessel that carries only two or three passengers, though you probably wouldn't make money. The increased costs of meeting inspected vessel criteria generally require a minimum of 16 to 18 passengers for profitability.

BIG AND LITTLE VESSELS

Until about a decade ago all passenger vessels under 100 gross tons or 65 feet in length were lumped into one category (46 CFR subchapter T). In recognition that size matters, "T-boats" were divided into "small" and "large." This system began to fall apart with the coming of gambling ships that were cleverly designed to admeasure under 100 gross tons but carry several hundred people on their unmeasured upper decks. In response, the coast guard revamped the whole system of regulations governing small passenger vessels. The old subchapter T was retained to cover what had been the "small" boats. A new subchapter K was created to handle the "large" vessels, and many of the regulations were revamped and updated.

Knowing the history of the two subchapters helps avoid confusion when looking up information. Some regulations that apply to both T and K boats are detailed only in subchapter K and then included by reference in subchapter T. Sometimes it takes a careful reading of both subchapters to decipher exactly what applies in your particular case.

Sub-T Vessels

Under 100 gross tons
150 or fewer passengers
No more than 49 overnight

According to subchapter T, vessels qualifying as "sub-T" are less than 100 gross tons, carry 150 or fewer passengers, or have overnight accommodations for 49 or fewer passengers. Prior to 2000, the wording was "fewer than 150 passengers," leading to some confusion. Older sub-T vessels still carry the certificates of inspection showing the previous wording, effectively limiting them to 149 passengers. Most people in the industry still think of 149 as the magic cutoff, although the wording has changed.

Captains holding 100-ton licenses find employment on sub-T boats. This category includes the ducks (World War II DUKWs) on the Wisconsin Dells, in Branson, Missouri, in Boston, and elsewhere. It also includes large headboats in the Florida Keys, gambling vessel shuttles, passenger ferries, dinner cruise vessels, and the like. Sub-T regulations are written to take into account the various services these smaller passenger vessels provide. Occasionally, such as within the gambling ship industry, a vessel is built that technically qualifies for sub-T, but which obviously does not fit the intention of the regulations. In such a case, the coast guard can prescribe the regulations applicable to that particular vessel.

A quirk exists with regard to offshore supply vessels (OSVs) for the petroleum industry. Those built before March 16, 1998, and that meet the sub-T criteria, continue to be inspected under this subchapter. However, inspections of all OSVs built after that date are governed by 46 CFR subchapter L.

Sub-K Vessels

Under 100 gross tons
More than 150 passengers
More than 49 overnight

Vessels qualifying as "sub-K" (46 CFR subchapter K [46 CFR 114.110]) are less than 100 gross tons, carry more than 150 passengers, or have overnight accommodations for more than 49 passengers. The obvious difference between sub-T and sub-K boats is passenger capacity. Within subchapter K there are additional differentiations made between vessels based upon size and passenger load.

CERTIFICATE OF INSPECTION

Each inspected vessel is issued a certificate of inspection (COI) by the officer in charge of marine inspections (OCMI) of the regional marine safety office (MSO). This is done on U.S. Coast Guard form CG-841 to ensure uniformity. A certificate is issued for a period of three years, but may be suspended and withdrawn or revoked at any time for noncompliance with the regulations. A COI may be obtained or renewed by application on form CG-3475: application for inspection of U.S. vessel to the OCMI of the zone in which the inspection will be made. An old COI is renewed by the issuance of a new certificate. Information on the COI includes:

- Vessel description including official number, hull material, year built, and propulsion
- The water or waters on which the vessel may carry passengers for hire
- Minimum manning requirements
- Survival and rescue craft that must be carried
- Minimum fire extinguishing equipment
- The number of life jackets required to be carried based on the total number of passengers and crew, plus children's life jackets equal to at least 10 percent of that total

Note: The vessel's COI must be posted under glass or other suitable transparent material in a conspicuous place on the vessel where observation by the passengers is likely. All pages must be visible. If posting is impracticable, such as in an open boat, the COI may be kept on board in a weather-tight container readily available for display on passenger request. To be on the safe side, many operators post copies of the COI for passenger viewing and keep the original in a dry location on the boat.

Number of Passengers

For either sub-T or sub-K boats, a key piece of information on the COI is the total number of people the vessel may carry. This number includes the crew and the passengers. A second critical number is the maximum passenger load. For most small passenger vessels, the maximum number of passengers is determined by one of three different criteria:

- **Length of rail:** One passenger is permitted for each 30 inches of rail space available to passengers at the periphery of each deck. Rail space in unsafe areas such as near anchor handling equipment or sail booms may not be included.
- **Deck area:** One passenger is permitted for every 10 square feet of deck area available for passenger use. The areas occupied by fixed seating, snack bars, toilets, and stairways are excluded.
- **Fixed seating:** One passenger is permitted for each 18 inches of width of fixed seating.

Some vessels have combined open areas and fixed seating. If the OCMI approves, the fixed seating and deck area criteria may be applied to the respective areas and the sum used as the maximum permitted number of passengers. The length of rail criterion may not be combined with either deck area or fixed seating.

Stability Letter

There is one other factor that affects the maximum passenger load of sub-T or sub-K vessels: intact stability. The undamaged (hence "intact") stability of a vessel is its ability to stay upright. A problem with small vessels is crowding of passengers on one side to witness something of interest. This is a common occurrence aboard whale watching and sightseeing cruises. To ensure safety, the coast guard requires stability calculations by a naval architect, an actual stability test using moveable weights, or both. The results of these calculations or tests are conveyed to the vessel owner in the form of a *stability letter.*

It is not uncommon for the stability of a small vessel to limit the number of passengers to well below the fixed seating or rail space. My pontoon water taxi could cram at least 24 people onto its bench seats. The interior floor space is 240 square feet, equal to the space needed for those 24 people. But the stability letter for this boat limits the total capacity to 18 passengers and one master, or 19 people. This lower number was arrived at by actually inclining the boat with bags of sand to simulate passengers moving to one side. The results of that test showed 19 people to be the maximum safe passenger load.

The stability letter may not just limit the total number of passengers. It may also limit the distribution of people on the various decks.

I know a fellow who has a 48-foot launch with a hardtop cabin suitable for passengers. The boat has a COI for 36 passengers and two crew. However, the stability letter sets a maximum limit of 12 people on the deckhouse roof at any one time. Limitations on the number of people permitted on upper decks are typical on vessels with narrow beams.

U.S. Coast Guard Routes

The U.S. Coast Guard uses the term *route* on the certificate of inspection and stability letters to mean something quite different from its everyday use. In bureaucratic lingo, a *route* does not specify the stops of a water taxi or the hot fishing spots of a headboat. It designates the geographic water or waters upon which the vessel may operate while carrying passengers. The vessel is free to operate to and from any port or dock within the geographic area specified by its route. The coast guard has created general definitions for certain types of waters based on the perceived roughness of waves and the swiftness of tidal or river currents. The following definitions apply to sub-T and sub-K vessels:

- **Great Lakes:** the waters of any of the Great Lakes and some of the St. Lawrence River
- **Lakes, bays, and sounds:** any lake other than the Great Lakes, an enclosed bay, a sound, or any other such waters designated by the local U.S. Coast Guard district commander
- **Limited coastwise:** a route that is not more than 20 nautical miles from a harbor of safe refuge
- **Oceans:** a route more than 20 nautical miles from a harbor of safe refuge on waters such as the Gulf of Mexico and either the Pacific or Atlantic Oceans
- **Partially protected waters:** a term used in connection with stability criteria that applies to (1) waters within 20 nautical miles of a harbor of safe refuge, (2) portions of rivers, estuaries, harbors, and lakes the OCMI deems to be not protected, and (3) waters of the Great Lakes from April 16 through September 16 (summer season)
- **Protected waters:** a term used in connection with stability criteria meaning sheltered waters presenting no special haz-

ards such as most rivers, harbors, and lakes that are not deemed exposed or partially protected by the OCMI

- **Rivers:** a route on a river or canal and any other similar waters designated by the Coast Guard district commander

A vessel's coast guard route is determined by both its overall construction and its stability. The obvious intent is to prevent taking passengers into waters for which the boat may not be safe. For example, fishing 30 miles offshore in a pontoon boat would not be safe. Limits are often placed on a vessel within its designated waters. For instance, I once served on a ferry with a Great Lakes route limited to the western end of Lake Erie from the west pier head light at Huron, Ohio, to Monroe, Michigan. When we needed to take passengers to Lorain, Ohio, which is east of Huron, we had to obtain coast guard permission. It was never denied.

There is a pecking order in the official route structure based on the expected severity of conditions that might be encountered. In descending order of severity, the order runs as follows: (1) oceans; (2) coastwise; (3) limited coastwise; (4) Great Lakes; (5) lakes, bays, and sounds; (6) rivers. It is permissible to operate a vessel on waters of lesser severity unless it is expressly prohibited on the certificate of inspection (COI).

STATE AND LOCAL REGULATIONS

The various states and many local governments also have regulations governing carrying passengers for hire. States have an interest in making sure that public transportation companies live up to their published schedules and services. Under most state laws, a ferry operation cannot deviate from its published schedule without first obtaining permission from the appropriate agency. Most states use the public's interest in consistent service as a justification for charging what are often called *franchise taxes* or *fees* on the gross incomes of ferry operations.

Under most state laws, a ferry sells one-way and round-trip tickets. Thus, if service is not maintained, a passenger holding a paid return ticket might be stranded if the boat line stopped operating on a whim. Water taxis, by comparison, do not have regular routes or scheduled service. Instead, they operate on a demand basis. Municipalities often impose franchise fees on water taxi companies, especially if the water taxis use public docks while serving their passengers.

REQUIRED INSPECTIONS

The date of each individual vessel's original COI determines when annual renewal inspections are needed on that vessel. Each year within 60 days of the original inspection date the vessel must be made available to the OCMI for an annual renewal inspection. This is done with the vessel in the water.

The inspection includes the structure, the machinery and equipment of a power-driven vessel, and the sails and rigging of a sailing vessel. All of the relevant documents must be on board, including charts of the operational area, the pilot book, light list, and (if applicable) tide tables. Each life jacket and all lifesaving apparatus will be carefully scrutinized. The inspector will ask to have the vessel get under way so that various safety drills can be performed. During most inspections the OCMI will conduct a man overboard drill.

If the vessel passes its annual re-inspection, the OCMI issues a sticker showing the next date upon which the vessel's COI expires. This sticker must be placed where passengers can see it.

Dry Dock Inspection

At regular intervals, every sub-T or sub-K inspected vessel must be inspected out of the water by the coast guard. This is termed a dry dock inspection, although it may be done at a marina using a traveling hoist. Vessels exposed to salt water must be dry-docked every two years. Those serving in fresh water are allowed five years between dry-dockings.

Metal hulls are inspected for corrosion, wooden hulls are sounded for signs of softness, and fiberglass hulls are visually inspected for damage. Hoses to through-hull valves (seacocks) are removed so the valves can be inspected. Special attention is paid to shafts, shaft logs, struts, and Cutless bearings. The inspector may require that part or all of the propeller shafting be withdrawn from the vessel for inspection of the shaft and stern bearing.

In contrast, no regulations require a formal survey of a six-pack boat, although one may be required to obtain insurance.

BUYING A VESSEL FOR YOUR BUSINESS

Few start-up businesses are financed well enough to purchase a new boat at from three to ten times the cost of an existing craft. Simple economics dictate that start-ups are more likely to succeed by purchasing an existing inspected vessel in good condition. The costs of paint and other cosmetic improvements are far less than a month or two of bank payments on a new vessel.

The big mistake most beginners make is to think that any boat can be easily transformed into an inspected vessel just by adding some safety gear. This approach fails to take into account the underlying assumption of coast guard regulations that commercial vessels should be built from the keel up for the purpose. Neophytes usually discover to their chagrin that the cost of rebuilding an existing boat to inspected standards far exceeds the price of a purpose-built passenger vessel. This expensive mistake has bankrupted many new businesses that were otherwise sound. If you intend to carry more than six passengers, start out with an existing inspected vessel with a valid COI that meets all regulations. At a minimum, look for the following:

- An existing certificate of inspection (COI) that has not expired
- Authorization for an existing route similar to the one on which you propose to use the vessel
- At least one working season before the next dry dock inspection

While it is not absolutely necessary, if you can find a vessel with one working season left before the required dry dock inspection, it makes good economic sense to give yourself a money-making season before incurring the expenses of hauling and blocking the vessel.

BUY USED

The urge to start a new business with a new boat is understandable. However, the smart money goes after a quality used vessel to avoid more than just the high price of new construction. It is a complicated undertaking to build a new inspected vessel from scratch. First, the plans have to be approved by the U.S. Coast Guard in Washington,

D.C. For smaller vessels it is theoretically possible to draw up your own plans, but plans done at home often get bogged down in the approval process.

To keep the project moving ahead, it is best to hire an accredited naval architect to draw the plans and get them approved. The coast guard monitors all stages of the construction of a new boat. Inevitably, this means delays creep into the process. Once the vessel is completed it may have to undergo stability tests before receiving its initial COI.

Buying a used inspected vessel eliminates the delays and costs of building new. You go straight to on-water operation because a used boat that holds a current COI comes complete with the life jackets, distress signals, radios, radar, fire pump, and other required gear. That's the good side. The bad news is that the boat also has the normal wear and tear on the cosmetics and engines. This is why you should never purchase a commercial vessel without a survey by an accredited marine surveyor.

Of course, it is too expensive to commission a survey of every boat you look at. A do-it-yourself inspection form is included in Appendix C. It will help you weed out boats unworthy of a professional survey and allow you to concentrate only on the best.

Selling prices of commercial vessels depend on factors beyond size and age. The location where the boat lies may add or deduct value. Also, the price will be highest just after a five-year dry dock inspection and lower as the years pass until the next one. Used sub-T vessels usually sell from $1,000 to $2,500 per authorized passenger. A similar new vessel can cost up to $5,000 per passenger.

The raw cost difference between new and used may not be as large as it first appears. The price of a used vessel must be adjusted upward to reflect any cosmetic improvements or replacement of worn-out equipment. Paint is inexpensive, but a worn-out diesel engine can be $40,000 or more, depending on its horsepower. Never bring a used boat into the market before the exterior cosmetics are completed. This means shiny new paint and bright graphics in place. The engines may still need an overhaul, but make sure that the boat looks great on its first public appearance in its home port.

The Ugly Duckling

William S. planned to improve the cosmetic appearance of his aging 149-passenger ferry. The plan was to update the exterior in June before going into service for the first time on the Fourth of July in the ferry's new home port. Before William could take action to repaint and clean the ferry, the local newspaper published a color photograph of it on the front page, which did great damage to his business at the new location. Sure, he got the boat looking good, but it took him more than two years to overcome the bad publicity of that first appearance.

CHAPTER 7

HIRING AND MANAGING EMPLOYEES

Human resources (HR) is a catchall term that has replaced *personnel* in the business lexicon. If you operate a sole proprietorship charter fishing business, you are the single human resource of your company. On the other hand, you may need to hire several captains and a handful of deckhands to operate an excursion service, and that's when knowing something about HR comes into play.

Laws and governmental regulations surrounding the hiring of employees probably cause more consternation for the owners of small passenger vessels than bad weather or mechanical breakdowns. It is impossible for you to be conversant with all of them while still having time to run your boat. The best way to handle government is to hire advisers in the form of an insurance agent, a good lawyer, and an even better accountant. Paying experts to do their jobs will save you time and money, and it will help reduce the chances of trouble down the road.

Fortunately, if you run a one-person charter fishing business, you don't have to worry about the issues described in this chapter. If you do plan to hire employees, then pay close attention to what follows.

The most onerous burdens of paperwork and record keeping do not begin until you have 15 employees. At that point, most businesses must comply with three different sets of laws: federal, state, and local (city). These tend to be quite similar, so that in meeting the most stringent requirements you will be in compliance with the others.

There are some quirks. For instance, many cities have living wage requirements that set hourly pay higher than state or federal minimum wage requirements. These laws usually do not apply to small one- or two-person companies or businesses that gross less than a set amount of income. However, a living wage requirement may apply if you conduct business with the city, such as renting dock space in a municipal marina. Check with an accountant or local lawyer to learn whether or not you fall under a minimum wage or fair wage mandate.

Do not confuse the hourly rate of pay with your cost per hour of hiring an employee. Because of government mandates, the worker only receives a portion of what you must budget for employing him or her. Keep the following costs in mind:

Agreed wage	$12.50 per hour
Federal matching payments	0.94 per hour
Injury compensation insurance	1.87 per hour
Payroll processing	0.44 per hour
Total cost	$15.75 per hour

HIRING BASICS

In the past, charter fishing captains did not formally hire a mate to help bait hooks and land fish. Anyone with the necessary skills could be picked up at the last minute. Their employment was for the duration of the trip and wages were typically paid in cash. Such informal hiring practices are impossible under today's network of interlocking federal regulations. U.S. Coast Guard regulations, such as those for drug testing, the Immigration and Nationality Act (INA), the Americans with Disabilities Act (ADA), and the Personal Responsibility and Work Opportunity Reconciliation Act (PRWORA) all set out requirements that must be met before new employees can go to work.

DO IT ONCE, MANY TIMES

The laws and regulations surrounding hiring employees can be intimidating. However, businesses create new jobs every day, so the task of hiring clearly can be managed. The key to easing the hiring process is to perfect it from the start. Keep detailed notes on what you need to do in terms of procedures, including what forms are necessary, as you go through your first hire. After that, instead of starting from scratch with each new employee, you just repeat a familiar procedure.

Create a hiring folder. This folder should contain blank job applications and a half-dozen packets with all of the government forms that either you or the new employee must fill out during the hiring process. These packets aren't available from any government office. You make them up yourself.

Each packet starts with an empty envelope. Into that goes a copy of each necessary government form that you gather from the appropriate agencies. Include a copy of your hiring procedures in each envelope. This becomes a checklist. Checking off the items on the list as they are completed prevents forgetting any steps. When someone comes to apply for a job, you know where to find an application. If you decide to hire that person, you simply take out one of your packets to speed through the red tape.

JOB APPLICATIONS

Owners of small one- or two-person businesses generally hire from within their group of friends and acquaintances. As long as you meet all of the regulations about reporting a newly hired employee, there is nothing wrong with this practice. However, as noted earlier, things change when you begin to employ more than 15 employees. Dozens of federal employment regulations become effective when that number of employees is reached. Even if your business does not have this number of workers, the public will judge you by the standards set by the various federal agencies and legislation. This is reason enough to be familiar with the various anti-discrimination laws.

Asking the wrong question on a job application form (or in an interview) can be costly in terms of fines. In addition, the federal Civil Rights Act of 1991 provides monetary damages in cases of intentional employment discrimination. Some areas to beware of include the following:

- **Age:** You can ask if someone is over 18 years of age, but the Age Discrimination in Employment Act of 1967 (ADEA) protects individuals who are 40 years of age or older.
- **Race, religion, color:** You cannot ask about race, color, religion, sex, or national origin.

- **Medical history:** You cannot ask about an applicant's physical or mental impairment or about an applicant's use of medication unless the questions directly apply to the work the employee will be expected to perform.

Perhaps the best way to avoid problems is to purchase pre-printed job applications from an office supply store. These forms are designed not to run afoul of federal regulations.

WRITTEN JOB DESCRIPTION

In addition to the questions on the application form, you may ask applicants if they can meet the requirements of the job description. It is a good practice to write a job description that includes not only those tasks normally done by a captain or deckhand, but which also outlines any coast guard requirements for drug testing and physical examinations for licensed personnel. Below is an example of a job description for a deckhand.

> *Deckhand:* **The applicant must be able to respond quickly to instructions, to handle docklines, and to manually recover an anchor and 200 feet of rope on a 30-foot powerboat; move about easily while the boat is under way; have corrected vision to 20/40; demonstrate night vision sufficient to maintain safe lookout; demonstrate hearing sufficient to maintain safe lookout; lift weights to 40 pounds; meet U.S. Coast Guard testing requirements for illegal drugs, and/or use of illegal drugs and alcohol on the job, and agree to the company drug and alcohol policy.**

A written job description like the one above can prevent a variety of problems. Informing applicants they will be tested for illegal drugs immediately weeds out anyone who uses them.

MEDICAL RECORDS

All medical information is covered by strict federal privacy laws. Avoid the chance of violating these strictures by separating medical records from job applications and all other related files. Medical files should be considered as secret and be kept in a secure location. Never discuss an employee's medical condition with any other employees or with your friends.

YOU'RE FIRED

On TV, Donald Trump can discharge an apprentice with a wave of his hand and the words, "You're fired." Except in the Virgin Islands, Puerto Rico, and Montana, you can do the same. Employers in those three areas must have "good cause" to fire workers who are not on probation. In the rest of the country, employees work "at will" for their employers unless there is a labor contract in place. Either party can end the employment at any time, with some exceptions. You cannot fire someone if the decision is based on the following:

- Discrimination on basis of race, religion, disability, or sex
- Worker becomes pregnant, has recently given birth, or has related medical condition
- Retaliation for worker taking advantage of rights under federal or state labor statutes
- Refusal to take lie detector test

In addition to the above, some states prohibit firings based on marital status or sexual orientation. However, in an "at will" state fairness is not required when an employer discharges an employee. For instance, you can discharge a hard-working deckhand just because your brother-in-law needs a job. Severance pay is not mandated by law.

Most of the prohibited reasons for firing an employee are open to interpretation. For instance, you may fire a woman for being incompetent, but she may claim it was because of her pregnancy. You may discharge a man for failing to show up for work, but he may claim it was because of religious intolerance. Who is correct in these cases? The employer seldom wins a case that turns on opinions.

To avoid problems, it pays to keep records of employee performance and to document specific instances where individuals did not perform to expectations. Keep these files absolutely private, except to review problem areas with the employee. Build a careful case for the necessity of discharging anyone and keep detailed records.

LAWS AGAINST DISCRIMINATION

A variety of federal, state, and local laws control your relationship with the people who work for you. Most of these regulations prohibit discrimination in the workplace. The complexity of these laws is such that it is possible to commit a technical violation of one while meeting the larger intention of the legislation. Fortunately, small businesses with fewer than 15 employees are exempt from most federal regulations. States and cities are usually as lenient, although some use the gross annual dollar volume of a business to set lower thresholds for compliance instead of the number of employees.

RACE, GENDER, AND AGE DISCRIMINATION

The Civil Rights Act of 1964 prohibited certain types of discrimination in hiring. A collection of anti-discrimination laws and regulations have grown from that landmark legislation. Today, the prohibited types of discrimination have been expanded beyond that original legislation. While I have already mentioned discrimination in terms of job applications and job interviews, it is worth repeating danger areas one more time. It is now *illegal* to discriminate on the basis of *any* of the following:

- Race, color, or national origin
- Religion
- Sex
- Age

Discriminatory practices under these laws include such things as denial of employment, unequal pay for equal work, or barring a person from job benefits or retirement plans. Employers are not permitted to retaliate against an individual for filing a charge of discrimination.

The federal laws prohibiting sex discrimination go well beyond just equal pay to men and women. All forms of sexual harassment are also prohibited. These include practices ranging from direct requests for sexual favors to workplace conditions that create a hostile environment for persons of either gender. Pregnancy, childbirth, and related medical conditions must be treated in the same way as other temporary illnesses or conditions.

Currently, there are no federal laws or regulations prohibiting discrimination on the basis of sexual orientation. However, 17 states and more than 180 cities and counties nationwide prohibit this type of discrimination.

Age discrimination laws target employees and potential employees over 40 years of age. An age limit may be specified for a job only in the rare circumstance where age is a proven occupational qualification. Benefits may not be denied to older employees based solely on their age.

AMERICANS WITH DISABILITIES ACT

The Americans with Disabilities Act, referred to as the ADA, and the federal regulations arising from it have set the minimum acceptable standard for fair treatment of disabled persons. Even if you do not come under the law, a publicized accusation that you have discriminated against a handicapped person may have a negative impact on your ability to attract customers.

According to the federal Equal Employment Opportunity Commission (EEOC), "The ADA strictly limits the circumstances under which you may ask questions about disability or require medical examinations of employees." Generally you may not require medical examinations of applicants prior to the time you offer them a job. There are some exceptions. For example, a medical exam is necessary to obtain a coast guard license, and any licensed employees will have had to submit to a medical exam before they are eligible for employment on board your vessel.

In addition, medical exams can be required after a job offer is made, provided that the same exam is required of all applicants in similar jobs. The EEOC says you may withdraw a job offer if the medical exam indicates the potential employee cannot safely perform the job. For instance, if you learn the applicant has frequent and unpredictable seizures that might cause a fall overboard, you can withdraw a job offer to a person who was to work as a deckhand.

Nothing in ADA is as clear-cut as it seems. The federal EEOC also says, "You cannot automatically prohibit someone with epilepsy from working around machinery. Some forms of epilepsy are more severe than others or are not well controlled. On the other hand, some people with epilepsy know when a seizure will occur in time to move away from potentially hazardous situations. Sometimes seizures occur only at night, making the possibility of a seizure on the job remote."

The ADA requires the employer to accommodate an employee's disability to a reasonable extent to enable him or her to maintain employment. It is reasonable to give an employee who is otherwise able to do the job, but who develops diabetes, regularly scheduled breaks to eat properly or to monitor blood sugar and insulin levels.

However, you are not required to continue to employ someone who becomes disabled and cannot meet the requirements in the job description. According to the EEOC, "You do not need to provide an accommodation that would pose significant difficulty in terms of the operation of your business." If you have the above job description in place, you would not have to remove the dockline handling requirement to accommodate an employee injured off the job. Doing so would remove one of the main duties of a deckhand.

TAX REQUIREMENTS

As a sole proprietor employing only yourself, you can use your personal Social Security number for all tax purposes. Once you hire an employee, however, you must obtain a separate employer identification number (EIN) from the U.S. Internal Revenue Service. This process can be done online and there is no fee. You use this number to make payroll tax deposits and to execute other transactions with the IRS. Most states follow the federal practice. You may use your own Social Security number for a sole proprietorship, but obtain a commercial tax identification number for filing state returns on your business.

W-4 FORM

Everyone you hire must complete a W-4 form. This form tells you how many withholding allowances to use when you deduct federal income tax from the employee's pay. Completed W-4 forms are kept in your files as verification that you are withholding federal income tax according to the employee's instructions. All W-4 forms on file must be made available for inspection should the IRS ever request it.

Employees often want to change the number of withholding allowances they claim. Marriage or the birth of a child can affect the employee's tax liability. If you receive a revised W-4 form, IRS regulations say it must be put it into effect no later than the start of the first payroll period ending on or after 30 days from the date you received it. Full information on W-4 forms is found in IRS Publication 15 and Publication 505.

Some states and municipalities that levy income taxes require employers to file a copy of W-4 forms, or have a similar form of their own. Check with your accountant on the reporting requirements where you do business. W-4 forms can be obtained online from the IRS website or they can be purchased in packages from office supply stores.

EMPLOYEE DOCUMENTATION

Employee documentation is yet another aspect of the hiring process. Don't take it lightly. The federal government takes it very seriously.

Social Security Number Verification

Internal Revenue Service regulations require you to identify employees by Social Security number. It is possible to verify employee Social Security numbers through a website operated by the Social Security Administration. Certain restrictions apply. This site can only be used to verify current or former employees and only for wage reporting (W-2) purposes. The URL is http://www.socialsecurity.gov/employer/ssnv.htm.

Immigration and Nationality Act

No matter how big or small the company, all employers are required by the Immigration and Nationality Act (INA) to hire only persons who may legally work in the United States. The employer must verify the identity and employment eligibility of anyone to be hired by having the prospective employee complete an employment eligibility verification form (I-9). To be eligible for employment, a worker must qualify in one of three ways:

- U.S. citizenship
- Lawful permanent residence
- Alien with authorization to work

For U.S. citizens, a driver's license establishes the identity of the new employee and a U.S. Social Security card is proof of eligibility to work. A U.S. passport is good for both purposes. Anyone holding a master's license has met these requirements to the satisfaction of the U.S. Coast Guard. However, a master's license is not on the list of acceptable documents for form I-9. Employers must retain all I-9 forms on file for at least three years, or one year after employment ends, whichever is longer. The I-9 forms are available as PDF files from www.uscis.gov/files/form/i-9.pdf.

New Hire Reporting

About a decade ago, Congress enacted welfare reform. This legislation also required employers in all 50 states to report their new hires to a state director. The purpose of this directory is to make it easier to collect child support from parents who frequently change jobs. The laws Florida passed to meet this federal requirement are typical. All newly hired employees in the Sunshine State must be reported even if they work for only a single day. Seasonal workers must be reported each time they return to work. Florida requires employers to provide the person's name, address, Social Security number, and date of hire. Reports must be filed within 20 days.

TAXES TO COLLECT

If you have employees, you are responsible for collecting and depositing a variety of federal, state, and local taxes. Employment taxes include:

- Social Security and Medicare taxes
- Federal, state, and local income taxes
- Federal unemployment tax act (FUTA)

Income, Social Security, and Medicare taxes are withheld from employee wages. The IRS claims that FUTA is not withheld from your employee's pay, but is a tax that is paid from the employer's funds. This is a political technicality, but beware that from a business standpoint FUTA is part of your cost of employing that individual. When hiring, you establish the total amount you can spend for an employee, then deduct FUTA from that. The result is the gross pay you offer the employee. In the end, FUTA comes out of the money you set aside for the employee's net pay, despite what the IRS says.

IRS Tax Deposits

Small businesses normally make quarterly payments to the IRS of all employee taxes collected. This is done on a 941 form (employer's quarterly federal tax return). The process is quite simple, but you should have your accountant walk you through it the first time. However, you may be eligible to make one annual payment, if you believe that your employment taxes will be under $1,000. This means your annual payroll will be under about $4,000. Use IRS Form 944 to claim this privilege.

DRUG AND ALCOHOL TESTING

The biggest hurdle to hiring new employees is the coast guard required pre-employment drug test. Everyone you hire to work on your boat who has anything to do with the safe operation of the vessel, including yourself, must be tested for illicit drugs prior to going to work. This requirement applies equally to six-pack and inspected vessels.

After being hired, employees must participate in a random drug testing program that meets regulations. The "whiz quiz," as drug tests are sometimes called, must be done by registered health care laboratories, and the results must be reported to the employer and to the coast guard. In addition, the employer is required to provide antidrug abuse instruction for the crew and to train supervisors how to spot persons using drugs or alcohol on the job.

Inspected vessel operators will deal with a representative of the local marine safety office (MSO) called the drug and alcohol program inspector, or DAPI. The DAPI conducts audits of marine employers' programs during each annual inspection. If they don't become involved in a serious marine incident, uninspected six-pack operators will probably never see a DAPI. For either an inspected or six-pack operator, however, failure to maintain a drug testing program can result in a $5,500 fine per calendar day of operation since last proof of compliance, suspension of your operator's or master's license, and/or removal of the certificate of inspection (COI) from the vessel.

DRUG AND ALCOHOL POLICY

As an employer, you must have a written drug and alcohol policy and you must give it to every new hire. The employee should sign and date either a copy of the policy or a separate receipt acknowledging that he or she has (1) received a copy of the policy and (2) read and understood the contents of that policy. The coast guard suggests a variety of topics to be contained within drug policies.

Policies

- **Prohibited:** Possession, sale, or use of illegal drugs or alcohol on company premises or use of illegal drugs or alcohol while on duty.
- **Prescriptions:** Statement from physician that prescription drugs will not impair employee's safe work performance.
- **Testing:** Required of all employees holding safety-sensitive positions before hire and randomly during employment.
- **Search:** In the interest of safety, the company reserves the right to search personal belongings of employees.

Discipline

- **Immediate discharge:** Testing positive for alcohol or drugs will be subject to immediate discharge from employment.
- **Failure to cooperate:** Refusing to undergo drug testing or cooperate with company drug and alcohol policies may result in termination of employment.

Administrative Procedures

- **Reporting:** The company will report the possession, sale, or use of illegal drugs and unsanctioned use of alcohol on its premises to public authorities.
- **Privacy:** Information concerning drug or alcohol testing, or violations of this policy, will be treated as confidential.

EMPLOYEE ASSISTANCE PROGRAM

You must offer your employees an employee assistance program (EAP) that at a minimum provides information on where to seek counseling and assistance. According to the U.S. Coast Guard, this section of the drug and alcohol testing program causes marine employers the most problems. Many fail to understand how their consortium or third-party adviser provides the required services. An acceptable EAP must include the display and distribution of informational material related to drug and alcohol counseling, with a community service hot-line telephone number. The employer's drug policy must be displayed in the workplace.

An EAP training program is also required for crew members and supervisory personnel. Four elements are required in the training program:

- The effects of drugs and alcohol on personal health, personal safety, and the work environment
- The manifestations and behavioral cues that may indicate drug and alcohol use or abuse
- Documentation of training given to crew members and supervisory personnel
- At least 60 minutes of training for supervisory personnel

BACKGROUND CHECK

Within 30 days of hiring a new employee, all marine employers must request drug- and alcohol-related information about that individual from all previous employers covered by the federal Department of Transportation (DOT) drug and alcohol regulations. To do this, you first must get the employee's written permission. The previous employer must provide information on these areas of concern:

- Alcohol tests with a result of 0.04 percent blood alcohol content (BAC) or higher
- Verified positive drug tests
- Refusals to test for drugs or alcohol
- Other violations of DOT drug and alcohol regulations
- Proof of completion of DOT return to duty requirements, if a violation was reported

You should receive a reply from an individual's previous employer within 30 days. If you do not, you may continue to employ that person in a safety-sensitive position, but keep written documentation that your request for the required information was not honored. As a marine employer, you are also required to provide this same information to another DOT-regulated company hiring one of your present or past employees. Never give out this information without seeing the individual's signature on a permission form.

DRUG AND ALCOHOL TESTS

The only drug test accepted by the coast guard is a "five-panel urine DOT test." Testing hair for evidence of drugs is not acceptable. Urine samples are tested for marijuana, cocaine, opiates, amphetamines, and phencyclidine (PCP). All samples must be collected under regulated conditions, generally in a hospital or independent medical facility. Collected samples then go to accredited laboratories where they are tested for the five illicit drugs.

Pre-employment and/or random alcohol testing is not required by the coast guard. Alcohol testing is only mandatory after a serious marine incident. The only acceptable tests for alcohol are either blood or breath analysis. A mariner is presumed to be "under the influence" for coast guard purposes with a blood alcohol content (BAC) greater than or equal to 0.040 percent while they are operating a vessel (33 CFR part 95). Note that coast guard regulations are different from state regulations on drinking while driving either a car or a boat. States now limit BAC to 0.08 percent.

One recent requirement mandates that vessels operating more than two hours from home port must carry one breath testing kit for each employee in a safety-related position on board. This regulation applies to six-pack and inspected vessels.

Part-Time Workers

Many small passenger vessels employ independent contractors as captains on a per-trip basis. Even though these people are technically not employees, they still must be part of the company's drug testing program. The reason is to make sure that you receive notification of any positive drug tests or refusals to test by that employee. If the person is not in your program, you might not be notified of either event, and so wrongly permit the individual to continue to work.

No pre-employment drug testing is required if you have proof the person has passed a pre-employment drug test for another employer within the last six months or has been part of a random testing program for the past 12 months (46 CFR §16.220). Volunteer crew members who work in safety-sensitive jobs must be drug tested even though they are not paid. The status of someone as a volunteer does not change the testing requirement.

Third-Party Administrators

The process of drug testing under DOT and U.S. Coast Guard regulations is complex. From a practical standpoint, a small marine employer simply cannot meet the regulations without outside assistance. A one-person operation like a sole proprietor charter fishing captain must meet the same regulations as a big, multi-ship cruise line. Yet, a self-employed fishing guide cannot conduct his or her own random selection because it would be impossible to have an "unannounced" test under the law. Even worse is the paper trail required of each individual test and the record keeping on individual employees and on your company.

The impossibility of "do-it-yourself" drug testing brought about the creation of consortiums and other third-party administrators (TPAs) that perform most or all of the work on a fee-for-service basis. The coast guard does not provide lists of these providers. It is up to you as an employer to find one suited to your business.

Some of these service providers are national businesses. Others are owned and operated by charter captain associations. Some hospital outpatient clinics located near high concentrations of maritime activity provide these services. Ask other vessel operators, or better yet, join a local captains' association to learn about third-party administrators that meet your needs. The costs of drug testing programs vary. Expect to pay about $65 to $95 per employee per year. Programs with lower per-person charges may have additional fees for each test administered.

Services Provided by Third-Party Administrators

- Approved collection process
- Substance Abuse and Mental Health Service Administrator (SAMHSA) accredited lab for testing

- Medical review officer to verify accuracy of testing
- Substance abuse professional (SAP) to evaluate violations and advise when employee is eligible to return to work
- Compliance record keeping and reporting

All agreements for third-party suppliers and service agents must state that services are being provided in accordance with 49 CFR part 40 and 46 CFR part 16. Get a written contract. A few years ago, I experienced a mix-up with my drug testing agency. I sent a list of employees to be deleted from our water taxi company. Instead, the testing service kept those names and deleted all of the current employees. At my next annual inspection, I discovered that my company had not been in compliance for almost nine months, exposing me to a whopping potential fine of $1,215,000. Fortunately, I had my contract with the provider and my copy of the written instructions regarding employees to be included. That got me off the hook.

Positive Tests

If an employee tests positive for illegal drugs, you must immediately remove that person from a safety-sensitive position. The individual may not return to work in a safety-sensitive position until a "return to work" letter is obtained from the medical review officer, or the employee has completed a drug rehabilitation program under 49 CFR part 40, subpart O. This means that either a doctor says the employee is "clean," or the worker has completed an approved rehabilitation program. You must also provide the crew member with the name of a service assistance provider (usually a licensed drug and alcohol counselor) who provides assistance in overcoming substance abuse problems.

If the person testing positive holds a coast guard–issued license, you must report the positive test to that agency. Failure to report a positive test can result in a civil penalty against you as the employer. Once the coast guard receives the report, an investigating officer will verify the validity of the test. If the test is validated, the process of suspending or revoking the individual's license will begin. Mariners may enter a consent agreement with the coast guard to settle the revocation process. For use of a dangerous drug, the coast guard will apply certain sanctions, usually suspension of the license, and it will list the following conditions that will be applied to reinstatement of that license.

- At least a 12-month suspension of credentials will be issued. Revocation of the credentials may be suspended if terms of agreement are met.
- Individual will be required to complete a bona fide rehabilitation program for reinstatement of credentials.
- At least 12 months of aftercare will be required, consisting of the individual's documented attendance at support meetings (average four per month). Not less than six unannounced random drug tests in 12 months, all negative. Obtain return to work letter from medical review officer.

It takes 12 to 18 months to complete the reinstatement process for suspensions resolved under a consent agreement. During that time the person may not work under the suspended license. Failure to complete the agreement in the specified time results in revocation of the license.

Refusal to Test

Anyone refusing to take a drug test must immediately be removed from any safety-sensitive job. The coast guard takes a dim view of a mariner's refusal to undergo testing. Persons refusing drug testing will be treated as if they had tested positive for drugs, and the same suspension and revocation proceedings will be initiated.

FEDERAL OSHA

Some confusion surrounds the federal Occupational Safety and Health Act (OSHA). According to the U.S. Department of Labor, "The OSH Act does not address the working conditions of employees on passenger vessels." The reason for this partially true statement is that OHSA cannot override safety regulations already on the books from other federal agencies. Worker safety on inspected vessels primarily comes under coast guard regulations. This means that OSHA doesn't apply because the coast guard has already implemented regulations that address safe working conditions on coast guard–inspected vessels.

However, recent court decisions and changes in legislation have allowed OSHA to regulate employee safety in areas not covered by coast guard regulations. This allows OSHA to become involved with uninspected six-pack vessels simply because they are not inspected by the coast guard. As of 2007, OSHA has issued no regulations specific to uninspected vessels. Even if such regulations are issued, small businesses with only one or two employees will not be subject to inspection unless an on-the-job injury occurs. Some aspects of operation likely to come under OSHA scrutiny if an accident occurs aboard an uninspected vessel may include the following:

- **Safety program:** Even if you have only one employee in addition to yourself, you should have a formal safety program, including training and a procedure for handling in-house safety complaints.
- **Walking surfaces:** Nonskid materials must be applied and maintained on decks and other walking surfaces likely to become wet.
- **First aid:** At least one crew member on each trip should be qualified to render first aid. Proof of passing a Red Cross or equivalent first aid class within the previous calendar year is sufficient. Qualification may be demonstrated by holding current Red Cross cards showing completion of first aid and CPR training.
- **First aid kit:** An uninspected vessel should have a first aid kit that meets coast guard standards for sub-T inspected vessels. This kit should contain equipment to protect from blood-borne pathogens, and it should be regularly inspected (you can do it) and refilled, and a record kept of these inspections.
- **Eating areas:** If a specific area is provided for consumption of food or beverages, there should be no exposure to toxic or potentially infectious materials.
- **Toilets:** The head should be cleaned regularly and kept in a sanitary condition.

To avoid a conflict with this federal agency, six-pack operators can only fall back on the OSHA requirement that employers must provide employment that is "free from recognized hazards . . . likely to cause death or serious physical harm."

CHAPTER 8

BUSINESS, MARINE, AND EMPLOYEE INSURANCE

Insurance has been described as a wager. You bet that something bad will happen, while the insurance company bets that it will not. Like all such witticisms, the statement oversimplifies the relationship you have with your insurance company. It only seems like you are getting nothing in return for your premium dollars because financial protection is an intangible. You can't store insurance coverage in your toolbox or see it on the shelf of your storeroom. Even so, you cannot afford to operate a marine business today without protection against lawsuits, accidents, pollution, wreck removal, and employee injuries.

The basis of insurance is an agreement ("policy") between you (the "insured") and the insurance company (the "insurer"). Under this agreement you agree to pay a specified premium. The insurance company agrees to pay ("indemnify") you if you suffer losses or damage specified in the agreement.

What follows is far from a complete discussion of insurance. It is intended to introduce the key types of insurance coverage you should consider as the operator of a commercial vessel. When it is time to purchase coverage, you should develop a solid working relationship with a trusted insurance agent or broker who has a full understanding of marine insurance and the issues associated with it.

BUYING INSURANCE

Broadly speaking, you will need to consider ordinary business insurance to cover your operations on land and separate marine coverage for your boat and on-water activities. Chances are you'll need more than one company, which means all your coverage won't be in one policy. Six-pack operators have the choice between true commercial marine insurance and yacht policies modified to allow limited commercial activities. Inspected vessels require full marine coverage. Both types of policies are based on the same concepts of marine underwriting.

Most of the time you will purchase insurance through an agent or broker who is not always an employee of the insurance carrier. The agent has nothing to do with the wording of the policy, and you should never trust an agent's word about what is covered in your policy. Read it for yourself. If the legal language is confusing, give the policy to a qualified maritime attorney for review.

As I said earlier, depending on the complexity of your business, you will probably need several different types of coverage. Insurance industry regulations often require you to buy separate policies for each type of coverage you require. Insurance companies use standard contracts for individual risks, allowing companies to jointly bundle risks so they are shared industry-wide. Thus, you will have to choose the coverage applicable to your needs from standard contracts.

OVERLAPPING COVERAGE

There is a potential problem that arises from having to purchase several different types of policies: the possibility of overlapping coverage, which wastes money and is unnecessary. In an overlap situation, you pay twice for the same coverage, but you can only collect once if you file a claim. Each policy will only pay a portion of the total loss.

On the other hand, sometimes gaps occur between policies, and you should read and study your coverage very carefully to identify any gaps that may exist. It is often possible to bridge these gaps with so-called umbrella policies that only pay after all of your other coverage is exhausted. A good agent should be able to help you steer clear of double coverage, or advise you when an umbrella policy is needed.

TRADE ORGANIZATIONS

There are a variety of trade organizations that service specific types of marine activities. One of the benefits of belonging to such a group is the ability to purchase insurance under a policy tailored to your particular type of operation. This eliminates a lot of the guesswork about what type of coverage to purchase. As an added benefit, the buying power of a trade organization helps cut costs. These policies often cost 10 to 30 percent less than the coverage you purchase on your own. See Appendix B for a listing of these organizations.

ORDINARY BUSINESS INSURANCE

Even though you work on the water, your business has a variety of land-based activities, and some or all of them may need insurance coverage. A six-pack skipper with an office outside the home will need to cover equipment and liabilities such as slip-and-falls. If the office is run out of the captain's home and the public doesn't go there, then the equipment may be covered under the person's homeowner's policy, but any loss of income to the business from a fire or theft would not be covered. He or she may need commercial auto coverage on a truck used primarily for business or additional liability coverage when renting a booth at a fishing or boat show.

Larger passenger operations often have offices on shore where employees keep the books and sell tickets. Six-pack or larger businesses may own or rent storage facilities. All businesses need to consider protection against claims arising from employee or passenger injuries, false advertising, trademark infringement, breach of contract, and unfair trade or employment practices. These risks are covered under various policies designed for businesses and include the following areas of concern:

- **Property insurance:** This type of insurance covers physical assets such as buildings, equipment, furniture, fixtures, and stock. Perils insured against include fire, windstorms, hail, explosions, riots, lightning strikes, and vandalism. It may also cover the cost of removing property to a safe place to prevent additional damage. Property insurance does not cover flooding or high-water damage.

- **Commercial auto insurance:** A car or truck used primarily for business is considered commercial and is usually not covered by personal auto insurance. Commercial auto insurance offers the same coverage for company vehicles. It may also cover the casual use of personal cars by employees on company business.
- **Liability insurance:** Business liability policies usually protect against claims arising from bodily or personal injuries to some other person. It may also cover damage to someone else's property. Most policies pay the cost of such damages, plus your attorney fees. Business liability insurance generally does not cover injuries to passengers on commercial vessels. That coverage must be obtained as part of the vessel insurance program.
- **Employment practices liability insurance:** This policy covers claims of employee wrongful termination, discrimination, or sexual harassment.
- **Lost income insurance:** This coverage repays you for income lost because of an event covered under your property insurance (e.g., a fire). It may also cover loss of income caused by actions of third parties such as the government.

OFF-PREMISES ACTIVITIES

Charter fishing captains typically participate in winter boat shows and sports shows. This involves renting booth space for the purpose of meeting the public and generating sales. Most show operators require proof of a minimum level of liability insurance covering booth activities, usually up to a million dollars. This coverage can be included in your basic business policy or you can purchase it separately on a case-by-case basis.

INLAND MARINE POLICY

For mariners, this is probably the most confusing term in insurance. *Inland marine* does not necessarily refer to boats or the water. It is a term that arose more than 150 years ago when most goods were transported by river and canal on the inland waterways of the nation. Today, it refers primarily to coverage on items that may be transported from place to place by any means of conveyance. You may need an inland marine policy to cover your laptop computer, tools, and other equipment.

BUSINESS OWNER'S POLICIES

The complexity of commercial insurance has motivated several carriers to create special products for small businesses called business owner's policies, or BOPs. One of these products combines property and liability coverage into a single policy that may also include specialized protection for different industries. A BOP is generally less expensive for the same coverage. The only problem is that one policy may not fit all businesses. Be sure the one you are offered really does protect you from all of your business risks.

MARINE INSURANCE

Marine insurance developed slowly over hundreds of years to meet the needs of commercial shipping on the high seas. It is intertwined with Admiralty Law and even the Rules of the Road. Much of the wording in your policy was originally hammered out at Lloyd's when it was still only a coffee shop in London. Because marine insurance is so different from ordinary business policies, you should consult only with agents or brokers who are experts in this field.

BASIC CONCEPTS

Because boats are so different from land-based businesses and business equipment, it should not be surprising that some insurance concepts that have evolved are unique to the marine field or are applied in different ways from their land-based counterparts. Similarly, there are unique types of coverage that apply only to boats or boat-based businesses. We'll address the basic concepts first.

Agreed Value

A typical yacht policy bases payment for loss of a vessel on its depreciated value. This is similar to car insurance. True marine insurance is based on an agreed value of the vessel for the duration of the policy. In most cases, you state the value of your boat and the premium for hull coverage is based on that amount. Hull coverage protects against damage to the vessel from grounding, fire, or other accidents. Claims are not depreciated. If your boat is a total loss, you receive the full agreed value (less deductible).

Seaworthiness

Perhaps the biggest differences between a marine policy and commercial auto coverage lie in the seaworthiness clauses. Auto policies do not demand as much of the owner, and they certainly do not demand that the insured car be seaworthy! A marine policy will require that your vessel be under the control of a qualified master (or operator, in the case of a six-pack vessel) at all times. Your vessel must comply with existing U.S. Coast Guard regulations and you must maintain the boat in a physically seaworthy condition at all times.

Finally, you may not exceed the passenger or crew limits set for your vessel by the coast guard. Violations of these provisions are usually grounds for policy termination or a release from liability on the part of the insurance company in the event of a claim; in other words, the company won't have to pay up.

Perils

Going to sea for any purpose is considered an adventure with a variety of associated risks. These are known as "perils" in the insurance world. In general, they include factors that may cause damage to the vessel or its total loss. Perils have traditionally been described as "wind and waves, fire and lightning, and pirates and kings." "Kings" referred to the seizure of the vessel by a foreign government. If you hire a captain and crew, the typical marine policy protects you against barratry, the deliberate destruction of your vessel by your employees.

It may not be immediately obvious, but a strict definition of perils confines them to forces outside the vessel or deliberate illegal actions by the crew. For instance, the crime of barratry (wrecking the ship deliberately for profit) by your crew is covered. On the other hand, negligence that is not necessarily a criminal act of your hired captain is not a "peril" under maritime insurance. A vessel loss through wear and tear, say from a broken propeller shaft, is not covered either. In both cases, these losses are the result of ordinary events related to the operation of the vessel.

TYPES OF MARINE INSURANCE COVERAGE

As the owner of a boat-based business, you will face a number of risks that are substantially different or altogether absent from those of land-based businesses, necessitating different types of insurance coverage. These include the obscurely named "Inchmaree clause," protection against the economic and legal dangers associated with collisions and pollution incidents, coverage for towing and wreck removal, and special coverage for accidents that occur "betwixt land and sea" on docks, piers, and gangways.

Inchmaree Clause

An obvious gap in coverage created a famous legal case that forced a new type of coverage named after the vessel involved. In 1887, the steamer *Inchmaree* gained lasting fame as the center of a dispute over insurance coverage of damage incurred through the negligence of its engineers. Today, an "Inchmaree clause" is part of hull insurance that extends coverage to damage on the vessel from a variety of causes ranging from human error to latent defects in machinery, including:

- Accidents from loading cargo or fuel
- Explosions on board
- Breakdown of machinery or latent defect in machinery or in the hull
- Negligence of the master or crew
- Being struck by a flying airplane
- A nuclear accident not on board the insured vessel

Inchmaree coverage requires that such losses do not result from "want of due diligence" by the insured. In addition, this coverage does not extend to ordinary wear and tear on machinery. If you try to get one too many trips out of a damaged transmission, your insurance won't cover an accident resulting from the failure of a worn-out part.

Collision and Running Down

Included in most hull insurance is a provision to cover liability incurred for damages done by your boat to another vessel. This portion of a policy does much the same job as automotive collision insurance but with one major difference. The principle of comparative damages applies.

On shore, one party in a collision is arbitrarily deemed "at fault." On the water, the two or more vessels involved are all held responsible to some extent. Usually, responsibility is assessed on a percentage basis. For instance, you may be held 40 percent responsible, while the other vessel is given 60 percent of the responsibility for an accident. This is sometimes called the "principle of cross-liabilities."

Protection and Indemnity

This is sort of a catchall provision of marine insurance that covers two main areas:

- **Loss of life, injury, or illness:** This covers people who may have a claim against your boat as the result of an accident. This coverage usually includes hospital and medical payments. A top limit for payments of this type is set by the policy.
- **Damage to another vessel:** Any liability not covered in the standard hull insurance clause is included here. Coverage may also be extended to damage to another vessel not caused by a collision. Damage done to docks, piers, and other structures along the waterway are included in this clause.

Pollution

A major economic threat to the business owner is the cost of preventing, containing, or cleaning up an oil spill resulting from an accident. The costs of deploying oil booms or hand-washing shorebirds are staggering. A marine policy should contain pollution coverage for such expenses. Typically, this coverage only applies to the cost of pollution remediation. It does not cover any civil fines imposed as the result of a pollution incident.

Towing and Wreck Removal

The owners of pleasure boats can purchase memberships in towing services. These memberships cover towing services in a breakdown or limited salvage in the event of a grounding. Commercial assistance towing companies serving the pleasure boat fleet do not offer similar coverage to commercial vessels. As a result, you must be sure that it is included in your marine policy. Whenever a commercial vessel needs assistance, it becomes salvage at a higher charge than ordinary assistance to a disabled pleasure boat.

Docks, Piers, and Gangways

Whether it is a six-pack charter fishing business or a 149-passenger ferry service, chances are your operation will be based out of a commercial marina. This means your passengers will use docks, piers, and even gangways provided by the marina. If someone is injured, it can be a nightmare sorting out who is responsible. "Docks, piers, and gangways" coverage extends your policy to cover customers using those boarding facilities. Most marinas will require proof that you carry such coverage before allowing you to load passengers from their property.

SAMPLE INSURANCE COSTS

The following list will provide you with a snapshot of what it would cost to insure a 24-passenger sightseeing vessel with an agreed value of $43,500:

Hull Coverage	**$575**
Hull and machinery	
Perils of sea	
Inchmaree perils	
Pollution hazard	
Collision liability	
Protection and Indemnity	**$920**
Loss of life, injury, illness	
Damage to other vessels	
Damage to docks	
Removal of wreck	
Pollution coverage	
Incidental longshore compensation	
Total Premium	**$1,495**

EMPLOYEE INJURIES

All states have some form of workers' compensation laws to cover employees injured on the job. Expect to be tied up in red tape when it comes to state compensation laws as they apply to mariners. Most state agencies are unaware of the Jones Act, which covers injured employees who work aboard a vessel. Think of the Jones Act as a sort of seagoing workers' compensation law. The difference is that instead of a state bureau of compensation, it is the employer who is responsible for payments due to injured mariners. Fortunately, you can purchase insurance to cover these expenses.

THE JONES ACT

Nothing is more misunderstood than the so-called Jones Act, the popular name for the federal Merchant Marine Act of 1920. This legislation deals primarily with big ship matters. It also controls *cabbotage*, the legal name for passenger and cargo voyages that begin and end in U.S. ports without an intermediate stop in a foreign country. This is the law that limits "cabbotage voyages" only to vessels built in the United States, owned by U.S. citizens or companies, and under command of a U.S. licensed master. However, for typical six-pack skippers or operators of small passenger vessels, the most important section deals with the employer's responsibility for mariners injured on vessels. The text follows:

> **46 USC 688(a) "Any seaman who shall suffer personal injury in the course of his employment may, at his election maintain an action for damages at law, with the right to trial by jury, and in such action all statutes of the United States modifying or extending the common-law right or remedy in cases of personal injury to railway employees shall apply."**

In general, an injured mariner has three types of protection under the Jones Act:

- **Maintenance:** This is a legal term for room and board payments. The law assumes that a mariner lives aboard ship and will need to be compensated for expenses incurred living ashore while recovering from an injury.
- **Cure:** Under maritime law, "cure" is payment for medical expenses paid to a mariner disabled by injury or illness. These

payments continue until the individual reaches "maximum cure," which is defined as when no further improvement can be obtained from medical treatment.

- **Wages:** The wages of an injured mariner must be paid as if an injured mariner were on duty for the duration of the employment contract.

Although you, as an employer, are responsible for payments required under the Jones Act, it is possible to purchase insurance to cover these costs. Jones Act coverage is normally included as part of your overall marine insurance package. Important concepts of Jones Act insurance are discussed below.

Unseaworthiness

Injured mariners are, in addition to the compensation outlined above, eligible to sue for damages caused by alleged "unseaworthiness" of the vessel if that condition contributed to the injury. To be seaworthy, a vessel must not only receive proper maintenance, but it must also have a trained crew and master. It is your duty as the vessel owner to maintain your boat in a seaworthy condition. As noted earlier, "seaworthy" in a legal context means more than just that the boat can float. It can be extended to include consideration of the training and experience of the captain or the injured person's direct supervisor.

Negligence

An act of negligence on the part of the vessel's owner or representative (your captain) can dramatically increase any monetary awards under the Jones Act. Legally speaking, in the maritime arena, *negligence* can be defined as taking or failing to take some action that another person exercising ordinary care would either have taken or not taken under similar circumstances. In other words, a reasonable person would fix broken steps leading to the bridge. If you or your captain failed to make those repairs and someone fell and was injured, your behavior would be judged as negligent.

Comparative Negligence

Often, when an injury occurs, it is partly the fault of the injured person and partly the fault of the employer. Under the doctrine of "comparative negligence," an award for damages under the Jones Act can be reduced by the percentage a court determines the injured employee contributed to the accident. If the court finds the mariner was 50 percent to blame, then any awards for injuries would likely be reduced by 50 percent.

LONGSHOREMEN'S COMPENSATION

Not all people who work on ships are considered "mariners" under the Jones Act. Under certain circumstances, if you operate an inspected commercial vessel, you can become an employer of dock workers under the federal Longshoreman's and Harbor Workers' Compensation Act (LHWCA). Employees such as line handlers, baggage workers, and even mechanics working on the waterfront but who are not vessel crew members often fall into the harbor worker category.

Covered workers receive medical and disability benefits as well as rehabilitation services under the act. Coverage of this liability can be included in your marine policy as well. A 2005 Congressional report found that LHWCA coverage costs up to three times the price of similar state workers' compensation insurance.

Uninspected six-pack vessel owners are not troubled by LHWCA. Employees who normally work on recreational vessels under 65 feet in length are exempt from LHWCA. This exemption applies even if they occasionally work on a commercial vessel, such as a ferry or dinner cruise boat.

STATE COMPENSATION LAWS

The real problem with Jones Act coverage is convincing state agencies that it supersedes state compensation coverage. You should not pay state coverage on workers already insured under your Jones Act coverage. The Jones Act only covers mariners and *certain* shore workers. It doesn't cover most of the people who work for you on land, such as ticket sellers, office staff, and boatyard crews. Instead, they come under state workers' compensation laws. You will have to pay premiums for state workers' compensation coverage on these employees.

In most states you will be required to either purchase workers' compensation coverage or contribute to a government fund covering your on-shore workers. Shop around if you operate in a state with an open market for workers' compensation insurance. The premiums for similar coverage can vary from one carrier to another.

Double-check that your company is correctly categorized by the state. For instance, our shore workers were first considered as "carnival workers" by the state workers' compensation agency. The premium for this group of workers was nearly three times that of the charge for the correct marina worker grouping. Had we not checked, we would have been paying hundreds of dollars every month in unnecessary premiums.

CHAPTER 9

MARKETING YOUR BUSINESS

M arketing and advertising are not the same. Marketing refers to an overall strategy to get your product in front of customers and induce them to purchase. Advertising is one of the tactics that may be used to achieve that strategic goal. A common, expensive mistake of beginning entrepreneurs is to rely on advertising in print media or on TV as the primary form of marketing. The money expended on this type of campaign is often lost because the effort lacks focus and direction. As a result, the entrepreneur falls into the trap of believing an old half-truth that "advertising doesn't work." The campaign stops and with it ends any marketing efforts. What comes next is predictable. Sales decline and the company fails.

Like it or not, we live in a media-driven world. People are constantly bombarded with messages. Some are unabashed advertising pitches aimed at convincing us to buy a specific product or service, often ones we don't even need. However, the majority of messages are more subtle. They come disguised as news stories or interview segments on the morning TV shows. They come in magazine articles and logos on baseball caps. Messages pile upon messages. Trying to get a potential customer to notice your company is a bit like trying to make them see white paper in a blizzard. In communications terms, the "noise level" is as high or higher than the "signal" (your message).

The good news is you can make your voice heard above all that noise. It just takes some thought, effort, and money. The following pages will help you figure out how to effectively market your business.

YOUR IMAGE

Image as a marketing concept is hard to define, but it is easy to demonstrate. Rock stars work hard to cultivate a hip image, and Wall Street investment bankers work hard to do the opposite, opting for the conservative over the flamboyant. The rockers and the bankers look, speak, and dress differently from one another, and that is no accident because image counts.

Each group projects an identifying image for a purpose. Few people would entrust their money to a musician, even though they might like the music. However, the polished shoes and fancy suit of a banker engender trust and foster a subliminal feeling that if the banker is prosperous he or she can make you wealthier, too. That may be the furthest thing from the truth, but the feeling arises anyway. In a similar fashion, your business must project an image that identifies both the service it provides and the customers it intends to attract.

The operators of sightseeing "ducks" usually paint their vehicles in bright, almost circus-like colors. They promote themselves as being "fun for the whole family." The fun aspect sometimes extends to passing out "quacker" noisemakers that passengers are allowed to take home. Advertising for these businesses usually features families and focuses on youngsters.

The owners of schooner cruise businesses project a more subdued image. The emphasis is on the beauty of sailing and being "at one with nature." Vessels are usually painted in traditional colors with lots of varnished brightwork to admire. History is often promoted as much as the actual vessel in advertising brochures. Some schooner companies go as far as putting their crews in period costumes. While families are not overlooked, the advertising is often aimed at a more mature audience with what are called "higher demographics" (meaning larger incomes).

If you plan to do fishing charters, consider your personal image. Ever notice how many successful captains have beards? The bearded look gives them an "old man of the sea" appearance, and that image helps customers believe those skippers can catch fish. There is no relationship between chin whiskers and fishing ability. When it comes to finding fish, some of the best skippers are women. At a fishing show, however, the bearded captain in the sun-faded cap has the attention-getting image even if he has yet to land a sunfish.

A typical failure of a new entrepreneur is to forget about cultivating a winning image. The result can be catastrophic. As that old saying reminds us, "you only have one chance to make a first impression." Developing the image you want to project to potential customers must be an important part of your marketing plan.

There are two key areas to consider. One consists of projecting the right image with the aesthetic appeal of your vessel, your home port, and even the clothes you wear. The other includes the collateral materials you use to communicate your message and image in print. These materials include your company logo, letterhead, business cards, and advertising brochures.

LOOKING GOOD

Keep the following in mind as you consider the essentials of your business image.

- **The boat:** Different areas of the country favor different types of boats for charter fishing. Your image will suffer if you choose an otherwise acceptable boat that does not "look like" a charter boat. Regardless of what marine business you want to operate, the boat you use must look clean and safe.
- **Home port:** An older marina with wooden piers may fit perfectly into the image of a fishing charter company, but such a facility projects the wrong image for an upscale dinner cruise. Do not underestimate the importance of the boat's location. It must convey the image you want to project to potential customers.
- **Crew dress:** What you wear at work tells potential customers how serious you are about your business. Fishing charter captains wear clothing suited to baiting hooks and hauling in fish that may be bleeding. Dinner cruise skippers are expected to appear in dress whites. Each costume projects an aura of confidence, but for different reasons.

COLLATERAL MATERIALS

The collection of printed matter you use to communicate with customers and to promote your business is called collateral material. It makes a statement about who you are, and it conveys your image subliminally. Cheap business cards and letterhead printed on copier paper convey a different image than embossed business cards and quality rag paper letterheads. You have to decide what is important to you and how much you want to spend on image. Whatever course you take, make sure every component in your collateral material package is professional. For example, spelling and grammar count.

- **Logo:** Every company needs a logo. This is an easily identified piece of artwork used on all company letterhead, business cards, and advertising materials. Don't go overboard on a fancy logo. Pick something simple that can be reduced in size without becoming unrecognizable. The logo should link to your business. For instance, a fish is a good symbol for either a charter or walk-on fishing business.
- **Letterhead:** This is the fancy name for blank paper used by businesses to write letters. It should have your company logo and return address information printed at the top. Today, it helps to include your website and e-mail address. Embossed letterhead with raised letters was formerly required to give the image of a successful company. You don't need it unless you are courting corporate charters or high-end weddings. It is perfectly acceptable to produce your letterhead on the same computer printer that does all your other printing jobs. Improve the image of computer-generated letterhead by printing it on heavier paper stock that has some "rag" content. Specialized papers in a variety of colors are available through office supply stores. Matching envelopes provide a finishing touch. If possible, match your letterhead paper with a similar stock for your business cards.
- **Business cards:** Computer-printed business cards are used by all small businesses. They are easy to produce and can be modified for specific purposes. You can have one card for fishing charters and another for sightseeing cruises. If

you are catering to a high-end market, such as corporate charters, consider paying the extra money for professionally printed embossed business cards.

- **Advertising brochures:** You will probably need to have a brochure printed. These are handy to send or hand out to customers who call to inquire about your service. The brochure should provide basic information about the company, and it should position the company within a given market. For example, if you specialize in corporate charters, that message should be prominent in the written text. Your local printer is an excellent source of information. He or she can give you a good idea of what you need and how much it will cost.

YOUR MESSAGE

After considering your image, the next step is to define your message. Do not answer too quickly. Saying that you want to tell people about your product does not go far enough. You do not just want to inform potential customers that your business exists. Thousands of charter boats, water taxis, dinner cruise vessels, tour boats, and DUKWs abound in every tourist area. Telling people that your company exists only confirms what they already know. They won't take action and buy your service unless you give them a good reason to do so.

Thus, your message must always go beyond just information. It must contain a motivational component. You want action. This is sometimes called the "sizzle." In my bird-watching endeavor, there were two big motivators. One was that my customers got to walk into an otherwise unreachable heron nesting ground. A second motivator was the multiple number of nesting bald eagles along the river. A fishing charter might use the size of walleye the captain can find as a motivator. If you operate a water taxi business, the motivator is usually some attraction at the other end of your route. Specifically, you want people to take out their wallets and hand over some of their hard-earned cash. Don't speak in general terms when structuring your marketing message. For example, say you catch monster fish, if you can prove it.

The next step is what salespeople call "asking for the order." It is not good enough to simply be enthusiastic about your product. You have to ask people to cross the line from *potential* customers to *actual* customers. Otherwise, they will merely nod their heads and go on with their lives. Never forget that the goal of marketing is to turn enough potential customers into actual, satisfied customers and, beyond that, to change those satisfied customers into *repeat* customers, so you keep on making a profit.

CREATING THE CUSTOMER

Let's look at each customer category in a bit more detail:

- **Potential customers:** When you researched and wrote your business plan, you identified your potential customer base, meaning you figured out who might be interested and able to use your services. In marketing terms, this is your "universe of customers." One of the frustrations of business is that no company ever achieves 100 percent penetration of its universe of customers because of factors ranging from competition to buyer apathy. A large universe of potential customers might help convince a banker to give you a loan or an investor to give you venture capital, but don't fool yourself. Potential customers do not put money in your bank account. Actual customers do.

- **Actual customers:** These are people who are currently on your boat and enjoying whatever service you are offering. They provide income you can bank.

- **Repeat customers:** This group is the real gold mine. They are people who routinely come back because they like your service and want to repeat a pleasant experience. As will be seen, these are the most profitable customers even though they take the most work to develop. Anglers obviously go back to where they catch fish. The same is true for other types of customers, such as bird-watchers and tourists.

A myth in tourism-related businesses is that all customers are new ones. In fact, people tend to repeatedly visit places they like because they know what to expect. Going to a familiar location reduces the risk of wasting money on an experience that fails to meet expectations. Customers and repeat customers may seem like the same group, but from a marketing standpoint they are quite different.

New customers have to be pulled from your universe of potential buyers by spending money on advertising and public relations. Getting a new customer is expensive. Some businesses spend as much acquiring a new customer as that person spends on the goods or services provided during the first transaction.

A repeat customer comes back voluntarily, so you do not have to spend large sums of money on advertising and public relations. As a result, dollar for dollar you make more profit off of repeat business than you do from new customers. Of course, nothing is free. Repeat customers have to be nurtured through a combination of your personal social skills and delivering the boat ride that the customer wants. That means finding bald eagles and heron nests if you are running a bird-watching tour or finding the right fish if you are running a fishing charter.

The overall process of turning potential customers into new customers and then converting them into repeat customers is the essence of marketing. Within marketing, advertising is just one of the many tools you use to get the job done. The first step is to get the attention of the people in your universe—the market segment you identified as potential users of your services. That takes more than spending money on advertising. You need a lot of hard work and creativity as well.

YOUR HOOK

What is your hook? In a marketing context, a hook is all-important when structuring your marketing message because it conveys the positive difference that sets your company apart from the competition. It is why people remember your business and come to it as new customers and, hopefully, return as repeat customers. Your job is to figure out what makes your service special and why it would appeal to your customer base and then fashion a message with an irresistible hook.

Let's take my bird-watching cruises as an example. One hook quickly became the promise of seeing bald eagles in their natural habitat. My promotion and advertising efforts stressed that we had a number of nesting pairs of eagles along the route. We frequently saw those majestic birds catching fish. Even birders who had added the bald eagle to their life-lists long ago were motivated by the promise of seeing the eagles. We often counted 35 or 40 other species of birds during a five-hour cruise, but it was the possibility of seeing a bald eagle in flight that drew customers to my boat.

In short, the eagles became a natural hook to include in all the marketing messages I wrote to promote the bird-watching cruises. If you think carefully about your business, you should be able to find a natural hook of your own.

Unfortunately, many hooks don't last forever. People have an innate desire for something new. That's why fashions and music change over time, and so a good hook for one season may seem outdated the following year. I discovered this with my bird-watching cruises. To keep my repeat customers interested, I had to offer them something new.

In my second season, I obtained special permission for my customers to go ashore. That was enough to keep my base of repeat customers happy, and, combined with the bald eagle hook, it helped build my base of new customers as well. Keep finding new hooks in mind as you plan your long-term marketing campaign. It may not always be possible to invent new hooks, but you should always be looking for ways to try.

My bird-watching cruises were easy to promote because they were a unique offering. Obviously, not every water business is as easy. Charter fishing skippers face a difficult challenge when it comes to setting their business apart and creating an effective hook to bring in customers. After all, every trip on every boat involves as short a ride as possible to a productive fishing ground, a period of hot fishing with lots of strikes, and a ride back to the dock.

So what do you do if you're a charter fishing captain? Where is your hook? The one thing you have that sets you apart is you. Your personality, your experiences, your ability to deliver the goods (fish) on every trip, that is where you should look for the hook in your marketing message.

Aunt Sandy Catches Anglers with Cookies

I first met Sandra as a student in one of my captain's license classes almost 20 years ago. Some of the men in that class were surprised to have a woman sitting with them as they plotted courses and computed tide tables. Sandy, as we knew her, had spent most of her life doing the traditional girl things, but she never hid her love of fishing. As she approached the second half of her life, she decided to make fishing her livelihood. She went straight for the master's ticket, bypassing the OUPV or six-pack license.

Today, Sandy operates a two-vessel fleet with the second boat operated by her retired husband. She has a large repeat clientele. Some of the guys call her "Aunt Sandy" because of the way she treats her customers on the water. Sandy is a natural-born hostess who bakes a mean chocolate chip cookie. She also has an uncanny knack for finding fish. This combination continues to be profitable year after year.

Walk the docks in any fishing marina and look at which boats are working constantly and which are not. Chances are the busiest boats are captained by a "rock star." These are skippers who have created a recognizable character within the fishing community. Most wear clothing that tells you immediately that they are a charter captain and a successful one at that. A good number have fishing contest trophies to prove their angling abilities. More than a few are spokespeople for fishing tackle manufacturers, boatbuilders, or outboard motor manufacturers. Their marketing plan is to make people want to go fishing with them. The boat, tackle, and even fishing grounds are secondary to the importance of wetting a line with a fishing rock star.

Never fool yourself into thinking that everyone in your universe of potential buyers has exactly the same needs and desires. No two people have exactly the same motivation for purchasing any product. The enticement for one buyer may not work on another. You cannot simultaneously tailor thousands of advertising and promotional campaigns so there is something for everybody. Instead, you will change your campaign from time to time so that over the years you reach maximum penetration of your universe of customers.

THE MARKETING TOOLBOX

Every skilled carpenter or mechanic has a toolbox full of chisels and saws or sockets and wrenches. Marketing has a similar toolbox. It is filled with a collection of clever techniques to bring in new customers.

These range from sending out news releases to making personal appearances and much more. We'll discuss some of them below.

PRICING

The price you charge, which was briefly discussed in Chapter 4 as you began researching your business, is a critical factor in your marketing plan. Some owners of start-up businesses price their products or services too low, usually out of fear that too high a price will drive customers away. What they forget is that low prices result in reduced income. Higher prices do result in fewer customers, but the profit margin is higher and should make up the difference in reduced sales volume (the banishment of bargain hunters). Of course, if your prices are too high you'll lose money because sales volume will drop. You need to find the right balance. Many factors should be taken into account when setting prices:

- **Competition:** The fees other businesses charge for similar services establish the market price in your area. Don't undercut it simply to gain business. You'll attract bargain hunters, not always a good thing, and you'll be throwing money away because most reasonable people expect to pay market price. If your service is comparable, you do not need to sell it for less.
- **Clientele:** Customers with higher incomes and expectations will pay more than those of lower incomes.
- **Location:** Even though you may fish the same reefs, the marina you depart from can influence the price of your trips. Better dockage (customer parking, closer to the fish, etc.) commands better prices.
- **Product:** A bare-bones fishing charter cannot command the same price as one that supplies poles, lures, bait, and lunch.

How to Lose Money

For five years we charged $2 per person for a one-way trip across the river on our water taxi. Mostly for our own convenience we did not sell round trips. Last year, increasing fuel costs forced us to raise our ticket prices.

Our decision was to begin offering a $5 round-trip ticket and raise the one-way price to $3. Since most customers took round trips, the rate increase amounted to just 50 cents over the old charge for a one-way ride across the river. Our number of riders dropped slightly, by a couple percentage points, but our income rose substantially. Looking back on it we realized that our price increase came a year too late. We actually cheated ourselves out of thousands of dollars in revenue by waiting too long to make the change.

Although rising prices forced our decision to increase ticket rates, the cost of operating your company should not be the sole determining factor in setting the price of your service. In years past, you could add up your costs and then figure in your percentage of profit to come up with the proper balance in terms of what you charged for the service you provided. That's no longer true. In the present business climate, market forces set the amount you can charge, not your costs.

If you cannot make a profit charging market price, the smart thing to do is get out of that market. Change from fishing to eco-touring, for instance. Move your business into a market that can support prices high enough for you to make a profit. That's easier said than done, of course, so it pays to have made the effort to do solid research before you even start your business. The last thing you want is to find out the market won't support your business after you started the enterprise.

Keep in mind that not all trips are worth the same amount of money. You can have a sliding price scale. A Saturday morning fishing trip during peak season is worth a lot more in actual dollars than one on Tuesday during the off-season. A private dinner charter is more in demand on Friday or Saturday evening than at lunchtime on Wednesday. Your pricing structure should reflect these differences.

COUPONS AND OFFERS

Strictly speaking, these are different marketing techniques, although they rely on the same buyer response—greed. People like to think they are getting something for nothing. The big difference is that an offer has no actual cash value, while a coupon is a valuable piece of paper in the eyes of your customers.

Offers are usually expressed in a percentage or dollar amount off the regular price. An offer is advertised widely and available to everyone who purchases during the life span of the offer. Everyone gets the better deal even if they do not request it. An example of an offer might be a charter captain who gives a 10 percent discount to anyone who books a trip during a fishing show.

Coupons also allow customers to get a percentage or dollar amount off. However, this discount is only available upon presentation of the coupon at the time of purchase. So coupons appear to have a cash value to customers. The same fishing captain as in the previous example might have 10 percent discount coupons printed for distribution through hotels, motels, and bait shops or on restaurant paper placemats and the like.

How do you make up the money you give away in offers and coupons? Sometimes it comes through increased sales volume. My water taxi benefits from weekday coupons that encourage people to use our service on days when our boats are not full. Each coupon represents "plus" business over what the boats would have done on that day, so there is no loss of revenue. My boats show a net gain in cash receipts. Another way to make up the money is to raise the regular price enough to cover the discount on the coupon. Sightseeing cruise operators who expect that the bulk of their customers will be motivated by coupons often do this.

NEWS RELEASES

Traditionally, a news release had only one purpose: to gain the attention of an editor. After that, a reporter was typically assigned to interview you and write a news story. In that case, nearly everything you wrote would be rewritten (if not discarded altogether), but that was okay, as long as your message got printed or read on the air.

Recently, however, news organizations have undergone the same kinds of personnel cutbacks as most other industries. As a result, they're a lot more willing to use what you send them, either lightly edited or even verbatim, if it's well written. Conversely, if it's not well written, it may not be used even if the subject matter was potentially of interest to the editor. He or she may not have the time or resources to turn a decent news idea into an actual news article.

The key to a good release is a "news peg." This is the reason why the story is "news." Good pegs for local newspapers or broadcast outlets are events like a customer catching a state record sturgeon or if your water taxi is about to hit the 10,000 mark in number of rides. Keep in mind that the definition of news is the reporting of an event of interest to a significant number of readers, listeners, or viewers. This means that a big-city newspaper will not view news in the same manner as a monthly fishing magazine.

E-mail is now the preferred method of sending out news releases. Most publications list an e-mail address for the editors on the masthead. This is the listing of names and titles usually found on or near the contents page of a magazine. Newspapers put the same information on their editorial page and sometimes on the front page. Do not send a "broadcast" release showing all of the recipient publications on the "To:" line. Instead, each publication should receive a release with only its name. If possible, get the address of the editor who will handle the story and e-mail it directly to that person.

If you send news releases via snail mail, type or copy the contents onto your letterhead. Use the old-fashioned Courier font that emulates a typewriter. Double space the entire document, not just the first paragraph. Center the headline about one-third of the way down the first page. Immediately below the heading put "For Immediate Release." This tells editors they can run the release as soon as they receive it. Start the text about one inch below the headline. The idea is to give plenty of "white space" for editors to make notes. In the upper right-hand corner of the first page put "contact" information. Give the name, phone number, and e-mail address of someone who can be contacted to verify the story.

Good photos always help sell a story. If you're sending hard copy, enclose a good-quality photo print of the boat and the angler with the record fish or whatever is the subject of the story. If you're e-mailing the release, check the publication's website for directions about attachments; they may not wish to receive attachments or may have specific requirements about the size of the attachments. The good thing about news coverage is that it is essentially free and has more value than a paid advertisement in the same media. It's always better for somebody else to blow your trumpet than to do it yourself.

GIVEAWAYS

These are the pens, key chains, coffee mugs, refrigerator magnets, and other inexpensive items with your company name, number, and logo printed on them that you give customers as a reminder of your company. This approach isn't necessarily effective and it can cost you a fair amount of money over the long run. However, putting your logo and phone number on the coffee mug a good client uses every day can be very smart business.

A special class of giveaway materials are those you pass out at fishing shows, travel shows, and the like. It is possible to go through thousands of these things in a few days. The vast majority wind up in a dumpster behind the convention center.

Another form of giveaway at show events is the brochure. Be careful about wasting big money on fancy four-color printing on glossy paper stock unless you cater to high-end customers. If that's the case, you must spend the money. In most cases, simple is better. Just be sure the brochure or single-page handout looks professional. A graphic designer, print shop, or small advertising agency is often well worth the added expense. Professional materials enhance your image as a professional captain and business owner.

PERSONAL APPEARANCES

One way to get publicity is to become known as an expert. Give presentations at fishing or boating seminars, make speeches to boating groups, or make appearances on local television or cable programs. Local radio talk shows are always looking for new experts who can speak with authority.

How do you become an expert? By definition, as a licensed operator or master, you are already an expert in boating. E-mail radio stations with your credentials just before Memorial Day and say that you can talk about boating safety. Or if you do a harbor cruise, take a local media personality on a private trip focusing on the history, ecology, or problems of the waterfront.

Watch the daily run of news to see a "news peg" developing. For instance, most states have a day in early summer when anyone can go fishing without a license. The idea is to promote the sport among people who might otherwise not take up a rod. Arrange to have a youth organization use your boat on free fishing day. Notify the media and let the magic of kids, fish, and the water draw TV cameras.

PROMOTIONAL EFFORTS

Promotion accomplishes many of the same things as personal appearances. It gets your name out there and enhances the visibility of your company. In a sense, you make the news. You use your business as its own promotional vehicle.

For instance, you might take handicapped kids fishing free of charge, give a free cruise to some retired nuns, or arrange to take the mayor on a waterfront inspection trip. Send out news releases to the local press and you are likely to get news coverage. Editors love fun stories, so the example of the nuns would be something an editor might want to cover. But be very careful. Taking handicapped kids or nuns fishing and then trying to get press coverage could backfire if the entire endeavor is seen as nothing more than a promotional stunt. Instead of good publicity, you'll get bad publicity that could harm your business.

HULL GRAPHICS

Every time your boat leaves or enters port, people on land see it. Make sure they know who you are and what you do by placing large, attractive, easy-to-read signs on the boat.

PAID ADVERTISING

This is the last resort when it comes to getting the word out to the public. Some beginning entrepreneurs think buying space in a newspaper or time on radio and TV will assure success. Without a marketing plan, they discover advertising is expensive and unproductive. The reason is wasted effort. Newspapers and broadcast outlets base their charges on the number of thousands of people an ad will reach. This is called "cost per thousand" (CPM). The M represents the Roman numeral for one thousand. Most media are skewed to attract people 18 to 37 years of age, and the demographic is predominantly female because conventional advertising wisdom holds this is the group spending the most money.

Fishing attracts mostly men slightly older than the conventional media audience. Bird-watching attracts the sexes about equally but mostly among senior citizens. Neither of these businesses will get good results from advertising in a regular newspaper or on broadcast radio and TV, because most of the audience for those media lies outside the universe of customers for these businesses. In either case, you pay for thousands of people but get only a handful of potential customers.

A close friend of mine runs a weekly "advertiser" newspaper. His competitor runs a summer-only paper aimed at tourism in our area. On a CPM basis my friend's paper was the best buy. But was it? To find out I purchased similar ads in both papers for my birding tours. My friend's paper produced virtually nothing. The competition drew in substantial business.

The reason for the difference was audience. One paper served residents who live in the county surrounding the river where my boat went touring. The other paper was read primarily by people from out of town who were looking for recreation. Not many local residents wanted to spend money on a boat to observe birds they could see every day from the highway. Out-of-towners, however, were looking for exactly the sort of adventure I was offering.

As the above example shows, the higher CPM paper was the more cost-effective for my business. Chances are you will find the same thing is true for yours. Instead of looking at CPM, a charter fishing or an eco-tour operator has to make advertising purchases based on productivity. The key element in a successful advertising campaign is to purchase space or time in media that penetrates your target market.

- **Print media:** Start with local publications aimed at your target market. Do not be enchanted by slick, four-color national magazines. A local fishing newspaper may be more effective. Similarly, local tourist publications will have more effectiveness for an eco-tour than a general-interest magazine. Avoid mass-circulation newspapers and magazines unless you can purchase space in a special section covering your target market.

- **Television:** This is the most expensive medium. It is also best suited for selling mass-appeal items. Some effectiveness can be realized by advertising on cable channels serving hotels and motels. Many cable companies have special tourist channels that promote local businesses. Avoid buying run of station (ROS) TV spots on broadcast stations unless your target market is primarily female and 18 to 37 years of age. ROS means your ad runs when it is most convenient for the broadcaster, which means it might run at 2:00 A.M. It costs more to buy a "position" spot, but you get to specify the time during which it will play. Broadcast TV can be effective, but only if you buy ads inside programs watched by your specific target market. An ad for a charter boat on a fishing show should work well. The same ad on a kid's cartoon program is a waste of money.
- **Radio:** Much of the advice about TV applies to ROS radio advertising. However, radio stations tend to target narrower segments of the listening audience. Spots on shows about your target market (e.g., fishing or outdoors shows) are likely to be productive. Study the *demographics*, the breakdown of types of people listening to various shows. A charter boat may have good luck advertising on a talk radio station at drive time when mostly men are listening. "Drive time" is radio jargon for 6:00 to 9:00 A.M. and 4:00 to 6:00 P.M. when people are in their cars either driving to work or back home.

WEBSITES

Websites are generally considered critical to marketing efforts. However, the Internet is still evolving so quickly and is so diverse that it is hard to make valid generalizations about its effectiveness beyond saying that every modern business should have a website. At a minimum, your website should explain what you offer in an engaging way to encourage visitors to become customers. Think of the website as an electronic sales brochure. Never forget to ask for the order. Your site should include some way for the visitor to send you an e-mail requesting more information.

There are strategies for attracting people to your website. Within the Web community this is called "search engine optimization." The goal is to make search engines like Google or Yahoo put your website in the top 10 listings when people query about your field. When most people do a Web search, they often limit the pages they actually visit to the top listings. You are not likely to get many visits if your site is listed as number 66 on page six of the search report. To achieve full optimization you need to know how the various search engines work. However, don't ask. The methods used to rank websites are carefully guarded secrets. Even so, some techniques have a proven track record. Here are a few of them:

- **Keywords:** Be sure to list as many keywords as possible on each page of your website. These are the words the search engines use to match search requests with your site.
- **Multiple pages:** Most search engines give higher rankings to sites with more than one or two pages.
- **Word content:** Keep the word content on each page high. The search engines seem to favor sites that appear to offer a great deal of information. They appear to judge the information content by the number of words per page.

Statistics show that most websites are not entered on the first, or home, page. It is far more likely that a visitor to your site will land first on an interior page. Use this tendency to your advantage. Provide Web browsers with content to attract them to your site.

For instance, had I been Web savvy during my bird-watching days, I would have included separate Web pages describing each bird likely to be seen along the route. Someone looking up bald eagles would have found my site for this information. Some of those people would have been motivated to find out how they could see an eagle in its natural habitat and that would have led to a percentage of them to become customers.

Another website feature that seems to boost ranking with search engines is a forum for viewer participation. The problem with this type of content is maintenance. You have to constantly monitor the website to be sure that all postings to your forum are in keeping with your company image. Or if you offer to answer questions, you have to do so in a timely fashion, which means spending time at the computer almost every day.

Another technique to help get into that coveted top 10 list is to encourage other websites to link to yours. A link means that a viewer of the other site can be transferred directly to your site by clicking on a keyword or URL in the first site. Finally, don't forget to self-promote your website. List the URL on all of your letterhead, business cards, and sales brochures.

GAME PLAN

As with your business, a successful marketing effort starts with a written plan. Many times, entrepreneurs find it easiest to write a full marketing plan and then cut it back to just an outline for inclusion in the business plan. Other times, the short marketing section prepared for the business plan is expanded later into a full-blown document. Either way, a formal written plan is needed to guide your efforts. It should include the following:

- **The hook:** Identify and fully develop your definable difference from the competition.
- **Timing of rollout:** In marketing vernacular, *rollout* means the process of introducing a new product or service.
- **Target media:** *Media* is the collective word meaning radio, TV, newspapers, billboards, coupons, signage, brochures, and the Internet.

The marketing plan identifies what you are going to sell (service or product) and emphasizes the key selling points of the service or product. The plan also outlines the timing of news releases and media purchases. A coordinated plan integrates each aspect of the marketing effort so that all components work together and build to accomplish the main objective: increase customer awareness of your business within a defined market segment to drive sales volume ever upward.

ROLLOUT

Marketing does not begin on the first day of boating season, nor does it begin on the day you launch a new boat. It should start months before the first day you take out passengers. Raising customer awareness takes time. Big advertising agencies say people do not even notice that a new product or service exists until they have seen or heard about it eight times. In the language of the business, each time a prospect sees or hears about a product or service is called an "impression." Awareness does not translate into purchases. Even more impressions are needed, sometimes dozens of them, to convert potential customers into paying customers. That's why rollout is important. Timing is everything in marketing.

A typical rollout starts weeks or months in advance with news releases about what is coming. It has a peak on the first day of operation with a flurry of news releases and purchased advertising. The campaign continues with advertising coordinated with promotional events and personal appearances. News releases are issued from time to time. Each season a new rollout campaign is planned and executed to keep the business fresh in the consciousness of potential customers in the defined market segment.

Every business has unique needs, so there is no single recipe for a successful rollout campaign. Watch what other companies do to learn what is successful and what fails. To illustrate a typical campaign, the following outline was for my new water taxi service when we were starting in business. Yours should be similar, but differ in the specifics.

Sample Water Taxi Rollout Campaign

6 months: News release announcing that a new water taxi company is coming to town. Not many specifics are given, just the basic information about service and how it will improve the local economy.

2 months: News release giving specific details of departure docks and hours of service.

2 months: Information packages sent to restaurants, hotels, and other local businesses that will benefit from water taxi service. Arrange with local dignitaries to attend the first-day ceremonies.

2 weeks: Give discount coupons to local businesses to pass out to customers. Coupons are good for first month of taxi operation.

I week: Make arrangements for news coverage of first-day event. Give editors best locations for photos, etc. Double-check that dignitaries will attend. Hire the band and catering.

First day: Water taxi makes first appearance, pulling up to dock with Dixieland band playing. The mayor is invited to handle first dockline. The band comes ashore and dignitaries go for a short ride on the taxi. Everyone comes ashore to enjoy refreshments. Free public rides on taxi are scheduled for the afternoon.

Second day: Special lunch cruise for operators of local businesses who will benefit from the taxi. Show them the route, have lunch, and get them back to work in no more than 90 minutes.

End of first month: News release saying how successful the new operation has been.

This process would continue throughout the life of the business. Note that it starts months before the boat arrives in the harbor. Also, this plan does not envision spending money on advertising because there are more effective ways of getting the message out through other people. The news media are courted with numerous "photo opportunities." Collateral businesses that will benefit from the water taxi are enlisted to promote the operation among their customers.

Advertising works for big purchases like a dinner cruise or a charter fishing trip, but water taxi customers are making a spur-of-the-moment buying decision. That's a bit different. When they are standing on the bank of the river, they are not going to be moved by an unheard radio spot or an ad in a newspaper they do not have. In this case, a coupon for a discount ride would be more effective and less costly than buying ads.

A new charter fishing boat faces a completely different set of problems in achieving the necessary customer awareness. It is difficult to make clever use of the news media because charter boats go in and out of business all the time. A new boat in town wouldn't be considered newsworthy. This means you have to find another way to raise customer awareness. Most often this involves buying advertising and paying for booth space at fishing and sport shows.

Sample Six-Pack Charter Rollout Campaign

Several years before: Become a noted amateur angler. Enter contests and gain bragging rights. Align yourself with manufacturers of fishing equipment and provide paid endorsements.

Winter before first summer: Join with one or more other captains in sharing the costs of booth space at fishing and outdoors shows. Print brochures or other sales materials promoting yourself and your new business, and hand them out at the shows. Get names and addresses of potential clients. Design and launch your website.

4 months: Visit motels and other lodging operators. At a minimum, get your sales brochures in the lobby. If possible, arrange for lodging operators to feed potential customers to you. Some fishing charter captains pay commissions to lodging operators who refer people to their boats. A few skippers also offer discounts to existing customers who refer other customers to the business.

3 months: Begin your advertising campaign in magazines that target your customer base. Tourism guides, free regional boating and fishing publications, and local newspapers are your best bets. Use money wisely. Ask to see readership survey data on the type of people reading the publication. Look at back issues over at least two years for editorial content related to fishing. Start by spreading your dollars over several publications until you learn which ones produce the best results. The campaign should run to the end of the fishing season.

2 months: Send postcards to all names acquired at fishing shows and elsewhere reminding potential customers of the new charter service. The card should include your telephone number and website address.

2 months: Contact politicians and other prominent people about fishing trips. Elected officials usually must pay for their trips to avoid ethics issues. TV, radio, and newspaper reporters may also have ethical standards that prevent accepting a free trip. Other TV personalities, radio disc jockeys, and sports stars are not so encumbered. Taking out famous personalities creates a news peg for reporters to cover your boat.

During season: Prepare and send news releases about unusual catches to fishing magazines. Include a photo. Big catches, record fish, etc., are grist for the mill in consumer fishing publications.

Looking at these two sample rollout campaigns illustrates how different types of businesses use different marketing approaches.

SAMPLE ROLLOUT MARKETING CAMPAIGNS: WATER TAXI VERSUS CHARTER FISHING		
TIMING OF ROLLOUT EVENT	**WATER TAXI**	**SIX-PACK CHARTER FISHING**
Years prior to start-up		Become noted angler. Win fishing contests.
6 months prior	Send news release saying that water taxi is coming to town.	Join other captains at fishing shows to get names of new clients.
4 months prior		Visit motels and place brochures.
3 months prior		Begin magazine and newspaper ad campaign aimed at anglers.
2 months prior	Send second news release with more specifics about service.	Send postcard to names acquired at boat shows to remind them of your new service.
2 months prior	Give informational packages to restaurants and other businesses on taxi route.	
2 months prior	Arrange for local dignitaries to attend a "first ride" ceremony.	Contact politicians and TV personalities about taking fishing trips.
2 weeks prior	Give discount coupons to businesses on or near the taxi route.	
I week prior	Make arrangements for news coverage of "first ride" ceremony.	
First day of operation	Have big ceremony with a band; invite public officials.	Catch fish and promote big catches or record fish during season to news media.

The water taxi will not benefit from the sort of advertising campaign necessary for the success of a start-up charter fishing business. Not mentioned in either of these plans is the basic package of marketing materials every company needs. These include business cards, brochures (usually the three-fold type), letterhead paper, invoice forms, and receipts. Invoices and receipts seem like mundane business forms, but they do go home with the customer. A sales "pitch" in the form of a photo or text becomes a reminder of the fun they had on your boat. Think of each bill, invoice, or receipt as a sales brochure sent directly to your best customers.

In the old days, all this material had to be ordered from a printer. Thanks to the computer it is possible to make most printed materials at home, as long as the quantity needed is not too large. In my water taxi operation, we combined professionally printed materials with those we generated ourselves on the computer. Print runs up to about 100 copies are homemade. Longer runs are more economically done by a commercial printer.

CHAPTER 10

CUSTOMER POLICIES

There is an old saying in business that is worth mentioning: "Good contracts make good friends." The idea is that a well-written contract spells out the benefits and responsibilities of all parties involved. There is no room for arguments of the "I didn't know" variety. Do not fear the idea of a written agreement between you and your customers. Technically, you enter into a contract with your passengers whether you write one out formally and have everyone sign it or whether you simply accept their money and welcome them aboard. Contracts can be oral as well as written.

AGREEMENTS

Contracts are a special branch of law. Depending on what you are doing and where you are located, your contracts may be governed by both state and federal laws. To get the best ironclad written document, find the best contract lawyer in your town and pay the fee. Nothing in this book should be considered as a substitute for competent legal advice. The concepts discussed here should help you get the most for your money out of a visit to a contract attorney.

Many small passenger vessel operations do not go to the trouble of entering into a formal contractual agreement with their customers. Instead, they publish a set of written policies regarding such things as the services they offer, charges, and cancellations. These policies are posted on their websites and made available to anyone inquiring about becoming a customer. Quite obviously, a fishing charter is different from a water taxi or dinner cruise operation. Still, there are several categories that appear in passenger agreements. The most common ones are:

- Services offered
- Price structure
- Payment terms
- Deposits
- Cancellation policy and refunds
- Boarding times

Things get more complicated when food and beverages are included in the package. The addition of catering often marks the change from informal agreements to formal written contracts. Food has to be purchased and prepared in advance of the departure, and it spoils if it is not used. Meal service involves considerable financial risk, which is why a formal agreement in writing is best. The document should cover:

- Food to be served
- Alcoholic beverages
- Extra boat time for caterer
- Cleanup fees

POLICIES

Before you open for business, it pays to give careful thought to the nature of the relationship between you and your customer. What can the customer expect for his or her money? Aside from money, what are the customer's obligations toward the business? The better you define these, the smoother the business relationship will go.

Because it is impossible to anticipate every situation that could result in an inconvenience for a passenger, a financial loss for the business owner, or a dispute between the business owner and the customer, your policies can never be totally comprehensive. When new types of situations arise for which your policies seem inadequate, you might consider modifying your policies.

After a certain point, too many policies can become self-defeating, scaring off customers and forcing every situation into a straightjacket of rules, when a bit of commonsense flexibility might be what is really called for. That said, most businesses should establish policies to manage at least the basics of the relationship between the business and the customer, as discussed below.

SERVICES OFFERED

Be specific about what you are offering but don't be wordy. The policy is not a sales brochure. A fishing captain might simply state: "Fishing trips of 4- and 6-hour duration for walleye on the reefs of the western basin of Lake Erie; lunch and bait provided." A bird-watching cruise might state: "Excursions of 4 hours' duration to the backwaters of the Little Muddy with a landing at a blue heron nesting area; lunch on return trip." Larger vessels may offer several different types of services ranging from wedding dinners to corporate outings and dance cruises. Each of these offerings should be explained, but avoid saying too much. A fishing captain cannot promise everyone will catch fish any more than I could promise to see bald eagles on every one of my birding excursions. Never contractually bind yourself to providing something beyond your control.

PRICE STRUCTURE

Your written policies should state your "rack rate" for each service offered. This is the maximum price you will charge without promotional considerations. Pricing can be by the person, by the hour, or even a combination of the two. If you charge by the person, you may want to consider setting a minimum charge to protect against a money-losing one-passenger trip. Customers should be informed of any taxes that apply in your state or municipality.

Pricing structures are often tiered. The highest charges apply to the most popular days, usually Friday evenings, Saturdays, and Sundays. Lower rates apply on weekdays. Some boats have an even lower rate for morning or lunch cruises. Setting too low a price is no different than putting money back into your customers' pockets. One way is to keep the published price high, but have lower "come-on" rates to make discount coupons available.

GRATUITIES

You may also specify how a gratuity for the crew will be added to the bill. *Gratuity* is a fancy word for tips paid to service workers. Mates on six-pack fishing boats traditionally have worked solely for tips. Food servers and bartenders usually receive a sub-minimum wage and so must depend on tips to earn a comfortable income. Customers are often unaware of how tips figure into the take-home pay of boat employees. It is only fair to these employees that you inform your passengers of the importance of tipping. Passengers who come aboard as guests of a wedding party or a corporate event are not expected to tip. This is why it is customary to apply a gratuity charge on these charters. Typically, the charge is between 15 and 20 percent of the total charter cost.

PAYMENT TERMS

Tell your customers how they will have to pay both the deposit and the final bill. There is nothing illegal or immoral in saying "cash only," but in this day of plastic banking you will probably turn away business. Credit cards are universal and many people no longer carry large sums of cash. If you do not take credit cards, they may not be able to purchase a ticket on your boat.

The problem for a watercraft operator is the cost and hassle of getting a card reader and telephone line to the boat. These sorts of physical constraints may make it impracticable for you to take credit cards at the dock. Check with your bank or card service about your options. Banking institutions do not all have the same policies when it comes to how credit card transactions can be handled. You may need to switch banks to get the services your business requires.

Unlike a merchant, a boat line has nothing to repossess if a customer fails to pay the bill after taking a cruise. You can't take back a boat ride. Extra charges for cleanup or overtime hours can be billed later. Make sure your written policy is to get payment in full for the basic charter and any food or beverage service before the boat leaves the dock. This is especially true of bachelor and bachelorette parties and other events where people will be drinking alcohol. Advance payment avoids a situation where the person with the money is too drunk to pay the bill at the end of the night.

SECURITY DEPOSITS

It is considered a normal business practice to require a security deposit from customers who charter your vessel. The amount of the deposit varies but is often 50 percent of the total charter price. Charging a deposit is needed simply to make sure that someone is serious when they book a particular date. This prevents holding a date open for a no-show when you could have a solid booking for that day.

You can do anything you want with deposit money but beware of the possibility you will have to return it to the booking party. Many companies place deposits in a separate fund so the money cannot be spent until after the charter trip takes place. If you choose this procedure, think about informing your customers of your good stewardship of their money. It may provide some people with a comfortable feeling that their money is not "lost" while they are waiting for the date of their charter.

CANCELLATIONS AND REFUNDS

Sometimes people have to cancel for good reasons, or you may not be able to run the trip because of bad weather or mechanical breakdown. Your written policies should explain the conditions under which refunds of deposits will apply and the methods by which they will be paid.

Most charter companies offer a 100 percent refund for customer cancellations until a stated number of days before departure. After that cutoff day, partial refunds are made. Typically, this date is from 14 to 28 days before the date of the charter. No refunds are typically given after a second drop-dead date from 7 to 14 days before departure. The idea behind this policy is to prevent people from reserving a charter on speculation and then pulling out at the last minute. It can be difficult or impossible to replace a cancelled charter on short notice. By retaining some or all of the deposit, the company avoids a total loss of income.

WEATHER CONCERNS

Passengers dream of having bright sunshine and calm seas during their outings, but it doesn't always work out that way. You will have to make money on overcast days when it spits rain and the sea is lumpy. Nature being fickle, the days passengers think are bad will always outnumber the ones they think are perfect. Yet most of the days passengers consider bad are really quite safe on the water. Obviously, you are going to have a fair number of disagreements with passengers over weather.

The days when the weather prevents a safe trip are easy to handle. You simply cancel. Once that decision is made, never be argued into changing your mind. Instead, follow the standard industry practice of giving full refunds of all deposits when the trip is cancelled by the owner of the vessel.

Sooner or later you will start a trip only to realize that the weather has deteriorated more than you anticipated. The only thing to do is get your passengers back to shore as quickly as possible, even if you cannot go to your own dock.

Any Port in a Storm

I recall one night when I was captain of an interisland ferry. We realized that it would take hours of bashing through head seas to get to our home dock. Our passengers were not enjoying the ride. Instead of extending their agony, we found a nearby harbor with a dock suitable for our boat. The ferry company owned a passenger bus used to take people to and from our remote parking lot. On this night, the driver was dispatched to pick up everyone at the unexpected termination point of our trip. Passengers voiced approval of our decision.

We did not have to give back any money because our passengers were returned to where they boarded the boat, and they had already received the full island cruise. Had this not been the case, we may have had to give the passengers some of their money back.

Most companies also have a policy covering reduced payment for trips that are forced to end earlier than scheduled because of weather or mechanical breakdown. No refunds are typically given in cases where the charter was terminated early because charter guests were violating U.S. Coast Guard regulations or participating in dangerous activities.

BOARDING TIMES

Passengers always want to board your boat earlier than the departure time. It's human nature. Even so, you must be firm about boarding times. You cannot properly care for passengers while preparing the vessel for the day's operation. Open engine hatches, boxes of snacks on deck, and the confusion created by getting ready are all open invitations to slips, falls, and other injuries. It's best to keep people safely on shore until your boat is ready to accept passengers. In your written policies, be sure to state how long before the scheduled departure time you will allow people on board. As a rule, 15 minutes should be enough time.

The one exception to the 15-minute rule comes on larger excursion boats offering private charters. A wedding party will want to decorate the boat. Anticipate this request with a formal policy about how many people can come aboard and when. Most excursion boats limit the number of decorators to four or six and give them 15 minutes of time prior to when regular guests are allowed on board. This allows the decorators a full half hour before the vessel departs.

EXTRAS AND OVERTIME

Customers often ask for extra services after they come aboard. They also sometimes alter the cruise itinerary so that the vessel spends extra time away from the dock. Both cases take money out of your pocket unless you state in advance that you charge for these extras. Charges commonly mentioned in passenger vessel policies include everything from cleaning up after drunks who lose their lunch or dinner to something called "demurrage."

- **Drunks:** Cleaning up is a messy business. Some charter companies charge for this service and then award special "combat pay" to the crew members who do the work. If your boat has a liquor license, you are liable for any mishaps that may occur because a person is drunk. If your boat doesn't have a liquor license, you are still required to maintain safety on board and that includes making sure an individual drinks responsibly.

- **Damage:** Some wear and tear on the boat is inevitable, but if expensive breakage or damage results from the customer or from the customer's negligence, the customer will be held financially responsible.
- **Demurrage:** This is a charge for "lay time" while the vessel is waiting for passengers. It may cover the late arrival of a wedding party or time while passengers go ashore at a distant location. Demurrage charges should be explained to customers in advance. Make sure customers have read and understood these charges by asking clients to initial and date the demurrage paragraph in your contract. If you use booking agents, make sure they understand demurrage charges and explain them properly to clients.
- **Extra time:** On occasion a customer may ask that an extra hour be added to a trip. If the vessel's schedule permits, this is a good way to earn extra income. Be sure to spell out in advance what you will charge for this extra time.

FOOD SERVICE

Some fishing charters expect customers to bring their own lunch. Others provide it. The choice is yours, but be sure to specify how meals and other food service will be handled. Excursion and sightseeing vessels traditionally do not permit guests to bring food aboard because they make a profit from hors d'oeuvres or sit-down dinners served while the vessel is under way. The same is true of walk-on headboats that can earn extra revenue selling soft drinks and packaged snacks. Fishing boats traditionally allow guests to bring food and beverages aboard even if snacks are sold on the boat.

Beware of catering food yourself. Most states require that all food preparation be done in a kitchen inspected by the local health department. Rather than go through the bother, form relationships with two or three different catering companies. Never depend on one source of catering. Just as your boat can be sold out, an individual catering company can have so much business that it cannot supply your food on a specific day. Also, each caterer has its own style of food and service. By having working relationships with several caterers you can offer a wider selection to guests.

Write a menu and price list for the various types of snacks or meals that will be served. Post it on your website and have menus printed to give to customers. Include at least a 15 percent markup over what the catering company charges as your profit for organizing the food service.

Some customers will demand to use their own catering service. Check your local laws first to be sure this practice is not prohibited. Many boats add a surcharge to the charter fee in these cases. Typically, a 15 percent surcharge is added when an outside caterer is used.

BEVERAGE SERVICE

This category applies to adult drinks that come under alcohol regulations that will be discussed in the next chapter. The question here is how to handle the consumption of alcohol. Tour boats and water taxis typically avoid the problem by forbidding alcoholic beverages. Fishing charters, dinner cruises, and excursion boats find that customers expect adult beverages to be available.

At a minimum, your written policies should include a statement to the effect that "Consumption of alcoholic beverages is at the discretion of the captain who may terminate the use of such beverages for the safety of the passengers, crew, or vessel." This allows the captain to cork the bottles should the party start to get out of hand. Some vessels also specify that no refunds will be paid if a charter is terminated early because of excessive drinking or the use of illicit drugs.

CLEANUP

The boat has to be cleaned after every trip. That is an unavoidable cost of doing business. Ordinary cleanup costs should be imbedded within your trip charges. However, some customers simply leave the boat a mess well beyond the usual spilled food or fish scales. It is fair to charge for extra cleanup if you tell customers in advance that an egregious mess will cost them extra money.

TIP SHEET

Charter boats find it helpful to send out a tip sheet prior to the date of departure. This is a friendly letter to customers explaining some "dos" and "don'ts" on the water. Examples of tips that might be included are suggesting soft-soled shoes, carrying a light jacket or sweater, wearing a hat and sunglasses for eye protection, and the use of sunblock.

Passengers subject to seasickness should be advised to contact their physicians. You can explain that certain prescription drugs are beneficial; do not suggest any particular product to avoid being accused of practicing medicine. Explain that over-the-counter medications are also available in drugstores but are not available on the boat. You cannot give out medications because you are not a pharmacist or a doctor.

The tip sheet should restate your alcohol policy, particularly any stipulations about termination of the charter should drunkenness become a problem in the opinion of the captain. Finally, be sure to remind them to bring a camera to record the fun.

The safest assumption when dealing with passengers is to assume they know absolutely nothing about you, your boat, your city, or being on the water. Consequently, you should be prepared to tell them everything.

GENERAL GUIDELINES FOR CUSTOMERS

Making sure customers know what to do onboard is critical, but it is also important that customers be guided before boarding.

DRIVING DIRECTIONS

Post full driving directions on your website and print them in your brochure. Send another copy of the directions with the charter agreement. This sounds like overkill but consider that time wasted while a lost driver finds the marina is money out of your pocket.

PARKING

Have signs telling your customers where to park. This is especially true of fishing charters based out of a public marina. Your customers have no right to block other dock holders from parking places close to their boats. Customers will not be upset if you allow them to unload at your dock and then park their cars somewhere out of the way. Use arrow signs to guide them to and from the parking area and your dock.

WAITING AREA

At the land end of the finger pier, install a sign explaining that customers should wait on land until receiving permission to come aboard. If the marina will allow it, it helps to dress up your waiting area. Providing a short-term storage place to lean fishing rods and a couple of benches will create a welcoming space for customers. Some skippers put up overhead signs across the finger pier beside their boats. Most have a nail rack for hanging the fish for the bragging rights photo at the end of the day.

TICKETING

An advantage of six-pack operations is informal ticketing. It usually amounts to collecting a check from whomever organized the trip. This single-payer situation also makes it easy to get paid for wedding parties, corporate charters, and the like.

However, you must have an organized system of collecting money when each individual passenger pays separately. This is particularly true during high-demand periods when more customers may want to board than your certificate of inspection allows. The answer is to issue numbered boarding passes for each trip. The number of passes is limited to the boat's legal capacity so that overloading is impossible. Tickets can serve as boarding passes so long as you can limit the number sold to the maximum legal number of passengers allowed on the boat. If this is not possible, make passengers exchange their tickets for numbered boarding passes.

The key to successful ticketing is not the office but the system. A folding card table and chair can be used as a "ticket office." I have one friend who operates a 49-passenger day sail schooner out of a cash box on his lap. The sales agent should do nothing except keep track of the money and hand out boarding passes. A second crew member should handle collecting boarding passes and allowing passengers to board the vessel.

Thanks to the terrorist attacks of 9/11, the U.S. Coast Guard and Homeland Security have instituted new regulations for boarding passengers on vessels carrying more than 49 people. These requirements mirror those for airlines. Vessel operators must first prepare a plan for handling passenger screening and security for coast guard approval. Boarding areas must allow for checking individual passengers as well as all baggage. It is difficult to give specifics about these regulations because they are being updated almost continuously. Check with your local coast guard station for current details.

MISSED THE BOAT

There are people who are always late, even for a scheduled departure. Nothing much happens if they get there after the boat has disappeared over the horizon. Big problems arise when tardy Tom shows up just after you have dropped lines and backed into the channel. The latecomer will expect you to return for him whether it is possible to accomplish or not.

Six-pack and other charters seldom depart without the full group aboard. Friends are usually willing to wait for the missing person to show up. Refunds are seldom granted to people who arrive after the departure time. Time spent waiting counts against the charter, so it shortens the duration of the trip for the other passengers.

A scheduled ferry or taxi with posted departure times must adhere to its schedule. This means the late one has to wait for the next boat. Refunds for missing a scheduled departure are seldom given. It is more often the practice to exchange the latecomer's ticket for a later departure on the same day at no extra cost.

HANDLING MONEY

Cash in the hands of employees has a tendency to disappear. Without getting into a discussion of employee dishonesty, it is just common sense to institute as many controls on your income as necessary to make sure it all goes into your bank account. "Controls" is a bookkeeper's word for ways of creating a trail of your money from the customer's hand to when you use it to write checks and pay bills. Options to consider include:

- Cash register
- Prenumbered tickets
- Inventory control
- Banking procedures
- Audit trail

Whatever controls you choose, they should be part of an overall income management plan. Even a one-person six-pack charter business needs a plan to manage money. It is very easy for a sole proprietor to pick the pocket of his own business by borrowing a few dollars here or there. There is nothing illegal about this because from a tax standpoint the company's money and the proprietor's money are the same. However, combining your business and personal finances in the family checkbook often results in a shortage of funds to pay company expenses. It doesn't seem to hurt if you buy a tank of gas for your car on the business until that day in midwinter when there is not enough money in your combined checking account to pay the boat mortgage.

CASH REGISTERS

Modern electronic cash registers allow you to keep track of different types of sales (tickets, food, souvenirs, etc.). At the end of the day, you can "Z out" the register, which means print out a full record of every transaction made on that machine. A cash register is absolutely necessary if you have large numbers of transactions each day. Cash registers are not expensive and can be purchased at any office supply store.

Lack of 120-volt AC power and the need to work in the open air force most small boat operators to use old-fashioned cash boxes. No record is kept of every transaction, so other methods of control must be instituted. Each cash box should be dedicated to a specific type of sale. The box for tickets should not be used for food or souvenirs. Each box should be assigned to a specific person who is the only employee allowed to put money in or to take it out.

The amount of cash placed in a cash register or cash box at the start of the day is called its "bank." Employees should count their banks before starting work and sign for the amount in their box or register. At the end of the day, employees are responsible for returning this "bank" plus all of the cash taken in. The total amount turned in, less the "bank," should equal the gross sales.

NUMBERED TICKETS

Prenumbered roll tickets are readily available. The numbers run sequentially, so they provide an easy check on the number sold each day. Keeping track of ticket numbers is one way to avoid a common scam used by ticket sellers to filch money from their employers: selling tickets but pocketing the money from some of the sales. Prevent this by noting the starting ticket number before each day's sales begin. Simple subtraction of that number from the next unsold ticket on the roll gives the total number of tickets sold that day.

A more complicated ticket resale scam involves two people: the ticket seller and the ticket taker. The taker collects whole tickets from boarding customers. He then gives them to the ticket seller who resells used tickets instead of giving out new ones off the roll. The scam artists then share the money collected from selling used tickets. When you compare the tickets sold off the roll to the cash box, everything balances. Crafty employees can take as much as 10 percent of your gross receipts this way with little fear of detection. A variation of this scam is for the ticket taker to redeem whole tickets for cash refunds, which are then split with the ticket seller.

To prevent these scams, ticket takers must be told to rip each ticket in half and give one half to the passenger. The ticket taker must give you the other half. The number of half tickets collected each day should equal the number of tickets sold off the roll, and both should equal the daily cash receipts.

INVENTORY COUNTS

Stealing inventory is another way that employees can take cash out of your pocket. Bar owners are particularly vulnerable to this problem. Without controls, it is easy for bartenders or waitresses to sell product and take the money but not report the sale. The cash goes straight into their pockets. This can be done with other products beyond alcohol. Soft drinks and souvenirs can also disappear in a similar fashion.

Employee Honesty Check

I worked with Captain Bill, who owned a small waterfront watering hole. His bar never seemed to make a profit equal to its popularity. So one night he paid his bartender and waitresses their base wage and a fair sum for tips they should have made. He sent these employees home while he and his wife tended bar and served drinks. That night, his gross sales were one-third higher than the previous Saturday evening. Captain Bill immediately installed inventory control.

The key to inventory control is obviously keeping count of the individual items on the shelf. Cans in an under-bar cooler are easy to count. Empty the cooler and put in a layer of cans. Draw a line at that level with a permanent marker and label it with the number of cans. Repeat this procedure layer after layer until the cooler is full. From then on, to count the cooler it is only necessary to check the line of the top full layer. Add the extra cans to get the total in the cooler. Similar creative counting can be applied to other merchandise.

BANKING PROCEDURES

Banking in this context is the physical handling of cash and checks from when you receive them until they are deposited in a banking institution. It is a process designed to protect your money against pilfering by employees or outright theft by criminals. As with so many things in business, it is important to establish a routine and follow it all the time.

Banks charge business accounts for each transaction. Study your banking fees before you establish your procedures. For instance, you may be charged less if you combine all of your checks into one deposit a week. Cash in small amounts can also be deposited once a week. However, even small amounts of cash are attractive to sticky fingers. If you keep cash, put it in a locked storage area and keep an accounting of the amount in a separate location.

Some operations like my water taxi business have big days when lots of cash is collected. Our biggest day is the Fourth of July, when people line up waiting for our boats from midafternoon until nearly midnight. Each of these passengers pays in cash and there is no way to hide the fact that each boat soon collects a large sum of money. We cannot stop some criminal from deciding to rob us, but we can limit our loss if that happens.

At regular intervals we make cash drops to a trusted person who carries the money off the boats to a secure location. This way, the boats only carry the receipts from an hour or so of operation and not the cash from the whole day.

AUDIT TRAIL

An audit trail is the paperwork that lets you track income from the hand of the customer to the bank. It includes the "Z tape" of your cash register as well as employee signatures on receipt of "banks." The audit trail on every dollar must be as complete as possible. People remain honest if they know they can be held accountable. The paperwork of the audit trail should be readily accessible for the whole fiscal year. After that, it should be kept with other business records as required by the laws of your state.

CHAPTER 11

PASSENGER SAFETY

Handling passengers is both frustrating and funny. A couple of years ago I was in the boarding lounge of the inter-island ferry I used to work for about 20 minutes before a scheduled departure. A rather flamboyantly dressed woman stopped me and asked, "Captain, are you going to drive me to the island?" Then, without missing a beat, she pointed both of her index fingers at me as if she was holding two pistols and said, "Click, click." She nodded, indicating I should respond to her question.

The whole conversation continued in this manner. Every time she finished a sentence there would be the two-gun gesture, the words "click, click," and the nod. It was as if she thought ordinary conversation was the same as a push-to-talk citizen's band radio. I had to stifle a laugh while watching my fellow employees snickering at my attempts to communicate with the woman. Later, one of the ticket sellers said, "I guess we should have warned you about Miss Click-Click."

Individually, passengers are saints and geniuses. They are mothers and fathers, dreamers and doers, diggers of ditches or tycoons of industry. Each person deserves to be treated with the dignity and respect due every human being, including even oddballs like Miss Click-Click. You have to develop in yourself and in any members of your crew who handle people a sort of formal kindness and professional politeness. Next time you travel by airplane, take time to study the cabin crew. They have been trained to separate their personal likes and dislikes from their professional demeanor. Everyone is a welcome guest on the flight.

Notice also how the airlines herd people with polite firmness. Flight crews know that when people are collected into a group they tend to lose the more ennobling characteristics of the human race. People in numbers become as stubborn as a herd of cattle and as unpredictable as a pack of cats. That is why the military has drill sergeants to march troops from place to place. To be successful in the passenger business, you must learn the fine art of discerning when to be "Captain Jovial" and when to be "Captain Bligh."

Something else that should influence your relationship with passengers is the realization that while they are necessary for your business success, they are always trying to put you out of business. Customers want you to go broke giving them the best possible price. They want you to spend yourself poor giving them the best amenities. If something doesn't go right, they have no qualms about extorting large sums from your business through the court system. So even though customers are necessary for your business to survive, you can never consider them as friends.

This admittedly dark and somewhat paradoxical view of passengers is the reason for developing and maintaining a formal business relationship with your customers. The purpose of this relationship is to extract as much money from your passengers as possible while pleasing them with your service to the extent they want to come back another day to spend more money.

Never forget, however, that you are legally required to carry your customers on the water without incidents such as falls, injuries, fires, or sinkings. Not taking care of your customers can eat deeply into your profits. This means you have to pay attention to a lot of dull stuff like safety preparation and legal paperwork before you have the fun of face-to-face interaction with customers.

SAFETY PREPARATION

These days it is not enough to simply meet U.S. Coast Guard regulations for a commercial vessel. There is an industry of victims, investigators, lawyers, and judges that thrives on the alleged safety violations and failures of companies doing business with the public. Make no mistake, if you are in business long enough you will be sued over some claimed failure on your part. This is a fact of modern business. While insurance may cover the financial costs of lawsuits, it cannot repay your lost time in court or loss of business caused by bad publicity. You cannot prevent all lawsuits, especially frivolous ones. What you can do is take action to avoid the failures and customer relation gaffes that lead to justified lawsuits.

Good Practices Prevent Lawsuits

Sometimes you do not even know you are about to be sued. Four years ago I picked up a solitary passenger who wanted to ride my taxi for lunch. His dark suit and suspenders told me instantly he was a lawyer. "Welcome aboard," I said. "Please watch your step on the stairs and be sure to use the handrails." As we crossed the river, he asked, "Do you always tell people to watch their step?" I assured him it was company practice. Then, by habit, I gave him another safety warning as he prepared to leave the boat.

Later, he identified himself as an attorney for a woman who claimed to have suffered a damaged ankle in a fall on our boat the previous Saturday night. The attorney asked about the incident. I recalled a woman with a badly sprained ankle who came to the boat to cross the river. She was in so much pain that I gave her a free ride. My "thanks" was that visit from her attorney. In the end, he declined her case because of our standard boarding safety practices. He said they made it highly improbable that she had been injured on our boat as she claimed.

A significant cause of litigation is claims arising from "trips and falls." This is why you see those yellow signs in stores and restaurants warning of slippery floors. Docks, piers, gangways, and boat decks are prime locations for an unwary person to lose his or her footing. Several things can be done to improve safety in these areas:

- **Trip hazards:** Any change in the level of a walking surface is a trip hazard. Whenever possible, these should be eliminated. The worst hazards are those of about an inch high that can be overlooked by passengers who are not paying attention. If a hatch or other small change in elevation cannot be removed, consider placing a small wedge leading up to it so that the toe-catching edge disappears.

- **Yellow paint:** Doorsills, dock edges, stair treads, and all other changes in elevation should be painted with bright yellow safety paint. This is a special color paint available from commercial paint dealers. An alternative is to use self-adhesive black and yellow warning tape.

- **Warning signs:** Post "Watch Your Step" signs warning passengers to be careful in all areas where they may normally walk. Self-adhesive, all-weather placards are available from office supply stores. Use them everywhere but particularly at doorways leading to exterior decks and in restrooms.

- **Nonskid surfaces:** All walking areas should be treated to reduce the possibility of slips, especially when wet. Ramps and other sloped surfaces should have aggressive nonskid treatment. Sand mixed in paint is one approach. Self-stick antislip tread material is also available. Some types of indoor/outdoor carpet retain enough friction when wet to be acceptable on horizontal decks and walkways. Do not rely on the nonskid surface molded into a fiberglass deck to do an adequate job of protecting commercial passengers.

- **Courtesy lights:** All walkways should be illuminated for safety when they are being used at night. Small LED courtesy light fixtures are now available for use in stairwells and other areas. These provide plenty of light without high current demand. Wide-area deck lights are a "must" when embarking or disembarking passengers after dark. These should be switched only from the helm station by the captain. This prevents the captain from being "night blinded" from the deck lights being accidentally turned on by an unknowing crew member.

- **Low overhead:** Signs warning of low deck beams are necessary in addition to verbal warnings from the crew. If possible, soften overhead beams with foam rubber padding. If a low beam cannot be removed, one idea is to place a "Watch Your Head" sign on the beam where people are most likely to bump their heads. It is hard for someone to claim injury due to your negligence if he or she bumps his or her head into a sign warning to be vigilant against just such an event.

- **Ramp and stairway handrails:** On ramps leading to the boat or on any stairways inside the boat the recommended height of handrails is 34 to 38 inches above the ramp or stair. Handrails serving stairs and ramps should be between 1¼ and 1½ inches in diameter.

Signs, yellow paint, and verbal warnings can only go so far. People still find ways to stumble. I have seen a passenger walk into a bulkhead (bloody nose) and another one trip over a sign warning of a slippery floor (twisted ankle).

BOARDING POLICY

There is no U.S. Coast Guard requirement to develop and implement a boarding policy. However, having a written policy goes a long way toward preventing incidents during what in some ways is the most dangerous part of a boating excursion. Each boat requires its own policy written to cover its specific circumstances. The document should be read and signed by every member of the crew to indicate they understand its contents. This should become part of the vessel's official logbook by reference. The term *by reference* means that you don't physically include the policy in the logbook. Simply referencing the policy in it is enough to establish that you have one.

A written boarding procedure is not intended for passengers. It is a private document primarily for use by the crew, and its purpose is to assure consistency in boarding practices from trip to trip. Some items to include are:

- **Boarding area:** Specify where passengers are to wait to board the vessel and which member of the crew is detailed to maintain order.
- **Required warnings:** Before opening the gate to let passengers aboard it is wise to explain any safety requirements that ap-

ply, such as only one person at a time on stairways or gangways. End each briefing with reminders such as "Walk, don't run; watch your step; hold children by the hand; and watch your head."

- **Prohibited items:** While passengers are still on the pier is the time to remind them of items that you prohibit on board. The list of items is up to you. It should obviously include dangerous items such as guns, but it may also include items unrelated to safety, like seemingly innocent GPS receivers to record your fishing hot spots.

- **Cell phones:** Passengers talking on cell phones are not likely to watch their step or hold on to handrails. Advise crew not to board anyone using a cell phone until the conversation is finished and the passenger can pay full attention to boarding.

- **Food and drink:** It is generally not a good idea for passengers to be distracted by food or drink in their hands while boarding. Advise them to finish consuming these items before coming up or down the gangway.

- **Departure procedure:** The boarding policy should specify what docklines must be connected during boarding as well as the placement of any gangways and other safety equipment. The contents should detail when any of this equipment is removed or when docklines are untied.

Writing and following a boarding policy go a long way toward preventing accidents. Any deviations from this written policy should be only by the captain's consent and done under special circumstances and conditions. Remember that in my experience with the slip-and-fall lawyer, it was our standardized boarding procedure that saved the day. It was not just because I happened to be running the boat that day. All of our captains are trained to go through the same boarding drill of warning passengers to be careful. It's part of the captain's job description.

MANDATORY SAFETY BRIEFING

All passenger vessels of every size must conduct a safety briefing before or shortly after departure. This coast guard briefing requirement applies whether you have one passenger or a thousand on board. It even applies to six-pack boats. Briefings can be done by the skipper at the dock, the captain over a public address system, or by individual members of the crew on the various decks of a larger vessel. The nature of this briefing varies somewhat among vessels, but all briefings contain the same key elements, which are discussed below:

- **Donning life vests:** If possible, actually demonstrate how to put on a life preserver. At a minimum, point out the placards showing donning procedures. Have your crew show passengers where the life vests are stored and the separate storage area for children's vests.
- **Life rings:** Point out the location(s) of life rings and other throwable lifesaving equipment.
- **Life floats and buoyant apparatus:** If equipped with either of these devices, explain their location and how passengers will be instructed to use them in an emergency.
- **Fire extinguishers:** Point out the location(s) of hand-portable fire extinguishers.
- **First aid kit:** On longer trips or on six-pack fishing charters where hook injuries are possible it can be helpful to point out the exact location of the first aid kit. Otherwise, notifying passengers it exists may be sufficient.
- **Cabin exits:** All exits should be plainly marked, but point them out as well. Include any "emergency only" exits such as kick-out windows, etc.

A professionally presented safety briefing tends to put passengers in a more confident mood. It does not frighten them because everyone is familiar with the "in case the cabin loses air pressure" speech made by airline cabin attendants. Safety has become an expectation these days, not a reminder that things can go wrong. Be sure to tell passengers that any member of the crew can answer questions about safety gear.

After the required safety items are covered is a good time to bring up other items necessary for passengers to know:

- **Smoking:** Make all smoking regulations clear. Most boats prohibit smoking inside cabins or on covered decks as a fire safety procedure.
- **Children:** If large numbers of children are carried, it is wise to remind parents that youngsters should always be kept near and watched closely.

- **Toilets:** Marine "heads" are notoriously cranky. Explain to passengers how the ones on your boat operate and any special problems.
- **Limited decks:** Some vessels have limits on the number of passengers on upper decks. Explain these limits and that they will be enforced by the crew.
- **Food service:** Explain any restrictions on where food can be carried from buffets and snack bars.

The end of the safety briefing is also a good time to welcome passengers aboard and remind them of places to spend their money, such as the snack bar.

FRIGHTENED PARENTS

There has been much publicity recently about wearing life jackets while boating. Many people think that it is mandatory to don a life vest when boarding any boat or at least that it is mandatory to put life vests on children. Sometimes you may encounter a parent who will grab the first adult life jacket he or she finds and try to put it on a preschool child. Be polite when this happens. Never embarrass the passenger. Instruct your crew to explain that children must wear smaller life vests and that it is only necessary for anyone to wear them when the captain says so. If the parent is adamant about a life vest for his or her child, tell your crew to simply make sure the child wears one of proper size.

SIX-PACK CHARTERS

Typically, the captain of a six-pack boat is the only trained person on board. As a precaution against sudden loss of that one trained person, it is a good idea to explain the location and operation of the ship-to-shore VHF-FM marine radio. Point out the distress call procedure placard. Also, explain where the first aid kit, distress flag, and flares are kept.

SAFETY WHILE UNDER WAY

Passengers can be trusted to do the strangest things. My most frightening experience as a professional captain came a few years ago on a ferry to an offshore island. We were making about 18 knots in perfect weather. I looked out the port side of the pilothouse to see a young mother holding her newborn baby outside the upper deck rail. "Look at the water," I could hear her say. "Isn't it pretty?" The baby dangled nearly 14 feet above the spray off the bow. All I could think about was the baby tumbling into that foaming water.

Fortunately, the senior deckhand saw this situation at about the same time. He went quickly but calmly over to the woman. "Please bring your baby inside the rail," he said in firm voice. "Captain's orders." In a moment, the potential danger was over, but my stomach kept churning for an hour after the mother and child were safely on shore.

The point of the story is that even good passengers do stupid things. It is your job to make sure your passengers return to shore in the same condition they were in when you took them on board. Sometimes this responsibility involves protecting them against themselves.

It is easier to discuss handling large groups of people such as passengers on small ferries and water taxis than it is to discuss handling six anglers who are already friends. On the bigger boat, there is a level of anonymity for both passenger and crew that allows for dispassionate interaction. Such is not the case when you are the only member of the crew and you know everyone in the boat by their first name. The following passenger-handling concepts apply to managing large groups, but six-pack skippers should find no difficulty in adapting these ideas to their specific needs, in spite of the more intimate setting of a small fishing boat.

CONTINUOUS HOUSEKEEPING

At all times and under all conditions, decks, corridors, stairways, and all walking surfaces must be kept clean and free of trip hazards. Train yourself and your crew to constantly clean up everything from loose ends of docklines to scraps of tickets. Water or spilled drinks on deck must be mopped up as quickly as possible. If weather conditions prevent keeping a deck dry, it should be closed to the passengers.

A special housekeeping situation applies to weddings. The tradition of throwing something at the lucky couple is deeply rooted. Most people have given up throwing rice because it hurts the recipients and is messy to clean up. Expect guests to want to throw either birdseed or confetti. Your passenger agreement should prohibit both practices since they raise the possibility of someone losing their footing on a moving vessel. Also beware of the practice of squirting the bride and groom with everything from water to red wine. Water just makes the deck slippery. Wine starts out slippery but quickly becomes a tacky mess that leaves behind permanent stains.

OBSERVING PASSENGERS

Guests on day boats should be kept in sight at all times with the one exception of when they are using the toilet. Six-pack operators are well advised to arrange seating so that everyone aboard can be seen from the helm station. At least one crew member must be stationed on each deck of multiple-deck vessels at all times to spot dangerous passenger behavior, as described below:

- **Children standing:** Beware of children standing on benches or moving chairs to the bulwark so they can look down on the water from open windows or railings.

- **Children playing:** Many parents see no reason to keep their offspring under control until reminded of their responsibilities. Be particularly aware of toys left in aisles and walkways where they can become trip hazards. Also, children should never be allowed to run on a boat.

- **Adult skylarking:** Adults on holiday are often as unruly as children. Beware of people who think it is funny to tie all of the life vests into a string or to plug a fire extinguisher hose with chewing gum (I've seen both happen).

- **Missing or damaged safety gear:** Most of the time you never know who mishandled safety equipment; it just shows up damaged or missing. Instruct your crew to restore equipment to working condition. If that is not possible, have them notify the captain, who should enter the discrepancy in the logbook. Missing or damaged equipment must be replaced before the next departure.

Do not rely too heavily on college-age and younger crew members to perform well at passenger-handling duty. I have seen a couple of college sophomores in a good-natured tussle on top of the buoyant apparatus rack of a high-speed ferry. Not only were they crew, but the wrestling match took place outside the safety rails of the vessel and beyond the view of the captain from the pilothouse. One way to prevent this sort of activity is to require crew members to make regular rounds of the vessel. Have them sign a sheet at each location and write down the time to prove they were there.

ROUGH WEATHER

Never forget that your passengers are in an unfamiliar environment on the water. They are not accustomed to the bouncing around normal in rough weather. Never let passengers guess how to be safe. Take charge by issuing a "rough water advisory" about where to sit and how to act. This will usually reassure most passengers by proving that you are aware of the situation and are taking action for their safety. Common precautions include:

- **Staying seated:** Be firm that passengers should remain seated in rough weather. This prevents slip-and-fall accidents. If someone is feeling queasy, bring the bucket to him or her. Never let passengers hang over the rail.
- **Moving passengers lower:** Motion is greater on upper decks, so for passenger safety and comfort it is wise to move them to lower levels. In smaller craft, such as a six-pack charter, this also improves boat stability.
- **Securing gear:** Passenger baggage should be secured so that it will not roll around in walkways where it can constitute a trip hazard.

Whenever the captain instructs passengers to remain seated for safety, the crew should be advised to make regular rounds to provide assistance to anyone requesting help. The idea is to avoid passengers moving about to fetch objects from suitcases or to take photographs. Discontinue all movement of passengers and crew in the cabin if conditions require such a precaution.

DONNING LIFE VESTS

Sooner or later, the time may come for donning life vests. Do not hesitate to break them out when the time comes. When is it time? The rule of thumb is that if you are wondering about life vests, it is already past time for having passengers put them on. Never scream at people to grab a life vest. Panic can be an ugly thing. Instead, be calm and speak in a firm conversational tone. A six-pack captain may find it effective to use his life vest to demonstrate the proper way to don the type of life jackets on board the vessel. It is always easier to lead by example. If you are wearing your life vest, what argument can anyone else have against donning theirs?

The following list covers the conditions when passengers should wear their life vests.

Conditions for Life Vests

- Rough seas and/or high winds
- Squalls in area or overhead
- Crossing a bar in rough seas
- Restricted visibility (fog)
- Your vessel is in any way incapacitated
- Your vessel is going to aid another in distress
- Whenever the captain deems life vests necessary

Keep in mind that life vest procedures are part of U.S. Coast Guard regulations. The mandatory emergency check off list (§26.03-2) discussed in Chapter 6 requires the use of life vests when crossing dangerous bars or in rough weather. Obviously, there is room for interpretation of when conditions go from unpleasant to dangerous. However, regulations are written to be interpreted by erring on the side of safety.

Fog is probably not as immediately dangerous as crossing a bar in breaking seas. However, risk of collision goes up dramatically in restricted visibility. You may be sounding fog signals and operating at a safe speed, but a fool in another boat may be running wide open and trusting to luck. If a collision occurs, the impact might hurl your passengers into the water or the boat might sink before they can don life vests.

If your boat breaks down, you will be unable to maneuver so as to ride the wind and waves correctly. This raises the possibility of capsize and swamping. Even though this is unlikely, protect your passengers by having them don life vests. Going to aid another vessel in distress also raises the possibility of something happening to your boat. This is why you are not required to aid anyone if you feel that by doing so you will put your passengers at undue risk. If you choose to help, first pause long enough to protect those people who are your primary responsibility. It should be noted in the logbook any time the captain requires donning of life vests.

NATURE CALLS

More men drown by falling overboard than women. In part, this is due to the fact that fewer women go boating than men. But the other obvious reason is men frequently stand at the rail to pee. Environmental concerns aside, as captain you must issue strict orders against it. A sudden lurch could send your male passengers toppling over the side. Instead of taking the risk, require men to use the head.

DOCKING PROCEDURES

The last part of your written boarding procedures should cover docking at the end of a voyage. Bringing a vessel into its berth raises a variety of special dangers that do not exist at sea. Chief among these are personal injuries from being caught either between the moving hull and the pier or in a bight of line when it is pulled taut by the boat.

PASSENGER INSTRUCTIONS

As the boat prepares to dock, passengers should be told to remain seated until the boat is safely alongside. Always tell passengers to keep hands, bodies, and heads inside the boat at all times, and tell them not to handle lines or to jump ashore. Both of these actions are likely to result in injuries. Displaying a placard reminding people to remain seated and not to attempt to assist the crew in docking is prudent. The language should be simple and direct.

> *Notice:* **Passengers must remain seated while boat is leaving or entering a dock. Keep hands, heads, and bodies inside the vessel at all times. Please do not handle docklines or attempt to assist the crew.**

Beware of jumpers as you near the dock. Young men, especially those who have had a few adult beverages, often think it will be funny to jump in, swim to shore, and be on the dock to greet their friends on the boat. The high fatality rate from this activity resulted in a federal law against jumping from inspected passenger vessels.

CREW INSTRUCTIONS

Docking is most dangerous for the crew. To minimize risk, organize docklines so that each docking is as similar to the previous one as wind and current allow. Making the same use of spring lines or fenders time after time does two things. First, practice makes perfect, so the crew is less likely to get hurt fumbling during an unfamiliar situation. Second, an organized system of docking helps prevent forgetfulness, such as not placing fenders or spring lines.

Shouting tends to upset passengers who associate raised voices with an emergency situation. Instead, use a system of hand signals. Whistle signals (try using a coach's whistle) can also be effective. Work up your own code of hand gestures or whistle toots to match the needs of your boat. Family radio service (FRS) walkie-talkies are also a good way of passing voice instructions.

CHAPTER 12

WHEN THINGS GO WRONG

Anything that can go wrong will go wrong—someday. This is especially true at sea where the environment is hostile to both people and the machines they build. Until now, we have been looking at how to prevent things from going wrong. In this chapter, we'll look at the other side of the equation by accepting that even good people doing their best get into trouble from time to time. Machinery fails. People fall and injure themselves. Other boats need assistance. These situations are just a few of the things that can go wrong on an ordinary day at sea.

By definition, you have a problem whenever things aren't going according to plan. It can be as simple as a burned-out instrument light on a night trip or it may be as life-threatening as a fire in the engine room. From a practical standpoint, trouble for an inspected vessel can be divided broadly into two categories: serious incidents and nonserious ones.

SERIOUS AND NONSERIOUS INCIDENTS

Serious incidents are events that require notifying the U.S. Coast Guard. All of the following events qualify as serious incidents:

- All accidental groundings and any intentional grounding that also meets any of the other reporting criteria or creates a hazard to navigation, the environment, or the safety of the vessel.

- Loss of main propulsion or primary steering or an associated component or control system, the loss of which causes a reduction of the maneuvering capabilities of the vessel.
- An occurrence materially and adversely affecting the vessel's seaworthiness or fitness for service or route including, but not limited to, fire, flooding, failure or damage to fixed fire extinguishing systems, lifesaving equipment, or bilge pumps.
- Loss of life.
- An injury to a passenger or crew member that requires professional medical treatment beyond first aid. An injury to a commercial vessel crew member that renders that individual unfit to perform routine duties.
- An occurrence not meeting any of the above criteria but resulting in damage to property in excess of $25,000, including labor and materials but not the cost of haulout.

Nonserious incidents, on the other hand, are all other events that do not require a report to the U.S. Coast Guard. With the exception of a grounding that blocks a channel, the dividing line between these two categories is determined by either the seriousness of injuries to people or the dollar value of damage to the vessel or vessels involved. Failure to report a serious marine incident may result in the coast guard taking action against your license.

Six-pack vessel operators also must report serious marine incidents to the U.S. Coast Guard. No distinction is made on the basis of a commercial passenger boat having uninspected status. The criterion (46 CFR §4.01 and §4.05) for requiring that a report be filed with the coast guard is based solely on the carriage of passengers for hire.

REPORTING SERIOUS INCIDENTS

All serious incidents must be reported to the U.S. Coast Guard marine safety office (MSO) having jurisdiction over the waters on which it took place "as soon as possible" after a marine casualty. This notice must include the name and official number (or state registration number) of the vessel, the name of the owner, and the nature and circumstances of the casualty including injuries and property damage. The last two items, injuries and property damage, are often difficult to assess, so just do your best. Telephone the local MSO with this information. Most have a 24-hour manned or answering service line for this purpose.

As an alternative, use the marine VHF radio to contact the nearest coast guard station. Request the station radio operator to inform the nearest MSO of the incident and that you will be filing paperwork later. This initial verbal notification should contain as few details as possible beyond what incident occurred.

Full details of the incident follow up this initial report. They are contained on the written U.S. Coast Guard form 2692. It is a two-part document. Although given the same form number, there are really two different pages designed to report completely different types of information.

One page covers just the accident, listing the vessel or vessels involved, the location, the names of operators, the nature of the incident (collision, grounding, fire, etc.), and any injuries to personnel. The other page of form 2692 covers only drug and alcohol testing of crew members involved in a serious marine incident. If the drug and alcohol form is filed, then certain items on the incident report are to be left blank. Fortunately, full details are printed on the forms to prevent confusion.

What to Say

Most of form 2692 consists of filling in blanks that require specific data. Section IV "Description of Casualty" is where you can get into trouble. This is a big, empty space in which you are supposed to write your description of how the accident occurred, what damage occurred, any alcohol or drug involvement, and recommendations for corrective safety measures. The block is large but usually not big enough to describe most major marine incidents. The easiest way to get around this space limitation is by typing or writing "See Attachment A" in block 44. Then write your full description of the accident on a separate sheet of paper.

At the top of the blank paper, put "Attachment A" and below that the name of the vessel, date of the incident, and your name, address, and telephone number. Should the attachment stray from the original form 2692, this header information will help the MSO get things back together again. Below the header tell your story in plain language.

Never try to change the facts to make you look better when you fill out the form. MSO investigators read a lot of these reports every year. They get pretty good at spotting puffery and falsification because it usually does not match what they have seen reported about other, similar accidents. If a full investigation follows, any stretching or altering of the truth can result in coast guard actions against your vessel or your license. The requirement to file a 2692 does not mean that you have to testify against yourself. Just present exactly what took place without voicing any opinions one way or the other. To prevent self-incrimination, a good rule to follow is "the less said, the better." Give only the basic facts.

Filing of form 2692 can be done by fax, mail, or hand delivery to the nearest MSO location. The time limit for filing a report is five days (46 CFR §4.05-10a) because the coast guard recognizes that aiding injured people and securing the vessel from further damage take precedence over paperwork. As a good rule of thumb, try to file form 2692 no more than 24 hours after a death and within 48 hours in other cases.

Obtaining Forms

Printed copies of form 2692 are available from all U.S. Coast Guard marine safety offices (MSOs). They are also available for download on the Internet. The following URL takes you to both the regular form 2692 and the special form 2692 for drug and alcohol testing reports: http://www.uscg.mil/hq/g-m/moa/repor.htm.

To File or Not to File?

Keep in mind as you fill out form 2692 that all information you supply becomes public record open for inspection by anyone who requests to see it. Sometimes you can avoid filing a report by making a phone call or you can just get lucky, as I did not so long ago.

Toward the end of the evening, one of my captains reported that his boat was not responding properly to the helm. I had him dock immediately and lay up the boat. The next day it was easy to see the hydraulic slave cylinder operating the rudder was binding. Since it was at least 20 years old, we decided to replace the cylinder. While I was working in the bilge, one of the local MSO vessel inspectors stopped by. He gave the old "I happened to be in the vicinity" excuse, but I know he can see me working on my boats from his office window. He obviously just got curious.

Rather than hide anything, I leveled with him. "We had to lay up the boat last night because the steering was getting stiff. I'm replacing the cylinder to fix the problem," I said. Then, without waiting for a reply, I added, "The captain had passengers on when he got worried about the steering, so he disembarked them and laid up the boat. There were no injuries."

Those last words were magic. Suddenly, a potential "serious" incident turned into ordinary maintenance. "This doesn't look like something you have to report," the officer said smiling. "Don't bother with a 2692." Had the officer not shown up, I would have gone through the drill of filling out a form 2692 and filing it simply to protect both my company and my captain. The coast guard can be lenient about things they know about, but they are generally hard-nosed about events they learn about only days or weeks later.

OTHER DOCUMENTS

Form 2692 isn't the end of it, however. There are additional federal requirements, possible state and/or local requirements, and your own need to document the incident for self-protection. We'll look at all of these below.

State and Local Reports

Laws vary from state to state about filing accident reports concerning commercial boats. Check with your local state watercraft law enforcement agency to learn what they expect. Be sure not to say one thing to the coast guard and another to local law enforcement officers. It is your responsibility to know the law and file the appropriate reports.

If you are required to fill out a state or local accident report, use the statement you made on form 2692 word-for-word on those other documents. Go out of your way to make sure that your story is exactly the same on every piece of paperwork. This avoids the embarrassing situation of being forced to explain why your story on one form is different than on another. You can expect somebody will compare the documents.

Records of Voyages

As the owner of a vessel involved in a marine incident, you are required (46 CFR §4.05-15) to retain all voyage records such as the logbook and other documentation. Upon request, the original copies of these records must be turned over to the coast guard inspecting officer.

Photographs

There is some debate over whether photographs help or hurt when it comes to defending against lawsuits arising out of marine accidents. At the moment, the tide has swung in favor of making a photographic record of the event. So many camera phones exist these days that somebody will have made a photograph anyway, so it is best to have your own photo documentation.

Many vessels carry disposable cameras sealed in food storage bags as protection from moisture and salt air. These cheap cameras are good enough to record the scene in sufficient detail. The zippered bag prevents moisture from attacking the camera and film. Be sure to purchase a camera with high-speed color film and a built-in flash. Replace the camera each season to be sure it will work if you need it.

The purpose of photographs is to show what was there at the time the image was exposed. Shoot straight-on without any attempt to get creative. Each location should be photographed at least three times: wide shot, medium shot, and close-up. The wide shot establishes the whole scene. The medium shot shows the area of specific interest. Close-ups are intended to look at one or more details of specific interest.

If possible, place something in each shot that helps give an idea of scale. This can be a yardstick, a foot-long ruler, or a person (in a wide shot). A hand in a close-up gives the needed scale to judge the size of the objects in the image. Among the things to photograph are:

- **Injuries to persons:** Take photos of personal injuries. Take photos of the absence of visible injuries, too. Either can be invaluable if that person suddenly develops an injury after receiving legal counsel, or a slight one becomes mysteriously serious. Technically, you can photograph anyone in the public areas of your vessel. However, you should get permission from the victim before you begin shooting close-ups.

- **Trip-and-fall locations:** The goal is to show that any stairways or other trip hazards were properly marked and that non-skid material was applied where necessary. Also, you want to illustrate that there was no water or other liquid or debris that might have caused someone to slip. An opposing attorney will eventually document conditions at the site of the accident. Your photographic record prevents any exaggeration of conditions, even if you did not take all possible safety precautions prior to the event.

- **Collision and allision damage:** It is amazing how much bigger damage can get when money is involved. Photos are a good way of preventing subjective memories. Photos should be taken of both your boat and either the other vessel or the object struck. Be sure to include enough of the undamaged hull or object so that it is easy to see where the damage ends. See Specific Incidents, below, for the definitions of *collision* and *allision*.

Make notes of what is included on each photograph. Sign and date your notes. Have the film processed by any commercial lab. Keep all the paperwork, including the processing envelope and the section of the negative on which the identification tag was applied.

Names and Addresses

It is obvious that you will need the name and address of anyone injured on your boat or of the operator/owner of another boat in a collision. Exchanging information with these people is required by law. Witnesses do not have to be so cooperative. It can be impossible to find witnesses of an event months or years later, so do your best to get information from any witnesses who are willing to give you their names and addresses.

ACCIDENT INVESTIGATIONS

All serious marine incidents are investigated by the U.S. Coast Guard and usually state watercraft officers. Government investigators will identify themselves as such before they ask questions. Private investigators will seldom be as courteous. Do not be surprised if you are the subject of an undisclosed private investigation arising out of an incident you are unaware occurred. Recall that I found myself in that situation when the attorney for the woman with the sprained ankle came aboard my water taxi.

Whether accident investigators show up in official uniforms or in civilian dress, they can never be considered as friendly. As you have heard in so many movies and TV shows, anything you say can and will be used against you. Aside from giving your name and address, make no statements to investigators until you have an attorney present.

This is particularly true with U.S. Coast Guard investigations where that agency serves as the investigating and prosecuting agency, the judge, the jury, and the executioner. Yes, there are procedural safeguards in the regulations. This does not change the fact that the same agency that investigates your actions in a marine casualty has the power to suspend or revoke your license, fine you, or send you to jail.

Your Defense Team

The need for prudence in dealing with coast guard investigators is obvious. You cannot get out of filing form 2692, but you are under no obligation to say anything to investigating officers beyond the minimal information reported on form 2692 until you have benefit of legal counsel. As they say on TV, you have a right to a lawyer. Take full advantage of this right. When dealing with the coast guard, hire an attorney who is skilled in such matters. The cost of the lawyer's service could be far less than letting the coast guard run the show unchecked.

Before you complete all the required government reports you should inform your insurance agent of the incident. Depending on the seriousness of the incident, your insurance company may want to become involved in what is placed on the official record. Also, if you think the incident may result in coast guard action against your license, obtain counsel from a qualified marine attorney before filing any paperwork. You must begin assembling your defense team and your defensive position before the official reports are completed.

SPECIFIC INCIDENTS

Collisions, allisions, and personal injuries are among the most common "serious" incidents reported to the U.S. Coast Guard by small passenger vessel operators. It is essential that your business have procedures in place to ensure the proper response to these incidents, and that you report them promptly and properly.

COLLISIONS AND ALLISIONS

Accident investigators distinguish between *collisions*, involving incidents between two or more moving boats, from *allisions*, which occur between a single moving vessel and a fixed object like a bridge abutment, light tower, or pier. In a collision, there is always some violation (or violations) of the Rules of the Road in addition to possible personal injuries, bent metal, or cracked fiberglass.

If you are involved in either a collision or an allision, your first response must be to check your passengers and crew for injuries. Almost simultaneously, you must determine if your vessel remains safe and functional. Check for water rising in the bilge and make sure the steering, throttle, and gearshift are in working order. After you determine that your boat is in safe condition, you have several other legal obligations:

- **Collisions:** By law, you must render assistance to the other vessel if you can do so without putting your vessel or passengers in peril. In addition, you must exchange information with the other skipper including your name, address, and phone number. You must identify your boat by name and official number or state registration. It also helps to exchange insurance company information at this point.
- **Allisions:** Unlike in a collision, there is no other vessel to assist. However, if you have struck a bridge or other safety-

related structure, you must immediately report the incident to the nearest U.S. Coast Guard station. If you collide with a buoy or strike any other aid to navigation, you are required to report the incident to the coast guard. Six-pack captains can simply radio the nearest coast guard station. Inspected vessel captains should do this and also file a report with the nearest officer in charge of marine inspections (OCMI).

Amtrak Bridge, Falling Down

The importance of quickly reporting allisions was made tragically apparent several years ago when a barge tow struck a railroad bridge in the bayou country of Louisiana. The towboat crew did not notice any damage, but they really could not tell because of a thick fog. In reality, they had knocked down a portion of a railroad bridge. A while later, an Amtrak passenger train dropped off that broken bridge with considerable loss of life.

Six-pack and small passenger vessels seldom have the power to knock down concrete and steel, but they can be a sort of "last straw" event that leads to catastrophe.

PERSONAL INJURIES

No matter how prudent the skipper, no matter how trained the crew, no matter how well prepared the boat, a time eventually comes when somebody gets hurt. Sometimes the injuries are serious and require immediate hospital attention. Other times, the injuries are of the bandage variety. Occasionally, the injuries are imaginary and invented to extort money from you and your insurance company.

Apologies and Kindness

In most of the country, the best advice is to treat any injured passengers with an overabundance of kindness. However, there are parts of

California and New York State where some case law has interpreted showing certain kindnesses to your passengers as an admission of guilt for injuring them. In those states, it is prudent for you to get legal advice on what to say to injured passengers and their families before you start your business.

Preventing marine accidents is the specialty of my water taxi partner, Rick Brown (who is not related to me in spite of our shared last name). "Saying you're sorry is not really an admission of guilt. You can express sorrow for the injury; just never say, 'it was my fault,' " Rick advises. "Kill the people with kindness unless you are in New York and California. Follow up afterward on the phone."

Rick has found a pattern in the types of people who file lawsuits arising from injuries. "The first group are really hurt and they can't go back to work," he says. This group of people usually must file a claim in court in order to collect a fair settlement from insurance underwriters.

"The other kind who sue are the ones who are just upset with you because you didn't go out of your way to assist them," he says. "You angered them." These are the lawsuits that you can prevent by helping injured parties in a courteous manner. For instance, you might arrange an overnight stay at your expense for the family of an injured person who is hospitalized overnight. You might cover the costs of the family's meals while the injured person is being treated. Before you have an incident, however, check with your attorney to determine what sorts of support you can supply the injured person and family under your state's laws.

Administering First Aid

When anyone is injured on your boat you must first determine the extent of those injuries and render first aid if necessary. This raises an immediate problem for six-pack operators. In most cases, the skipper will be the only person on board with first aid training. Yet the skipper's responsibility is not just for the injured person but for everyone on board. There is no good solution to this problem. The best thing to do is to demonstrate quickly to other passengers how to aid the injured person so you can go back to running the boat.

Getting Passengers to Help

A few years ago, one of my captains faced a situation in which his reliance on a passenger in an emergency saved a life.

While making an upriver pickup with my pontoon water taxi, he spotted a rider spill his personal watercraft in what looked like a particularly vicious spinout. The rider waved feebly in the direction of the taxi instead of swimming back to his stopped machine. My captain altered course to investigate and found the rider in obvious physical distress. He was hauled aboard where he immediately began to reassure everyone he was OK. To cover himself, my captain reported the incident by VHF marine radio to the nearest U.S. Coast Guard station.

The station operator asked for a condition report on the man. The captain was in the midst of saying, "He says he's all right," when one of the women aboard shouted, "He's falling!" Fortunately, she was a practicing nurse and managed to ease his fall to the deck. "Check that," the captain said into the microphone. "He just collapsed. Send an ambulance to the riverside launch ramp. Tell the rescue squad to back down the ramp."

The nurse arranged the man's body to prevent shock. Our taxi headed for the ramp faster than my captain might otherwise have driven through a harbor. As he arrived, the rescue squad was backing down the ramp. "His heart stopped," the nurse said, her voice reflecting the seriousness of the situation. Without hesitation, my captain drove the taxi up on the ramp, leaving the aluminum pontoons high and dry. The rescuers grabbed red cases and swarmed aboard over the foredeck. Moments later, the man's heart was beating and he was breathing again.

Several important lessons can be learned from this incident:

- Never hesitate to involve professionals on shore whenever you have a possible serious injury on board. By contacting the coast guard early, my captain saved several precious minutes getting the rescue squad to the launch ramp.

- Be willing to deviate from normal procedures in an emergency. Both my captain and the coast guard operator knew to send the taxi to a launch ramp the rescue squad could reach quickly and easily, and they knew not to attempt to bring the victim back to our home dock.

- Be willing to delegate responsibility to a passenger. Although you cannot always have a trained nurse aboard, anyone with some basic first aid knowledge might be helpful if someone is injured. Likewise, passengers might be able to help out in mechanical emergencies or in situations in which someone is needed to manage unruly or panicky passengers while you run the boat.

First Aid Kit

Inspected vessels are required to carry an extensive first aid kit (46 CFR §184.710). The coast guard specifies the type of container, its contents, and even how the kit is packed (46 CFR §160.041). A full listing of the required contents can be accessed at http://www.access.gpo .gov/cgi-bin/cfrassemble.cgi?title=200446.

The regulations were written a long time ago when steel boxes were the standard containers for first aid supplies. More practical are the soft-sided kits offered by Adventure Medical Kits and Orion. Both companies use waterproof nylon bags better suited to six-pack boats and smaller inspected passenger vessels. Under the regulations 46 CFR §160.041-2(a), alternate arrangements of materials meeting the performance requirements of metal boxes will be given special consideration.

Six-pack operators are not required by coast guard regulations to carry first aid kits. Safety expert Rick Brown advises not to be fooled. "You have to keep your vessel in 'seaworthy' condition, and that generally means you have to meet inspected vessel standards when it comes to safety gear," he says. The cost of a kit that meets regulations is currently under $100, so there is really no economic reason not to carry one.

You must inspect your first aid kit at the start of each season. Check the dates on any medications and replace those that are out of date, or will become out of date during your operating season. Keep a written record of these annual inspections and updates.

Heart Attacks on Board

In two decades of commercial operation, I have seen only one case in which a passenger had a heart attack, and that was on another boat. It happened on a six-pack fishing charter. The skipper had his hands full because all of his passengers were from the man's family. He started cardiopulmonary resuscitation (CPR) and then passed it off to two family members before calling the coast guard for a rescue squad. Under different circumstances the CPR might even have been successful, but this victim was probably dead before he fell to the deck. The emergency medical technicians took the man to a nearby hospital, where he was pronounced dead.

That skipper handled the situation well. He did as much as possible to save the victim, but his actions also protected his other passengers from potential harm. Having family members perform the CPR kept them occupied and hopeful. To everyone aboard, the victim was still alive as the boat raced for shore. This prevented any panic that might otherwise have developed. The family did not have to face their grief until after they arrived at the hospital where trained professionals were standing by to help them cope with their loss.

Over-the-counter heart defibrillation machines are now coming on the market. They first appeared on commercial aircraft, where they literally proved to be lifesavers. Yacht clubs are buying these machines in greater numbers, as are racing organizations, in spite of the high cost of the equipment. Defibrillators are not required, and it is therefore up to you whether to equip your boat with one or not. If you do decide to carry a defibrillator, check with your attorney regarding any legal liabilities. In addition, you will require training in the proper use of defibrillators.

Refusal of Treatment

Always offer to have anyone injured on your boat the opportunity to receive treatment at a nearby emergency room. Be sure to document it if they refuse treatment. The best documentation is a signed statement by the injured person stating they have refused treatment. This statement should also be signed by at least one witness. The witness need not have seen the incident that caused the injury, just that he or she saw the injured person sign the statement. If the injured person refuses to sign the document, when you describe the incident in your logbook be sure to note that the injured party refused treatment. Sign and date your entry and have that signature witnessed by at least one person.

AID TO OTHER VESSELS

As a professional mariner, you will spend more of your time on the water than nearly all pleasure boaters, which means you are more likely to encounter other boats in distress. The law and common decency require you to give whatever assistance you can provide without putting your vessel or passengers in jeopardy (23 U.S. Code §2304).

While there can be no quibbling with the intent of the law, there is no good Samaritan clause protecting you from liability for damages resulting from rendering assistance. Strangely, though, there is a good Samaritan clause in the law (23 U.S. Code §2303) requiring you to provide all assistance possible to another boat involved in a collision with yours.

Not having spelled out good Samaritan protection is really of little consequence. The clause is flimsy legal protection easily wiped away by claiming you did not act as an *ordinary*, *reasonable*, and *prudent* individual would have acted under the same circumstances. During an emergency on the water you have to make real-time decisions with no chance to analyze the alternatives. In court, an opposing attorney will take months or years to develop a "what-if" case to show that if you had been acting more reasonably and prudently the injuries to his client would not have occurred.

Keep in mind, however, that by holding a U.S. Coast Guard license you can be held to a higher standard of seamanship than an ordinary weekend boater. That opposing attorney's job is made all the easier by the fact that as a licensed mariner you are by definition a professional and should know what to do and how to do it without injuring others.

Each captain has to reconcile the potential legal ramifications that could arise when aiding others in distress with his private conscience. For me, I rescue people in peril without reservation and in the most expeditious way possible. This includes towing another boat if that is the prudent way to preserve the lives of those aboard. However, I draw the line at towing disabled vessels when there is no threat to life. Instead, my procedure is to contact the coast guard with information about the disabled craft. I offer to stand by if necessary, but I also inform the radio operator that I am operating a commercial vessel with passengers on board. With that, the problem belongs to the coast guard. Most of the time, the operator has released me from the scene to continue my route.

CHAPTER 13

FOOD AND BEVERAGE SERVICE

Peiople like to eat and drink on the water, and a great way to
increase your business is to provide "good eats." Big cruise
ships know this. The most valuable member of the crew is not
the captain or navigator but the head chef. A small charter
fishing or excursion boat may not be able to do ice sculptures and serve
flaming baked Alaska desserts like big cruise ships, but it is possible to
capitalize on food and drink to boost the bottom line. The trick is tailor-
ing food service to match both the boat and the clientele it serves.

There is a dark side to food and beverage service. Handling food
brings the twin problems of spoilage and contamination. The atmosphere aboard a boat is often damp, hot (above 40°F), and dirty compared to a commercial kitchen. These conditions make your boat an
ideal breeding ground for bacteria that can cause food poisoning. Di-
arrhea and vomiting associated with this condition quickly dehydrate
the victim, making the boat ride an unpleasant experience at best,
and, at worst, food poisoning can be life-threatening, especially for
kids and the elderly. A sick customer will also ruin the boat ride for
other passengers. Food-borne illnesses are the reason for public health
laws governing the way in which food is served and the requirements
for food service licenses.

People drink a lot on boats, and fortunately it is mostly soft drinks
and water to replace water lost due to sweating. Adults are also fond of
beer and hard liquor. Be aware, however, that serving alcoholic beverages puts you in a very strange area of the law where things are not
always what they seem.

The disastrous attempt at prohibition in the United States was instituted and repealed by Constitutional amendments. As a result, each state has its own laws governing alcoholic beverages; it's not a federal issue. Localities in some states have "home rule" power over the sale of alcohol. Because of the Constitutional repeal of prohibition, you do not enjoy federal constitutional protection against entrapment by law enforcement officials if you violate the regulations. Entrapment involves the police forcing you into an illegal act to provide cause for an arrest, and that's usually not allowed. With alcohol, things are different. It is legal for liquor agents to use a minor to buy alcohol just to test that you are obeying the law.

If all of these negatives sound intimidating, they should. But do not lose hope. Food and beverages are served on small passenger vessels every day without incident. As with anything else related to boating, you simply have to learn the ropes. This means gaining an understanding of both the laws governing food and beverages, and the practicalities of serving them. In the end, the result should be a substantial increase in your net profits.

Laws and procedures governing soft drink sales are so similar to other packaged foods that from here on pop, iced tea, and water will be included with "food service." Alcoholic beverages will be considered under "licensed beverage service."

PREPACKAGED FOOD SERVICE

There are two broad legal categories of foods that can be served aboard a boat. Prepackaged foods, bottled drinks, bagged potato chips, and candy bars are the easiest to handle because they are sealed at the factory and protected against contamination. The other broad category of foods are those requiring an on-site kitchen to prepare. Foods such as fresh cheese trays, snack dips, and chicken wings fall into this category, and they spoil quickly in the heat.

BUYING PREPACKAGED FOODS

A food service license is seldom required with prepackaged foods. However, most states require you to acquire a vendor's license to sell these items. The reason for requiring this license is not food safety but to make sure you pay your sales tax. However, it also allows you to make purchases at wholesale prices. The net result is an increase in your profit for the price of filling out regular tax reports.

Some boat-based businesses are too small, however, to qualify as customers of food distributors, so true wholesale pricing may not be available. If that's the case with your business, "wholesale clubs" such as Costco and Sam's Club are a good alternative, selling snacks and soft drinks in bulk at close to wholesale prices.

Individual serving bags of snacks come in variety or single-product packages. Buy the variety pack because having a choice often stimulates sales. Pop does not come in variety packs, so you have to settle on a few popular flavors. Year after year, colas are the top-selling soft drinks. Lemon-lime drinks are a favorite flavor among women. Root beer is no longer a top-selling item. Iced tea is a good alternative to carbonated beverages. People like this product with or without sweeteners and with or without lemon. At least half of the soft drinks in your cooler should be diet.

If possible, serve snacks in lunchbox-sized, single-serving bags. There are several advantages to providing these small bags rather than opening a large family-sized package. First, you can't charge for chips by the handful. Individual bags can be sold for a dollar or more each, adding a tidy income to your operation. Small bags also do not go stale the way chips and pretzels do when a larger package is left open in the moist air. Small bags make considerably less mess when they spill than a family-sized package. Good choices include:

- **Potato chips:** These are everyone's favorite. Get plain and flavored varieties. Avoid serving potato chips when winds exceed about 10 knots because of the "blow around" factor.
- **Pretzels:** These don't blow around much, so they are good in most weather conditions. The salt and dough help to settle queasy stomachs.
- **Corn chips:** Corn chips are good alternatives to potato chips. These often stay fresher longer than potato chips. But some corn chips leave greasy hands.

One snack food to avoid is that all-American favorite, popcorn. It just does not work well on a boat. The individual puffs are so light they tend to blow out of the bag. If a bag spills, you'll be sweeping popcorn out of the oddest corners of the bilge for years to come. But the main reason to avoid it is that popcorn gets stale almost instantly in the moist marine environment.

BEVERAGES

Beverages are considered a "food" in this discussion, because they are something you serve that goes into your passengers' digestive systems. Even if you choose not to sell prepackaged solid food, passengers should have access to beverages on all but the shortest of boat trips to prevent the possibility of dehydration.

Drinking Water

Potable water tanks on boats are not always the most sanitary containers. Adding bleach or other chemicals to kill bacteria can produce an "off" taste, and unless you have an onboard laboratory, you have no way to know if the purification chemicals have done their job.

Why take a chance on your tanks causing illness? Instead, provide your customers with commercially bottled water. Purchase water in single-serving bottles and keep them on ice in a special cooler. A steady supply of cold, fresh water really helps make a successful trip. Six-pack charter fishing skippers often find that including water in the overall package goes a long way toward turning customers into repeat business. Charging for bottled water is more common on excursion boats and ferryboats where passengers are not spending long hours in the sun and exposed to the wind.

Soft Drinks

Cans chill faster than bottles (glass or plastic), and they do not break. It is also possible to cram more cans in a cooler than other types of containers. This is why canned pop and iced tea are preferred by most boat operators. If real aluminum cans are not available, the next best thing are single-serving plastic bottles. Don't even think of bringing glass containers aboard due to the possibility of breakage.

If you operate an excursion boat on a hot day, you will need to keep a steady supply of cold pop on hand. To do so requires two coolers. Cans can be chilled quickly by immersing them in ice-cold water in the first cooler. Mix up a slurry of water and ice, then dump the cans into this chilling cooler. Once they are cold, transfer them to the second service cooler. The second cooler only needs a layer of ice across the top to keep the cans cold.

As with family-sized bags of snacks, those big two-liter bottles of pop present problems. You can't sell pop by the swallow or the cupful. Spilling a big bottle makes a bigger mess than spilling a small one. The one time to use two-liter bottles is for a reception where drinks are served by bartenders.

Conventional soft drinks are sweetened with corn syrup. A spill quickly becomes a sticky mess if it is not wiped up immediately. Diet drinks are sweetened with chemicals that do not become sticky as they dry. The advantage of serving only diet drinks is obvious, but at least half the population still prefers the corn syrup version. The only solution to spills is to quickly mop them up. Keep a mop handy at all times to prevent slip hazards in the event of spills.

Homemade Drinks

Iced tea and lemonade are favorite homemade drinks. In particular, a lot of skippers put a jug of water and tea bags on deck to brew "sun tea." At home, these drinks are fine. However, making your own soft drinks puts you into the food preparation business with all of its inherent liabilities. Unless you are planning to get into the catering business, don't take the risk. Purchase all your soft drinks in factory-sealed containers and simply resell them to your customers.

SELLING PREPACKAGED FOODS

You do not need a formal snack bar and clerk to sell these items on a six-pack or excursion boat. Simply put them out where they are accessible to the passengers, and put a sign up to give prices. Place a cash box nearby so customers can pay for what they take. I've been doing this for about a decade on my river excursions without any problems. The vast majority of people are honest.

Of course, I do not follow this practice when operating regular taxi service. The confusion of boarding and rapid turnarounds would make it easy for a thief to steal a lot of product or the cash box. The more controlled atmosphere of a boat with no way to escape seems to prevent petty theft. Perhaps the fact that many of the people on an excursion are either friends or family makes a difference too.

Pricing

Never forget that you have a captive audience once the boat leaves the dock. Your customers can't go anywhere else to buy a snack or soft drink. From a practical standpoint they have to pay your price or remain hungry or thirsty. They are not expecting to find any bargains on your boat, which means you are giving away money if you do not put a healthy markup on these items. Typically, charge no less than double your actual cost on each product. This is called a 100 percent markup.

The top price you can charge is determined by the local market price for similar items. For instance, if pop is going for $2 per serving ashore, you can charge at least that on your boat, plus a small amount for being afloat without making people mad at you. Most people expect to pay perhaps $2.50 on a boat for the same $2 drink ashore. Selling below market price is stupid business practice. In effect, you are subsidizing your customer by the difference between your low price and the market value of the product. Remember, the money is always better in your pocket than in your customer's pocket. That is why you are in business.

The actual price you charge also depends on the situation. A harbor tour or excursion boat can charge a higher price for food and soft drinks than a six-pack charter. Few people take a harbor tour more than once in a lifetime, and so it makes sense to maximize profits on concessions because you aren't counting on building repeat business. However, as a six-pack operator you are trying to build repeat business and maximize profits over time. In this case, charging below a 100 percent markup can make a lot of sense. You don't want customers to think you're gouging them for nickels and dimes.

CATERED FOOD SERVICE

In this context, "catered food" is fresh cheese, meat, and vegetables prepared for a specific voyage and paid for by the customers of that voyage. It may also include hot food such as Swedish meatballs, Buffalo wings, or hot dogs. You'll have to decide who's going to do the catering.

While running the whole show may seem like an attractive way to maximize profits, there are serious impediments to running what amounts to an on-board restaurant that should give you pause, unless you have experience in food service. Other options include having your company provide the food on board with the help of a shoreside caterer to prepare it or renting space on your boat to a third-party food service provider.

RUNNING YOUR OWN CATERING SERVICE

Unlike prepackaged products, voluminous health regulations, licenses, and laws are associated with catered food. Serving catered food that has not been prepared in an approved kitchen can lead to fines and even jail time if a severe outbreak of food poisoning develops.

Food Preparation and Handling Licenses

Laws governing the preparation and serving of fresh food vary widely by state. In general, you need to have at least one license for the kitchen. Most jurisdictions require an additional catering license to serve food at a site remote from the kitchen, such as aboard a boat. In some areas, there are different forms of licenses depending on the food and method of preparation.

The best thing to do is contact your local or county health department to learn what licenses they require and to acquire a listing of regulations for kitchens and food service. You will probably discover that cooking food at home or in your boat's galley is impractical due to health regulations.

Some people try to create a loophole in the laws by claiming that homemade food was a "gift" and not part of the cruise or charter package. Giving a tin of homemade cookies to charter guests as a "thank you" for their patronage is not likely to cause problems. However, providing homemade meatballs, baked beans, or other picnic fare consumed during the voyage would probably be viewed as food service within the context of the ticket price and not as a gift. When in doubt, get legal advice from a professional.

Kitchens on Boats

Requirements for an approved kitchen are decidedly unfriendly to a boat. Most jurisdictions are now requiring at least a three-basin dishwashing sink. Some have upgraded to a four-basin sink. These are known as "three-hole" and "four-hole" sinks at restaurant supply houses and by health inspectors. Even the smallest approved sink is bigger than the average boat galley. In addition, you will have to have a completely separate sink for washing your hands. Hot water must be provided at a specified temperature over a specified period of time. Supplying so much hot water requires a sizeable electric tank powered by at least a five-kilowatt generator.

Go into any commercial kitchen and you will notice that everything from the prep table to the deep fryer and the grill carries an "NSF" sticker. This means that the particular item meets the standards of the National Sanitation Foundation. Most health departments require NSF labels on all appliances used to store, prepare, or cook foods. The requirement to use approved equipment makes it very difficult to get a home kitchen or boat galley approved by local health departments. Even when buying used equipment, an all-NSF kitchen for a small restaurant represents an expenditure in the tens of thousands of dollars.

HIRING OUT FOOD SERVICE

Instead of spending a lot of money going into an unknown business (remember, you know boats, not food preparation), the best thing to do is hire somebody else to do the food work. There are several ways to do this depending on the volume and complexity of the food involved.

For big jobs, the only real solution is to hire a professional caterer to do everything from buying the first tomato to cleaning up the last of the spilled food afterward. Let the caterer worry about licenses, equipment, and even hiring the serving staff. Smaller jobs can sometimes be handled with take-out catering: have a pro prepare the food in an approved kitchen ashore and then pick up the food, bring it aboard, and serve it to your customers.

Be aware that few caterers have ever prepared food that will be served aboard a boat. They are unaware of the effects of wind on potato chips or the safety hazard of barbecue sauce drippings on the deck. As the operator of the boat, it is up to you to work with your caterer on menus that are both tasty and workable at sea.

Caterers typically supply a variety of specialty crackers to eat with cheese and meat cubes. Invariably these crackers go stale or are blown around on open decks. Few get eaten. Forget the crackers unless they can be kept in a damp-proof container out of the wind. Standard buffet items such as Swedish meatballs and wieners in cocktail sauce are also difficult on board a boat. Not only is it hard to keep them warm, but there is always a slip hazard from sauce dripped on deck. Caterers can reduce the amount of sauce in these items to make them work better on your boat without sacrificing product appeal.

Foods That Work Well on Boats

Cheese cubes

Meat cubes

Dry meat pasties

Roumaki

Buffalo wings (without sauce)

Pretzels

Fruit, either cut or whole

Foods to Avoid on Boats

Crackers

Foods in sauces (meatballs, wieners, etc.)

Soupy dips like salsa

Potato chips in open bowls

Salads served in bowls

Never allow caterers to bring glass cups or dishes aboard the boat. Even though you may (and should) require all passengers to wear shoes, somebody is always going to go barefoot on deck. Glass shards are hard to find and today's broken drinking glass can become next week's injured passenger. The one exception to glass comes during a wedding celebration when friends toast the happy couple. Let the bride and groom use real glass, but serve the guests from plastic barware champagne "glasses." Nobody will complain.

Catering Discount

You should make money on any catering, even though you do not actually touch the food. Caterers typically offer a percentage of the retail price of the job to the owner of the hall where an event was held. These discounts usually range from 10 to 20 percent, and that should be your take of the catering bill. Many customers prefer to hire their favorite caterer. In these cases, halls usually tack a surcharge on the rental bill of about 15 percent, so you should add a surcharge of 15 percent to your fee. Substitute "hull" for "hall" and you can apply these standard industry practices to your boat. Be sure that customers are aware of your catering policies (see Chapter 10).

Flying Chips and Falling Guacamole

I learned about the difficulties of dealing with caterers who aren't experienced in boat work a few years ago when I was a fill-in captain on a schooner during a corporate sales party.

The evening started with a catered meal of finger food. One particular item was a guacamole-based salad that was as juicy as it was delicious. Our guests scooped it up with little regard to the drips and splats on the cabin top and the deck. One crew member had to be detailed with a mop for the whole meal to keep the slip factor to a minimum. This same party started with a huge bowl of potato chips. One gust of wind and the harbor gulls thought they had died and gone to potato chip heaven. Fortunately, the meal was served before we got under way. We had time to deal with the mess, and we didn't have to worry about passengers moving about on pitching decks made slippery by crunched chips and dripped dip.

Chafing Dishes

Caterers use chafing dishes to keep hot food warm on a buffet line. These are a pan within a pan. The inner pan holds the food, while the outer one holds hot water kept hot by the flame of gelled alcohol. Only you can decide if a chafing dish is safe for use aboard your particular vessel and under what conditions. If you decide against chafing dishes, tell the caterer in advance so the menu will not include food that requires heat.

TAKE-OUT CATERING

For smaller events, purchase prepared foods designed for take-out from deli counters and restaurants. This relieves you of the need to have a licensed kitchen, but you are still responsible for preventing the food from spoiling. Toward that end, purchase this sort of food as close to departure time as possible. Put it in a cooler at the deli and keep it on ice until the moment it is served. You cannot be too careful with fresh food when it comes to preventing food poisoning, especially during the summer months. Food-borne bacteria grow best at temperatures from 90°F to 110°F in a moist atmosphere. These conditions are not hard to find in the cabin of a boat under the summer sun.

Ice chests for food and soft drinks must be kept separate. Cross-contamination from people grabbing a pop can easily infect food with bacteria. Store the food cooler in the coolest part of the boat and keep it out of the sun. Make sure there is sufficient ice on top of and around all perishables to keep the food at or below 40°F. Once food is taken off ice, the spoilage clock begins to tick. The rule is that food stored at room temperature must be eaten or thrown away within two hours, according to the Food Safety and Inspection Service (FSIS) of the U.S. Department of Agriculture. Cut that to one hour if the temperature exceeds 90°F.

Hot Food Safety

Safety experts at the U.S. Food and Drug Administration advise that hot foods must be kept at or above 140°F to retard bacteria growth. This is easy to do ashore in a gas-fired oven or on an electric steam table. Few boats under 100 gross tons are equipped to maintain hot food at a safe temperature. Your boat may be able to handle a household slow cooker, but be aware that it is probably not NSF approved. If you do use one, make frequent checks of the contents to be sure they are above 140°F at all times. Keep a written record of these temperature checks, just in case.

Food Server Cleanliness

Anyone who has gone on a cruise liner recently knows the hand-sanitizing drill. All passengers coming to a buffet table are given a squirt of hand-sanitizing liquid before they are allowed to begin grazing the buffet. The purpose of this drill is to prevent disease from being passed among the passengers from contaminated serving utensils on the buffet. The cruise ships use the hand-sanitizer liquid because no hand-washing sinks exist in the dining rooms. This same concept of cleanliness must be part of your food service routine.

Few small passenger boats provide a proper hand-washing area. Yet the hands of anyone touching food should be sanitary. It is possible for your crew to use the same sanitizing liquid as the cruise lines, or you can provide inexpensive disposable food service gloves. Either way, don't let anyone touch food without gloves or before a wash with a hand sanitizer. Be sure to put a sign in each restroom saying, "Employees must wash their hands thoroughly before returning to work." This sign is now required by most state sanitation regulations.

Plates and Utensils

China plates and fancy silverware add a touch of class to any dinner. However, china and silver are best left ashore. In their place, use high-quality plastic dishes, knives, forks, and spoons. By using plastic you eliminate the possibility of dirty dish contamination caused by improper washing after the last meal. Place a plastic trash can lined with a plastic bag near the buffet table. Cleanup becomes a matter of hauling the bag to a trash bin on shore. Use a "contractor" trash bag. The thicker plastic won't rip or tear while you are hauling garbage off the boat. Never let empty beer containers remain on the boat overnight during the summer. Beer dregs in trash barrels quickly go "skunky" and develop a powerful stench.

When to Serve

Lunch aboard a six-pack fishing boat comes sometime around noon, unless the fish are biting. When it comes to catered affairs such as weddings or corporate outings, however, a more organized approach is needed. Vessels of the size within the scope of this book may not be stable enough for a buffet line under way. The possibility of an upset chafing dish or a plate of cheese cubes on the deck is too great. This means you have to do some planning with your customers to ensure a successful party.

Shared Fun

Six-pack operators and skippers of small excursion boats that serve "box lunches" can do well following a concept employed in the U.S. Army's

C-rations during World War II. While each individual ration package contained enough food for one good meal, no package was really complete. The idea was to force soldiers to have a communal meal at which sharing was expected.

This shared meal technique worked extremely well on my bird-watching cruises. Everyone got a catered meal consisting of a sandwich, chips, fruit, and a cookie. At least four different sandwiches and an equal number of different cookies were supplied. We also put an orange in half the meals and an apple in the other half. Each noon I "deputized" a steward to pass out the meals. Of course, not everyone got exactly what they wanted. Pretty soon there was a flurry of activity trading half of a ham sandwich for one with turkey or swapping an oatmeal-raisin cookie for a chocolate-chip cookie. This got a lively conversation going even among people who had previously been strangers. An ordinary box lunch became a lasting memory of the trip.

Leftovers

Make an unbreakable rule that leftover food can never be served to passengers aboard your boat. Nearly everything will have been exposed to the air for about the two-hour limit set by the Food Safety and Inspection Service (FSIS). Spoilage may have begun even if you get the food on ice again. You cannot afford the liability consequences of a food poisoning outbreak. Also, beware of letting your crew take it home if you have another trip the next day. No boat sails when the crew is suffering from food poisoning. So, as FSIS suggests, "If you have any doubt, throw it out."

LICENSED BEVERAGE SERVICE

Nothing gets murkier than laws surrounding the sale and consumption of alcohol. There are only two legal ways to serve alcohol aboard. One is to completely avoid selling alcohol yourself. Instead, allow guests to bring aboard closed containers of beer and wine that they purchased elsewhere for their private consumption. The other way is for you to obtain the license or licenses necessary to sell alcoholic beverages.

Some charter companies attempt to skate around the problem by "giving" alcoholic beverages to customers. This practice is prevalent in the Florida Keys during sunset cruises where adult guests are often served either mimosas or champagne as the sun dips below the horizon. Whether "giving" champagne away is legal or not in Florida is immaterial to your operation. City and county law enforcement often turns a blind eye toward activities that help the local economy. But never assume that you can do something just because it is being done successfully somewhere else.

CARRY-ON ALCOHOL

The easiest way to deal with alcoholic beverages on your boat is to never touch the stuff. Let your customers bring, serve, and consume their own adult beverages. In most jurisdictions, a boat is considered "private property" under liquor laws, and people are free to enjoy their own drinks as they see fit. As the owner of the boat, you do not come under laws regulating alcohol as long as you do not sell or give it away.

Be aware, however, that you may become liable if you allow someone in the party to give alcohol to an underage person. A posted warning that persons under your state's minimum drinking age are not to be served or to consume alcoholic beverages may be helpful in preventing prosecution should underage drinking occur. This is serious business. Under some state laws your boat may be seized if an underage violation is deemed to have occurred. Make sure your policy of no underage drinking is stated in your passenger agreement. Finally, never allow any underage crew members to handle closed or open containers of alcohol until they have been discarded in the trash.

LIQUOR LICENSE

To sell alcohol you must have a license that defines what types of products you can offer, the hours of operation, and whether or not you can sell for off-premises consumption. The process of obtaining a license varies from state to state. Generally, the license is issued to the owner of the boat and is valid only for sales aboard the vessel. Much like captain's licenses vary by tonnage, liquor licenses vary according to the beverages to be served. "Small" licenses limit sales to lower alcoholic content beverages (wine and beer), while "big" licenses allow high-proof whiskey (spirits).

Many states have quota systems or other means of distributing licenses to prevent the proliferation of bars that occurred prior to Prohibition. Finding an available license can be expensive. Instead, check to see if boats are covered by these quota restrictions. Often a boat that travels between two or more jurisdictions (cities or other political subdivisions) may be eligible for a "quota exempt" license. This can save the tens or hundreds of thousands of dollars it can cost to purchase an existing license, depending on location. Once you get a license, the fee charged by the government is usually only a few hundred dollars per year.

Just holding a license does not relieve you from the constant spying by liquor control agents. An example of this cost one dinner cruise operator a hefty fine for selling to a minor. He was caught in an entrapment scheme done quite legally by the Ohio Department of Liquor Control. The agent arrived with his wife and underage son. The son claimed he was taking his parents out to dinner. The couple enjoyed adult beverages while the son drank a soft drink. At the end of the meal, the boy paid for everything. That triggered an arrest and conviction for selling alcohol to a minor. Even though the boy did not consume the beverages, he had *paid* for them under the guise of an anniversary celebration.

Server Age Restrictions

Most states have age restrictions on not only the purchase and consumption of alcohol but even the handling of closed containers of these products. The typical minimum age is 18, but some states specify 19 for handling closed containers of alcoholic beverages. Some states require that the person who actually conducts the sale (operates the cash register) must be over 21 years of age.

Dram Shop Insurance

One of the biggest reasons not to handle alcohol is the liability if someone gets hurt. Ordinary policies do not cover lawsuits arising from the commercial sale of alcohol. "Dram shop" insurance is required. Like all specialty insurance, this type of policy is expensive, so it may make serving alcohol prohibitive unless you sell a sizable quantity of alcoholic beverages each season.

OPEN CONTAINER

Whether you sell alcohol or not, you should find out the exact regulations in your state regarding open containers. In most places, it is legal to walk around with an open beer or a mixed drink as long as you are on private property. This is typically illegal on public property. Expect your customers to have forgotten everything when they come to your boat. They may know about open-container laws at their neighborhood bar, but you can trust them to forget around your boat. Nothing ruins a day faster than having a customer be arrested on an open-container violation for just stepping ashore from your boat. So advise your customers as necessary to keep them happy and coming back year after year.

APPENDIX A

Pro Forma Business Plan

The following pro forma projections are for a hypothetical six-pack charter fishing operation. It is based on the purchase of a $52,500 boat using a conventional mortgage of $45,388 at 9 percent interest. This plan assumes the owner intends to invest a total of $15,000 in paid-in capital to get the business operating. The total start-up investment is therefore $67,500.

The owner anticipates making a total of 20 fishing trips during the first season. His anticipated average income per trip is $350. This average income represents both the higher-paying spring and fall trips and the lower-cost midsummer trips when fishing is at its poorest. The operator anticipates burning 24 gallons of fuel per hour at cruising speed for one-third of the operating hours. Gasoline is figured at $2.64 per gallon.

This pro forma shows a small net profit the first year that declines to a loss in the second year. Despite this operating loss, the company is able to maintain nearly $4,000 in available cash at the end of the operating year. It is this positive cash flow that keeps the business going despite the loss during the second year.

While this pro forma shows a profitable business by the third year, it is not a gold mine. The owner invested $15,000 of his own money. The business's net worth does not grow substantially beyond that investment until the third year of operation. The initial investment (net worth of business) does not double in value until into the fifth year. At the end of the fifth year, the business is worth $36,880. That represents a cash return of $21,800. Divided by the five years of operation, this skipper has made an average of $4,376 per year for his efforts, or about $25.95 per hour for going fishing.

Note that the numbers are not adjusted for annual inflation.

FIVE-YEAR INCOME/EXPENSE PROJECTION					
	YEAR 1	YEAR 2	YEAR 3	YEAR 4	YEAR 5
PROJECTED INCOME					
Charter sales	31,102	48,208	60,260	63,273	66,436
COST OF SALES					
Fuel	4,827	5,069	6,843	8,211	9,032
Maintenance	1,645	2,549	3,186	3,346	3,513
Insurance	2,363	2,363	2,363	2,363	2,363
Dockage and storage	1,888	2,171	2,497	2,871	3,302
Advertising	886	930	1,255	1,506	1,657
Equipment	350	368	1,496	795	875
Licenses	150	300	300	300	300
TOTAL EXPENSES	13,338	14,218	18,829	20,937	22,908
GROSS PROFIT (LOSS)	11,962	12,347	17,034	22,098	24,431
OPERATING EXPENSES					
General and administrative	474	996	2,690	3,228	3,550
Professional fees and services	500	500	500	500	500
Loan interest	3,858	3,598	3,316	3,010	2,677
Depreciation	4,539	7,943	6,808	5,673	5,673
TOTAL OPERATING EXPENSES	9,371	13,037	13,314	12,411	12,401
NET PROFIT (LOSS)	2,591	(690)	3,721	9,688	12,030

Cash Flow Projection

	YEAR 1	YEAR 2	YEAR 3	YEAR 4	YEAR 5
Yearly income	25,300	26,565	35,863	43,035	47,339
Cost of sales	13,338	14,218	18,829	20,937	22,908
Operating expenses	4,832	5,094	6,505	6,737	6,728
Loan principal	3,059	3,320	3,602	3,908	4,240
GROSS CASH	4,070	3,933	6,927	11,453	13,463
All taxes	863	0	1,240	3,229	4,009
NET CASH	3,206	3,933	5,687	8,224	9,454
CUMULATIVE CASH	3,206	7,139	12,826	21,050	30,504

Pro Forma Balance Sheet

	YEAR 1	YEAR 2	YEAR 3	YEAR 4	YEAR 5
CURRENT ASSETS					
Cash available	6,860	10,793	16,480	24,704	34,157
Pre-paid expenses	7,781	6,917	8,157	10,146	10,927
FIXED ASSETS					
Vessel	56,735	56,735	56,735	56,735	56,735
Equipment	350	718	2,214	3,009	3,884
SUBTOTAL	57,085	47,452	58,948	59,743	60,618
Less depreciation	-4,539	-12,482	-19,290	-24,963	-30,637
TOTAL ASSETS	67,186	62,680	64,295	69,631	75,066
CURRENT LIABILITIES					
Loan payment	6,917	6,917	6,917	6,917	6,917
Unpaid taxes	863	0	1,240	3,229	4,009
TOTAL	7,781	6,917	8,157	10,146	10,927
LONG-TERM LIABILITIES					
Boat loan	42,328	39,009	35,407	31,499	27,259
OWNER'S EQUITY					
Paid-in capital	15,000	15,000	15,000	15,000	15,000
Retained earnings	2,077	1,754	5,731	12,985	21,880
TOTAL	17,077	16,754	20,731	27,985	36,880
TOTAL EQUITY and LIABILITY					
TOTAL	67,186	62,680	64,295	69,631	75,066

BUSINESS RATIOS

	YEAR 1	YEAR 2	YEAR 3	YEAR 4	YEAR 5
Debt to equity	2.5:1	2.4:1	1.7:1	1.1:1	0.7:1
Current ratio	1.9:1	2.6:1	3:1	3.4:1	4.1:1
Quick ratio	0.9:1	1.6:1	2.0:1	2.4:1	3.1:1
Return on assets	0.4:1	0.4:1	0.6:1	0.6:1	0.6:1
Return on equity	1.5:1	1.6:1	1.7:1	1.5:1	1.3:1
Working capital	(921)	3,875	8,322	14,558	23,231
Net worth of business	17,077	16,754	20,731	27,986	36,880

APPENDIX B

Online Resources

The Internet is a powerful research tool, and I encourage you to take full advantage of it. Below you will find a variety of excellent resources to consult as you plan your business. Every effort has been made to ensure the accuracy of the Web addresses. However, websites undergo redesigns, links are eliminated or moved, and sometimes websites are no longer active. If you encounter a problem with a specific Web address, chances are it is due to the ever-changing nature of the Internet.

U.S. GOVERNMENT AGENCIES

U.S. Coast Guard
www.uscg.mil

U.S. Coast Guard Office of Boating Safety
www.uscgboating.org

U.S. Coast Guard National Vessel Documentation Center
www.uscg.mil/hq/g-m/vdoc/poc .htm

U.S. Coast Guard *Marine Employer's Guidebook* (for drug testing)
http://drugfreevessel.com/public _regulations/meguidebook.htm

U.S. Department of Labor
www.dol.gov

U.S. Equal Employment Opportunity Commission
www.eeoc.gov

U.S. Federal Communications Commission
www.fcc.gov

U.S. Federal, State, and Local Geographic Data
http://gos2.geodata.gov/wps/ portal/gos

U.S. Food and Drug Administration
www.cfsan.fda.gov

U.S. Internal Revenue Service (IRS)
www.irs.gov

U.S. Occupational Safety & Health Administration
www.osha.gov

U.S. Small Business Administration
www.sba.gov

U.S. Social Security Administration
www.socialsecurity.gov

FOR THE ENTREPRENEUR

GENERAL

AllBusiness
www.allbusiness.com

Business Nation
www.businessnation.com

Entrepreneur **(print and online)**
www.entrepreneur.com/bizstart
ups/index.html

Marriott School, Brigham Young University
www.marriottschool.byu.edu/cfe/
startingout/test.cfm

Quicken (start a business)
www.quicken.com/small
_business/start

SCORE (Counselors to America's Small Businesses)
www.score.org

Startup Journal **(***The Wall Street Journal* **Center for Entrepreneurs)**
www.startupjournal.com

Steps to Starting a Small Business
www.businessguide.net/starting
.htm

U.S. Internal Revenue Service (articles)
www.irs.gov/businesses/small/
article/0,,id=98810,00.html
www.irs.gov/businesses/small/
article/0,,id=99336,00.html

U.S. Small Business Administration (excellent resource)
www.sba.gov/smallbusiness
planner/index.html

INSURANCE, PROFESSIONAL AND MARINE

Aon Risk Services, Inc. (general marine and passenger vessels)
www.aon.com

Atlass Insurance
www.atlassinsurance.com

Blackadar Marine Insurance
www.blackadarmarine.com

Bonek Agency, Inc.
www.bonek.com

Brown & Brown Flagship
www.flagshipgroup.com

Loomis & Lapann, Inc.

MOPS Marine License Insurance (captain's license insurance)
www.mopslicenseins.com

Paul Lynch & Associates, Inc.
www.insuremarine.com

JOBS

JOB HUNTING ADVICE
Career Journal (The Wall Street Journal Executive Career Site)
www.careerjournal.com/job hunting

www.careerfair.com

www.forbes.com

EMPLOYMENT OPPORTUNITIES
American Crewing
www.americancrewing.com

N. Shaw Associates (marine delivery employment)
http://deliveryskipper.com/employment.html

Rent a Captain
www.rentacaptain.com

Ride the Ducks
www.phillyducks.com/about/career_opps.asp

YACHT CREW AGENCIES
Carole Manto, Inc.
www.carolemanto.com/home/index.cfm

Crew4Yachts
www.crew4crew.net

Crewfinders International, Inc.
www.crewfinders.com

Crew Unlimited CU Yacht Charters
www.crewunlimited.com

Elite Crew International, Inc.
www.elitecrewintl.com

Palm Beach Yachts International
www.yachtcrew.com/crew.html

The Crew Network
www.crewnetwork.com

EDUCATION

MARINE EDUCATIONAL INSTITUTIONS
Chapman School of Seamanship
4343 S.E. St. Lucie Blvd.
Stuart, FL 34997
(772) 283-8130
www.chapman.org

Marine Education Textbooks
124 North Van Ave.
Houma, LA 70363
(985) 879-3866
www.metbooks.com

Maritime Professional Training
1915 South Andrews Ave.
Ft. Lauderdale, FL 33316
(888) 839-5025
www.mptusa.com

National Captain's Institute
P.O. Box 11834
St. Petersburg FL 33733
(800) 345-6901
www.captains.com

MARITIME ACADEMIES
Cal Maritime (California State University)
200 Maritime Academy Dr.
Vallejo, CA 94590
(707) 654-1000
www.csum.edu

Great Lakes Maritime Academy at Northwestern College
715 East Front St.
Traverse City, MI 49686
(800) 748-0566
www.nmc.edu/maritime

Maine Maritime Academy
Pleasant St.
Castine, ME 04420
(800) 227-8465
www.mainemaritime.edu

Massachusetts Maritime Academy
www.maritime.edu

Seattle Maritime Academy (Seattle Central Community College)
1701 Broadway
Seattle, WA 98122
(206) 587-3800
www.seattlecentral.edu/maritime

State University of New York Maritime College
6 Pennyfield Ave.
Throgs Neck, NY 10466
(718) 409-7200
www.sunymaritime.edu

U.S. Merchant Marine Academy
300 Steamboat Road
Kings Point, NY 11024
www.usmma.edu

MARINE SURVEYING

The National Association of Marine Surveyors, Inc. (NAMS)
www.nams-cms.org

Navtech U.S. Surveyors Association
www.navsurvey.com

Society of Accredited Marine Surveyors, Inc. (SAMS)
www.marinesurvey.org/contact.html

FIRST AID INSTRUCTION
American Red Cross (classes)
www.redcross.org

ONLINE CPR/FIRST AID COURSES
www.firstaidandcpr.com
www.firstaidweb.com
www.cprtoday.com
www.profirstaid.com

ORGANIZATIONS
GENERAL MARINE ASSOCIATIONS
National Association of Charterboat Operators (NACO)
www.nacocharters.org

National Marine Charter Association (NMCA)
www.marinecharter.org

New York State Tour Boat Association
www.cruisenewyork.com

Passenger Vessel Association
www.passengervessel.com

CHARTER FISHING ASSOCIATIONS
Connecticut Charter and Party Boat Association
www.ctsportfishing.com

Eastern Lake Erie Charter Boat Association
www.greatlakesfishing.com

Indian River Captains Association (Chesapeake Bay)
www.indianrivercharters.com

International Big Fish Network
www.ibfn.org/whoweare.asp

Kona Charter Skippers Association, Inc. (Hawaii)
www.konabiggamefishing.com

Louisiana Charter Boat Association
www.louisianacharterboat association.com/

Michigan Charter Boat Association
www.micharterboats.com

Mississippi Charter Boat Captains Association
www.mscharterboats.org

Montauk Boatmen's and Captain's Association
www.montauksportfishing.com/ mbca.htm

Pennsylvania Lake Erie Charter Captain Association
www.plecca.com

Port Washington Charter Captain's Association (Washington State)
www.portwashingtoncharter fishing.com

Rhode Island Party & Charter Boat Association
www.rifishing.com/charter.htm
www.rifishing.com/tour.htm

Solomons Charter Captains Association (Chesapeake Bay)
www.fishsolomons.com

Upper Bay Charter Captains Association, Inc. (Chesapeake Bay)
www.baycaptains.com

Virginia Charter Boat Association
www.fishva.org

Waukegan Charter Boat Association (Illinois and Lake Michigan)
www.wcba.info/index.html

BOATS

NEW VESSEL CONSTRUCTION

Canal Boats II, Inc. (water taxis, glass bottom, excursion, and ferries)
www.watertaxiboats.com

Cooper Marine, Inc. (catamarans)
www.coopermarine.com

Corinthian Catamarans
www.corinthiancatamarans.com

Scarano Boatbuilding, Inc.
www.scaranoboat.com

Scully's Aluminum and Fabrication (customized aluminum boats up to 60 feet)
www.scullysaluminumboats.com

Sea Hawk Industries, Inc. (fiberglass commercial vessels)
www.seahawkboats.com

SkipperLiner (steel and aluminum passenger vessels)
www.skipperliner.com

Tour Craft Boats (25- to 49- passenger catamaran hulls)
www.tourcraftboats.com

BROKERS, USED VESSELS

Boats & Harbors, Inc. (monthly trade advertiser newspaper)
www.boats-and-harbors.com

CAT Financial Services
www.cat.com/catmarinefinance

Pinnacle Marine Corporation
www.pinnaclemarine.com

Scruton Marine Services (Canadian)
www.scrutonmarine.com

SkipperLiner
www.skipperliner.com

MISCELLANEOUS

American Association of Retired Persons (AARP)
www.aarp.org

Boat U.S. Links
www.boatus.com/links/default.asp

Coastal Boating
www.coastalsailing.net

CREWfile (database of jobs and crewing information)
www.crewfile.com

Dream Jobs to Go
www.dreamjobstogo.com/titles/djtg0020.html

eSmallOffice
www.esmalloffice.com

Neptune Group, Inc. (crew housing and computers near Ft. Lauderdale, FL)
www.theneptunegroup.com

WestGroup Research
www.westgroupresearch.com

What's Cooking America
www.whatscookingamerica.net/summersafetytip.htm

Working on a Boat
www.workonaboat.com

APPENDIX C

Prequalification Form for Purchasing a Used Inspected Vessel

GENERAL INFORMATION				
Vessel name:			Year built:	
Builder:		Where built:		Gross tons:
Official number:				
No. engines:		Fuel:	Gen sets:	
Current location:				
Previous names and locations:				
CERTIFICATE OF INSPECTION				
Route permitted:				
Crew required: master	deckhands		other	
Total persons:		Total passengers:		

Next annual certificate of inspection:		Next drydock:	
No. PFDs:		No. fire extinguishers, B-I: B-II: B-III:	
Other lifesaving equipment:			

WALK-THROUGH CHECK OFF LIST

Item	Check	Item	Check
Navigation lights		Anchor and rode	
Anchor light		Docklines	
Whistle		Hand bilge pump	
Compass		Powered bilge pumps	
Distress signals		Bilge high water alarm	
First aid kit		Fire suppression system	
Adult PFDs		Fire buckets	
Child PFDs		Fire pump, hose, etc.	
Life ring and line		VHF marine radio	
Water light on ring		Radar	
Fire axe (sub-K only)		EPIRB	
Fuel shutoff valves		Valves marked on deck	

General appearance:

Hull and running gear:

INDEX

CPSIA information can be obtained
at www.ICGtesting.com
Printed in the USA
LVOW04*1824031116

511529LV00012B/184/P